COLLEGE OR MARIN LIBRARY
KENTFIELD, CALIFORNIA

P9-EDV-348

Nicaragua Under Siege

Edited by
MARLENE DIXON and SUSANNE JONAS

SYNTHESIS PUBLICATIONS
San Francisco

CONTEMPORARY MARXISM SERIES

Series Editor: Marlene Dixon
Volume Editors: Marlene Dixon and Susanne Jonas

Editorial Assistance: Ed McCaughan, Rod Bush, Elizabeth Martínez, Nancy Stein

Translation provided by a team of translators at the Institute for the Study of Labor and Economic Crisis, including Mercedes Coto, Jerry Dekker, Magally Huggins, Ester Madriz, Mimi Méndez, Martha Miranda, Ole Poblano, Mark Richey, Rebecca Schwaner, Roberto Talavera, and Jaime Vanegas.

The Contemporary Marxism Series consists of book editions of *Contemporary Marxism*, a journal of the Institute for the Study of Labor and Economic Crisis, San Francisco. This volume includes materials from *Contemporary Marxism #8*, 1984.

"The FSLN Position on Religion" was published in *Sandinistas Speak*, by Borge et al. (New York: Pathfinder Press, 1982) and is reprinted here by permission.

Cover photo: Nicaraguan firefighters battling the disastrous fire resulting from the CIA-directed attack on fuel storage tanks at Corinto on October 10, 1983. Photo by Leo Barreto, published in *Barricada*, October 12, 1983.

Cover design: Vanda Sendzimir

Synthesis Publications, 2703 Folsom St., San Francisco, CA 94110

Library of Congress Cataloging in Publication Data
Main entry under title:
Nicaragua under siege.

 (Contemporary Marxism series)
 Includes index.
 1. United States—Foreign relations—Nicaragua—Addresses, essays, lectures. 2. Nicaragua—Foreign relations—United States—Addresses, essays, lectures. 3. Nicaragua—Politics and government—1979- —Addresses, essays, lectures. 4. United States—Foreign relations—1981- —Addresses, essays, lectures.
I. Dixon, Marlene, 1936- . II. Jonas, Susanne Leilani. III. Series.
E183.8.N5N53 1984   327.7307285   83-24184
ISBN 0-89935-036-4 (pbk.)

Copyright © 1984. Synthesis Publications. All rights reserved.
Printed in the United States of America.

Contents

Introduction: The Reagan/Kissinger Assault on Central America

Marlene Dixon and Susanne Jonas

On July 19, 1983—the same day that the government of Nicaragua presented a far-reaching six-point peace proposal to the United States (see Section III of this volume)—President Reagan announced the formation of the National Bipartisan Commission on Central America, the Kissinger Commission. Its formal mandate was to advise the President and Congress on U.S. interests in Central America and the threats now posed to these interests, and on the building of a "national consensus" for U.S. policy for the region.

Underneath its formal mandate, the Commission's unstated purposes were: 1) above all, to provide a justification for increased military aid ("security assistance") to Central America, particularly El Salvador, and to persuade Democratic congressmen to vote for such aid; and 2) to gain bipartisan support for Reagan's Central America policy, thereby removing this divisive issue from the 1984 election—in effect contributing to Reagan's re-election campaign.

In this Introduction, we focus on the Kissinger Commission and its Report for several reasons: first, because of its importance in the 1984 U.S. presidential election; second, because it is an expression of and a touchstone for understanding Reagan's policy toward Central America and the debates over that policy; and third, because it illuminates the broader and longer-range options and limitations of U.S. policy toward the region.

A. The Formation of the Kissinger Commission And the U.S. Escalation of July-November 1983

The formation of the Kissinger Commission in July 1983 took place amidst a sharp intensification of Reagan's aggressive policy in Central America. A high-level policy paper prepared for the July 8 meeting of the

National Security Council, which was leaked to the press, proposed a 40% increase in military aid to U.S. allies in Central America, among other measures.[1] The administration no longer even pretended to rest its case against Nicaragua on the grounds that Nicaragua "exported arms to El Salvador," but rather began to argue openly that the Nicaraguan government *itself* was the source of the problems in Central America.[2] Shortly following the July 8 NSC meeting, Nicaragua was surrounded by 19 U.S. ships carrying over 16,000 crew members; 4,000 U.S. troops were sent to Honduras for military maneuvers. At this time, the CIA began to take over direct control of the operations of the Nicaraguan counterrevolutionaries *(contras)* and step up sabotage attacks against key economic targets in Nicaragua.[3]

Also in July, the House of Representatives held an unusual secret session prior to voting on covert aid to the *contras*. After hearing the administration make its case, Rep. Bill Alexander (D-Ark.) expressed his concern that the Reagan administration "has a hidden agenda, undisclosed to Congress and the American people, and while talking about peace in the region, it is seeking a military victory."[4]

Within this context, administration hard-liners, including Jeane Kirkpatrick, U.S. Ambassador to the U.N., were instrumental in pushing for the creation of a bipartisan commission on Central America. As Reagan's representative on the Commission, Kirkpatrick is an advocate of putting maximum military pressure on Nicaragua and has openly called for the ouster of the Nicaraguan government.[5] Administration hard-liners on Central America also urged that Kissinger, who has played an important role in past U.S. interventions, be appointed to head the Commission.[6]

Kissinger was in charge of planning the credit blockade and the CIA operations leading to the overthrow of Chilean President Salvador Allende in 1973, which resulted in the deaths of 40,000 people and the imposition of the brutal right-wing Pinochet regime. In 1972, at the same time as he was negotiating with representatives of North Vietnam in Paris, Kissinger sent urgent cables to Nixon to renew the bombing of the North.[7] Thus, he has a history of pursuing "two-track" policies, using diplomatic negotiations to cover for military solutions.

Regarding Central America today, Kissinger has been on record as opposing any cuts in military aid to El Salvador, supporting covert aid to Nicaraguan counterrevolutionaries, and approving a U.S. military presence on the Honduras/Nicaragua border if necessary[8] — all of which are in line with Reagan's policies.

Aside from Kissinger himself, the Commission was stacked with conservatives (some of them nominally Democrats), and run by a conservative staff, headed by Harry Shlaudemann, who has been closely linked with covert intelligence operations, and was part of the U.S. team in the 1973 coup against Allende.[9]

The Kissinger Commission was not designed to achieve a genuine peaceful reconciliation of interests between the revolutionary forces in Central America and the Reagan administration. This became clear from

CIA activities in Nicaragua and from the Commission's conduct during the six-day, six-country trip to Central America in October 1983. During the very week before Kissinger's arrival in Nicaragua, for example, the CIA directed a wave of devastating sabotage attacks against strategic economic targets — a significant escalation over previous *contra* operations. Moreover, the CIA, recognizing the ineffectiveness of the *contras* on their own, took direct charge of *contra* activities.[10]

While in Nicaragua, the Commission showed no disposition to listen to the government's point of view, and in some cases Commission members displayed open hostility and disrespect toward Nicaraguan government leaders. In addition, the Commission met with *contra* leader Alfonso Robelo in Costa Rica and with opposition leaders inside Nicaragua. In no other country did the Commission meet with groups in opposition to the existing government.

Upon the Commission's return to Washington, Kissinger summed up the situation in Central America as "graver than most of us had expected," and stated that a military program had to be a fundamental aspect of U.S. strategy; and, while recognizing the economic crisis affecting Central America, he emphasized the overriding need to send military aid to the region.[11]

In November, in the wake of the U.S. invasion of Grenada, the Reagan administration openly warned Nicaragua: according to one U.S. State Department official, "if [Nicaragua] had any doubts about our willingness to use force, those doubts should be erased."[12] Further, at the instigation of the United States, military leaders in Honduras, El Salvador, Guatemala, and Panama called a meeting to revive the Central American Defense Council (CONDECA). Press accounts indicated that at a secret meeting CONDECA representatives discussed the legality of a joint military action to "pacify" Nicaragua.[13] Although the CONDECA option could not work as a *military strategy*, because the armies of Guatemala and El Salvador are in no position to be diverted from their own domestic insurgencies (as was bluntly stated by Guatemalan officials),[14] it is *politically* dangerous because of its potential role in a Grenada-style scenario — a *contra* invasion, backed up by a request from a "regional organization" for direct U.S. "assistance," i.e., intervention. This option, according to well-informed sources in Washington, has by no means been permanently discarded.

B. The Kissinger Commission Report: An Extreme and Reactionary Document

The context for the formation and activity of the Kissinger Commission, then, was the interventionist escalation of July-November 1983 — a dynamic which was halted in late 1983, primarily, as we shall argue below, in response to practical re-election considerations. The content of the Kissinger Commission Report laid the foundations for another form of escalation: long-term militarization, military build-up, and a geometric increase of U.S. involvement in Central America.

The Report, delivered to President Reagan on January 11, 1984, is one of the most profoundly reactionary and extremist statements on Central America to have appeared in recent years. Over all, the Report is based on the premise that the conflicts in Central America present a threat to the security of the U.S. because "hostile outside forces—Cuba, backed by the Soviet Union, and now operating through Nicaragua" are exploiting the revolutionary conditions in the region.[15] Nicaragua is characterized as "totalitarian" and "a crucial steppingstone for Cuban and Soviet efforts to promote armed insurgency in Central America."[16] No serious evidence for this thesis is presented, but it forms the basis for the major recommendations of the Report.

In regard to Nicaragua, the Report takes the position that a consolidated revolutionary (in their terms, "Marxist-Leninist") government in Managua cannot be "contained" without a permanent U.S. military presence, and therefore represents a permanent security threat to the region (i.e., to U.S. interests and allies in the region).[17] Therefore, the majority of Commission members recommend continued U.S. support for the *contras*—although, because of the dissent by two Commission members, Mayor Henry Cisneros of San Antonio and Professor Carlos Díaz-Alejandro, the Commission was unable to make a unified recommendation on *concrete* support (i.e., funding) for the *contras*.

In effect, without stating so explicitly, the Commission comes down against political (negotiated) settlements of conflicts in Central America, with its rejection of "power-sharing" agreements with the FDR/FMLN in El Salvador.[18] The one concession made in regard to El Salvador (as a result of pressure from the Democrats on the Commission) is the "conditioning" of U.S. military aid on human rights improvements, specifically, the cessation of death squad activities. Kissinger, together with other conservative Commission members, makes clear in his individual commentary on the Report that he personally (like Reagan) disagrees with this limitation of U.S. military aid to El Salvador; and the Report's overwhelming emphasis on the *need* for vastly increased U.S. aid calls into question the commitment to human rights *"conditions"* on such aid.

The Commission's recommendations on the amounts of U.S. military and economic aid to be poured into Central America are, in themselves, extreme. The Commission proposes not just continuing U.S. aid at the present level or gradually increasing it—but "significantly" increasing it. In regard to U.S. military aid to El Salvador, no concrete figure is recommended outright, but the Defense Department's figure of $400 million for 1984–1985 is cited approvingly.[19] In addition, the Report calls for increased military aid to the other Central American governments (minus Nicaragua) and the restoration of U.S. military aid to Guatemala (cut off since 1977, because of Guatemala's gross human rights violations). It calls for resurrection of U.S.-funded "public safety" assistance to Central American police forces—a program discredited throughout Latin America and ended in the mid-1970s after revelations that it was a cover for U.S. training in torture.

The Report also proposes that the U.S. pour $8 billion into Central America in economic aid over the five-year period beginning in 1985.[20] This "Marshall Plan"/"Alliance for Progress"-type proposal is based on the assumption that somehow, in the midst of the wars raging in the region, U.S. funding and counterinsurgency programs will resolve the deep-rooted social and economic problems, without any basic reforms or political settlements. Given that this assumption was already proven incorrect in the 1960s with the Alliance for Progress (even when Central America was not in a state of revolutionary turmoil), the Kissinger Commission proposal cannot be regarded as reflecting any serious concern about basic social change or reform.

Over all, the Report is a rubber stamp for Reagan administration policy in Central America, and the Kissinger Commission turned out, as one critic put it, to be a "house organ" for the administration.[21]

C. The 1984 Presidential Election

Within the context of the 1984 presidential election, Reagan's main foreign policy problems as of early 1984 are the Middle East and Central America. In Central America there is little possibility of a "military solution" that will not ultimately force the U.S. to intervene directly. Even if, as some informed observers in Washington believe, the Reagan administration will play out all options short of sending U.S. ground troops into a land war (in Nicaragua or El Salvador)—these options being full U.S. military aid, use of *contras,* the Honduran Army (which the U.S. has been fortifying massively), CONDECA, and U.S. air and naval attacks—the logic and the material necessities of these options lead ultimately to overt U.S. intervention, most likely involving U.S. ground troops.

The problem for Reagan is that, for all his anticommunist propaganda campaigns, he has not mobilized American public opinion to support such an intervention in Central America; there is widespread fear of "another Vietnam," involving U.S. troops in combat. According to a *Washington Post* poll of November 21, 1983 (*after* the invasion of Grenada), only 30% of people surveyed would approve of U.S. involvement in the overthrow of the Nicaraguan government;[22] and opinion polls since 1979 have consistently shown strong public opposition to U.S. intervention in Central America generally.

Since the administration's main concern at this time is re-election, those within the Reagan camp who know how to count votes have their eyes on the public opinion polls. Therefore, they want to postpone any major military action in Nicaragua or El Salvador (if possible) until after the 1984 election—and meanwhile to continue destabilization efforts against Nicaragua and a general military build-up in Central America. Within the U.S., they want to avoid a major public debate over Central America.

In this regard, their concerns were well served by the Kissinger Commission. According to the analysis of *Washington Post* polling director Barry Sussman,[23] the Reagan administration has successfully used other "bipartisan commissions" (on Social Security and MX missiles) to neutralize public opposition, in preparation for a battle with Congress. In this case, the objective of pushing Reagan's increased aid requests for Central America through Congress, in the absence of sufficiently *organized* popular opposition, required that the Kissinger Commission produce a unified "bipartisan" report.

In addition, Kissinger's own future career as a top-level policymaker (some say, Secretary of State in a second Reagan administration) would be greatly enhanced by a unified Commission Report, making Kissinger appear to be the architect of a consensus defining U.S. policy toward Central America. This is generally believed to be another reason why Kissinger did everything possible to avoid a minority report.

In the short run, Kissinger was successful: he managed to bludgeon (or to out-maneuver) dissenting Democrats on the Commission into participating in a unified report (i.e., no formal minority report), confining their statements of dissent to a section of individual opinions at the end of the Report. This was no small achievement; and the fact that he was able to do it will undoubtedly help Reagan's re-election effort. (One is left with the question of why the Democrats on the Commission were willing to go along with it, given the implications for the 1984 election: Were they afraid of being blamed for "losing" El Salvador—or advocating policies that would lead to such an outcome? Do they, in the end, have more agreement with Reagan's policies than they would care to admit? Are they too divided to define a clear alternative policy?)

However, the fact that Kissinger managed to produce a unified Report should in no way be interpreted to mean that a consensus actually exists. Even before the Report was published, it was already well known that there was no consensus within the Commission. Four of the Democrats on the Commission expressed opposition to Reagan's policies: Carlos Díaz-Alejandro, professor; Henry Cisneros, mayor of San Antonio; Lane Kirkland, president of the AFL-CIO; and Robert Strauss, former national chairman of the Democratic Party. In particular, these Democrats were threatening to write a minority report or to walk out of the Commission altogether if a clause on "conditioning" aid to El Salvador on human rights improvements were not included.[24]

More importantly, in the longer run, the Kissinger Commission Report cannot serve as the basis for a genuine bipartisan consensus on Central America or remove Central America as an issue in the election. Within the first two weeks after its publication, leading Congressional Democrats attacked various aspects of the Report, particularly the recommendation that the U.S. pour massive amounts of money into Central America over the next five years—both on the grounds that it is throwing good money after bad, and on the grounds that the U.S. economy, with its $200 billion annual deficit, can in no way afford it.[25] In fact, because the recommendations of the Report are so extreme, the effect may well be to further polarize U.S. public and congressional opinion, despite administration objectives.

However, beyond the Commission's role in attempting to counter democratic debate over Central America, the Report is already having a substantive effect in shifting the spectrum of public debate to the right. The *real* issue of *U.S.* intervention in Central America is eclipsed by the Report's emphasis on the Soviet/Cuban threat; and the real issue of whether the U.S. ought to continue propping up regimes like those of El Salvador and Guatemala with U.S. taxpayers' money is eclipsed by the furor over imposing human rights conditions on such aid. In this regard, whatever the outcome of the debates in Congress, the Report is already serving the Reagan administration well in defining the issues of the 1984 election.

D. A Latter-Day "Truman Doctrine": A Permanent Threat to the Peoples of Central America

From a longer-range perspective, the Kissinger Commission Report represents, restates, and justifies the key aspects of Reagan administration policy toward Nicaragua and Central America since 1981. To briefly summarize the process of escalation: in 1981, Reagan policy, according to State Department officials, was one of "strangling" the Sandinista government economically and financing the *contras*.[26] It began in early 1981 as a cutoff of U.S. aid to Nicaragua and U.S. pressure on international aid agencies and banks not to lend to Nicaragua—even as Nicaragua was complying with its agreements to repay the huge $1.6 billion debt left by Somoza.[27] This was followed in 1982 by a 90% reduction of Nicaragua's quota for sugar imports to the U.S. (which has traditionally been the principal market for nearly all of Nicaragua's exports), thus creating a serious shortage of foreign exchange earnings.[28] Combined with the restricted access to loans and the U.S. refusal to sell replacement and spare parts to Nicaragua, the hard currency shortage in Nicaragua has devastatingly cut into reconstruction programs, as detailed in Section I of this volume.

Simultaneously the CIA engaged in an ever-expanding program of training, financing, and equipping *contra* groups and launching clandestine destabilization measures against the government. At the same time, the U.S. launched a huge military build-up in Honduras and the creation in Honduras of a military base and infrastructure for *contra* attacks against Nicaragua (as well as air and naval facilities which would give U.S. forces access).[29] This military build-up forced Nicaragua to divert scarce resources to defense purposes; and the CIA-directed sabotage against key economic targets in July-October 1983 was clearly intended to bring Nicaragua to its knees economically. The combination of economic warfare in its various forms and building up the *contra* forces can only be seen as part of a long-range effort to destabilize and eventually overturn the Nicaraguan government.

This process of escalation is given a justification in the Kissinger Commission Report. First, as seen above, it enshrines Cold War, anti-Soviet politics and the crudest version of the "domino theory," which has been the ideological basis for the administration's steadily escalating war against

Nicaragua. Nicaragua is depicted as "a base for Soviet and Cuban efforts to penetrate the Central American isthmus, with El Salvador the first target of opportunity."[30] The Report revives the portrayal of Nicaragua as the crucial link in the export of arms to, as well as the training of, the Salvadoran FMLN.[31] The Reagan administration tried for years to prove this thesis, only to discredit itself totally in the international community when its desperate efforts yielded no "proof," and were exposed as propaganda manipulations.

What the Reagan administration has always distorted (and the Kissinger Commission Report distorts) is that, to the extent that a "domino theory" is operative in Central America, Nicaragua's role lies not in the export of arms but in the power of setting an example. In the words of Nicaraguan government leader Sergio Ramírez Mercado (see "The Unfinished American Revolution and Nicaragua Today," below in this volume):

> We export the news that in Nicaragua the revolution has brought with it literacy, agrarian reform, an end to poliomyelitis, the right to life and hope. . . . How can one prevent a peasant from another Central American country from hearing, from finding out, from realizing that in Nicaragua land is given to other poor and barefoot peasants like him?

Beyond its ideological dimension, the Kissinger Commission Report recommends spending up to $8 billion in U.S. economic aid to Central America in the next five years—a proposal that has been compared to the 1947 Marshall Plan of massive aid to postwar Western Europe. Even though it is not invoked by name, the real referent of the Marshall Plan is the Cold War Truman Doctrine, a *military* strategy for the containment of the Soviet Union and the socialist bloc. In fact, this is the application of the approach that the Reagan camp has taken toward Central America since the 1980 presidential campaign. In 1980, Reagan advisers openly proposed the Truman doctrine approach for Central America, spelling this out to mean massive military and economic aid, possibly including military advisers, the training of Nicaraguan *contras,* and so on—everything short of overt U.S. troop involvement.[32]

This military approach is reproduced in the Kissinger Commission Report (even using the Cold War terminology of "containment"). The Report's elaborate language about economic aid and economic development should not obscure the fact that what is really being proposed is a long-range U.S. commitment to a very costly militarization of Central America—everything short of direct U.S. intervention, Vietnam-style.

In fact, while acknowledging that the deployment of U.S. forces would be very costly,[33] the Report does not even totally preclude the direct intervention option:

1) In regard to Nicaragua, the Report makes clear that "the consolidation of a Marxist-Leninist regime [i.e., the present one] would be seen by

its neighbors as constituting a permanent security threat,"[34] *implying* that the only kind of government in Nicaragua that is really tolerable to the U.S. is a new, non-Sandinista government. And more explicitly, it states that while direct U.S. military action should be "only a course of last resort," "Nicaragua must be aware that force remains an ultimate recourse" for the U.S.[35]

2) In regard to El Salvador, Kissinger states in his individual dissent that "conditionality [of U.S. aid] should not be interpreted to mean tolerating a Marxist-Leninist victory in El Salvador." Moreover, the Commission rejects "power-sharing" (as it calls the basis of negotiations proposed by the FMLN), making a serious negotiated setlement impossible;[36] the most likely alternative over time is intensified military confrontation, leading ultimately to direct involvement of U.S. combat troops.

The implications of this approach for Nicaragua and for the revolutionary movements in El Salvador and Guatemala are clear: to the extent that the U.S. is not presently engaging in open military attacks, the Kissinger Commission Report provides the rationale for a permanent U.S. club held over the heads of the peoples of Central America, with the implicit threat of direct U.S. involvement if it becomes necessary.

E. Divisions Over Central America Policy

One of the principal obstacles to Reagan's Central America policy, and now to acceptance of the Kissinger Commission Report, is a lack of unity at the level of corporate/government policymakers. As a background for understanding some of the major divisions within U.S. ruling circles, and as an instructive example, we shall review briefly the debate within the Carter administration over policy toward Nicaragua.[37]

The victory of the revolutionary forces over the Somoza dictatorship in 1979 sparked a serious debate within U.S. ruling circles over whether to extend aid to the new Nicaraguan government to reconstruct its devastated economy. While all sections of the ruling class were unwilling to tolerate *permanently* a sovereign revolutionary state in Nicaragua, there were serious tactical differences among them over how best to maintain control over Nicaragua while simultaneously destabilizing the new government. Within the Carter administration this debate pitted those representatives of transnational monopoly/banking capital who advocated extending minimal U.S. government aid as a mechanism for controlling the situation in Nicaragua (and for keeping Nicaragua "in line" in regard to repayment, *on commercial terms,* of the $1.6 billion foreign debt left by Somoza) against representatives of competitive industrial capital, e.g., the military-industrial complex and their political spokesmen, who advocated no aid at all except to the Somocista counterrevolutionaries and favored direct action to overthrow the Nicaraguan government.

Under Carter, himself a member of the Trilateral Commission, the transnational bankers won the day; yet we should not forget that the Carter administration supported the Somoza regime until it literally could no longer do so within the logic of its "human rights" policy. Carter accepted the defeat of Somoza as a fait accompli, but was determined at all costs to avoid "another Nicaragua" elsewhere in Central America. (The October 1979 coup in El Salvador was part of this strategy.) Thus, while extending minimal aid to the Nicaraguan government, at the same time he also increased aid to El Salvador to $72 million to prop up the pro-U.S. regime, and generally adopted a more hard-line policy toward El Salvador. Furthermore, in its last days, the Carter administration, using the pretext that Nicaragua was supplying arms to the guerrillas in El Salvador, suspended aid payments and food shipments to Nicaragua and gave Nicaragua 30 days to "stop the arms flow."

In a sense, then, the Carter administration was constrained from following a policy of monolithic interventionism, both because of the influence of competing interests in making policy and because of the contradictions of its "human rights policy." Both of these factors have been eliminated (human rights policy, even as rhetoric) or substantially altered (the balance of power within ruling circles) under the Reagan administration.

But the divisions over policy have persisted, impeding Reagan's attempts to carry out his interventionist designs. Specifically, some representatives of transnational corporate interests have opposed Reagan's open militarism *because it could involve the U.S. in a Vietnam-type land war in Central America*—an unpopular venture, in terms of U.S. public opinion, and ultimately a losing venture. The most explicit statement of a position critical of Reagan's policy was the Linowitz Report of April 1983. Signed by such transnational and Trilateral Commission representatives as David Rockefeller, (former Secretary of State) Cyrus Vance, and Sol Linowitz, this report asserts that the U.S. can best achieve its long-range interests in Central America through a "many-sided dialogue" and a more "restrained approach" by the U.S.—not through intervening in the region by overt or covert (military) action.[38]

Furthermore, representatives of transnational corporate interests within the Reagan administration, the prime example being Secretary of State Shultz, do not necessarily agree with all of Reagan's Central America policies (for example, Shultz has stated that he favors "conditioning" aid to El Salvador); they are more concerned about the Middle East, where transnational capital has material interests to protect (oil), than about Central America, where Reagan's openly militaristic and aggressive policies are too costly and too risky, in terms of jeopardizing other objectives.

The above should not be oversimplified to mean that those sections of the ruling class linked to transnational interests favor peace worldwide and oppose militarism across the board (in fact, Carter's "human rights policy" was essentially a different brand of anti-Sovietism). Many of them simply believe that the U.S. empire might be damaged more by a Vietnam-type land war in Central America than by a policy of isolating, neutralizing, influencing, and destabilizing revolutionary governments and movements.

More generally, transnational interests, lesstied to the policy of any *one* single nation or U.S. administration, have the ability to play out more than one option at a time: they can very easily acquiesce in Reagan's military build-up and escalation, while *simultaneously* criticizing Reagan from time to time and not tying themselves down to the short-sighted interventionism of a Reagan.

We may expect that the tendencies outlined above will emerge in some form or other in the debate over the Kissinger Commission Report in the coming months. Although the voices of opposition, both within and outside the U.S. Congress, are multiplying as of the end of January 1984, most opponents (including dissenting Commission members) have taken exception to the more controversial and extreme recommendations of the Report, rather than to its underlying premises and analysis. A coherent alternative to the Report has yet to crystallize from within transnational corporate/government circles opposed to Reagan policies. Whether such a view does crystallize (as may be expected) and whether it is reflected in the Platform of the Democratic Party and its candidate in the 1984 Presidential election is, of course, a crucial question.

One early indication of the direction for a critique of and alternative to the Report by representatives of more transnationally oriented interests is the report issued by the Carnegie Endowment for International Peace at the end of January 1984. It is clearly intended as an alternative to the Kissinger Report, with many of the contributors being ex-officials of the Carter administration;[39] the extent of its influence remains to be seen. At this level within the U.S. political arena, then, the debate over the Kissinger Commission Report will serve as a kind of test or weathervane to measure the real unity or disunity that exists within U.S. ruling circles over the issues of Central America policy.

The other crucial arena of debate will no doubt be the U.S. Congress, where the financial and political implications of the Kissinger Commission Report's recommendations will be translated into legislation (or modified or rejected). In this regard, to the extent that Congressional debate is at all responsive to U.S. public opinion, it is relevant that, according to a *Washington Post*/ABC poll taken soon after the Report was released, 62% of the general population believed that the policies proposed by the Kissinger Commission have a "not so good" or "poor" chance of improving the situation in Central America.[40]

Viewed from a broader perspective, however, and keeping in mind that U.S. public opinion has been viewed by policymakers as a factor to be manipulated more than as a determining factor, we should not simply conclude that criticisms of the Kissinger Commission Report would automatically translate into a noninterventionist policy in Central America under a Democratic administration. As we shall see, there are real issues and real stakes in Central America that will face any administration in power in the U.S.; and there is a large gap between an alternative to

Reagan's interventionism and a genuinely noninterventionist U.S. policy for the region.

F. The Decline of U.S. Hegemony

From the foregoing, it is clear that the course of present U.S. policy as reflected and projected in the Kissinger Commission Report is extremely dangerous. The danger stems, we believe, from the conjuncture of three factors: the tenure of a reckless and reactionary Reagan administration; the rise and development of the revolutionary movements in Central America; and the decline of real U.S. hegemony (political and economic) in the international capitalist order. The divisions over foreign policy among different sectors of the U.S. government/corporate ruling class are, in a sense, different responses to the realities of U.S. decline. In this Introduction, we shall not dwell at length upon an analysis of this decline, as the following article by Marlene Dixon and Ed McCaughan, "The Suez Syndrome: U.S. Imperialism in Decline," makes the case eloquently and convincingly. However, *it is critical to understand that the dangers of U.S. interventionism in Central America today stem fundamentally from U.S. weakness, not from U.S. strength.*

To broadly summarize the argument: since the crisis of the capitalist economy and in particular the erosion of the hegemonic position of the U.S. in the world-economy, beginning in the mid-1960s (after two decades of unchallenged hegemony)—and even more sharply since the political and military defeat of the U.S. in Vietnam—the U.S. has been losing its ability to impose by political or economic means its preferred solutions upon the peoples of the world. The U.S. government has been decreasingly able to discipline its European "allies" (which have their own interests to pursue, for example, in developing closer economic ties with the socialist bloc). And domestically, the "Cold War consensus" has been shattered by the Vietnam experience, and to this day has not been restored, despite intense propaganda campaigns by the U.S. government.

Coming from a position of relative economic decline, and of international and domestic political isolation, the U.S. government—beginning with stepped up Cold War anti-Soviet policies in the last year and a half of the Carter administration, and much more markedly with the ascension of the Reagan administration—came increasingly to employ military measures and military solutions to situations that it defined as "threatening U.S. interests."

More broadly, in the present period, naked force, open militarism, and interventionist policies are becoming the rule; this is a consequence of imperialism under attack—as has been true since the end of the Vietnam War. An "age of imperialism" is also by necessity an age of militarism. The ruling class has always comprehended the real meaning of the Bolshevik Revolution: that capital could no longer rule in peace; it could no longer rule without opposition. A revolutionary age is, thus, a militarist age for the ruling class, because only by force of arms is it able to protect and to perpetuate its rule.

We have seen the evolution of this dynamic in Central America today, where the U.S. has been unable to contain the explosion of revolutionary movements in an area once considered the "back yard of the U.S." In Nicaragua, the U.S. was unable to prevent the victory of the Sandinistas in 1979 through any means short of a massive military intervention. Over the past four years, the *contras* trained, funded, and equipped by the U.S. have been able to inflict very serious damage on the country's economic infrastructure, but are no match militarily or politically for the Sandinistas, who have organized, mobilized, and armed the Nicaraguan people.

In El Salvador the weakness of the army, despite years of training by U.S. military advisers, has reached a critical point, and many believe that the fall of the U.S.-supported Salvadoran government is only a question of time. In Guatemala one right-wing dictatorial regime after another has unleashed devastating attacks on the base of the guerrilla movement that has been operating for over 20 years in that country, but they have been unable to inflict substantial damage on the guerrillas themselves. In fact, the pressures of the Guatemalan counterinsurgency state itself constantly regenerate a base for the guerrillas, especially among the severely oppressed Indian population. And while the prospects for victory by the revolutionary forces are not short-term in Guatemala, no measure short of another direct U.S. military intervention (like the one in 1954) can stop the movement there. Finally, in Honduras, the massive U.S. presence, turning the country into a virtual U.S. military base, could well generate a revolutionary response where no such movement previously has existed.

Given the very likely evolution of the revolutionary situations in Central America, it is also to be expected that the effects will be felt in Mexico; this is already the case on Mexico's southern border, with the influx of thousands of Guatemalan refugees, and the generalized impact of the crisis in Guatemala. Moreover, Mexico itself is undergoing a severe internal economic crisis, with half of its work force underemployed, and with an $80 billion debt to the transnational banks. Over the longer range, Mexico's stability cannot be taken for granted—a situation that could eventually have repercussions within the United States itself.

Furthermore, in Guatemala, and far more in Mexico (as contrasted with Nicaragua and El Salvador), the economic stakes (in terms of U.S.-based and transnational corporate investment and trade and in terms of resources such as oil) are very real and very high. It is for this reason, many believe, that the policy of "drawing the line in El Salvador," one way or another, has support among many sectors of the U.S. and the transnational bourgeoisie.

From this perspective, the long-range threat to Central America goes far beyond the policies of one U.S. presidential administration or another. Putting aside the crude domino theory that informs the policies of a Reagan or a Kissinger, we are in fact witnessing an era of revolutionary change in Central America. Sooner or later—very likely in El Salvador—the line will have to be drawn, the decision will have to be made either to "lose"

El Salvador (and in the future, progressively Guatemala and Mexico) or to intervene to "save" the region for U.S. and transnational bourgeois interests. Despite the divisions currently existing within U.S. ruling circles over Reagan's Central America policy because it is so extreme, the issue of a comprehensive alternative policy remains unresolved. Actions such as the massive, long-range U.S. military build-up in Honduras, designed to establish a permanent U.S. military presence in the region, have not received significant opposition within policymaking circles. There is no indication that transnational corporate interests, when forced to choose, will ultimately let Central America "fall."

Nevertheless, there is no question that the most *immediate* danger to Central America remains the policy of President Reagan, who represents and whose interests are so closely tied to those of U.S. *national* bourgeois interests. To the extent that the loss of *U.S.* political and economic hegemony is combined with a reactionary party in power, tied primarily to national (as opposed to transnational) corporate interests, any attempt by the peoples of Central America to assert their sovereignty is taken as a "threat to U.S. interests" and incurs implacable hostility from the U.S. government. And within the context of growing revolutionary movements in Central America, there is a growing likelihood that this hostility will take the form of a direct military confrontation.

G. Conclusion

The perilous course of Reagan administration policy toward Nicaragua and Central America generally can best be understood as a long-range tendency, intensifying over time, toward direct confrontation with revolutionary forces in the region. At a particular moment in time—as happened from July through November of 1983—it can escalate so dramatically as to raise the specter of a direct invasion by U.S.-backed or even U.S. forces. Subsequently, the immediate danger of military confrontation may subside—for example, at a time when election-year realities (i.e., anti-interventionist public opinion in the U.S.) take higher priority. While the immediacy of overt military U.S. intervention varies, the interventionist logic of Reagan administration policy over time does not. This is the lesson we draw from reading the Kissinger Commission Report.

During one of the periods of unprecedented escalation, in October 1983, the editors of *Contemporary Marxism* were in Nicaragua, as well as two delegations organized by U.S. Out of Central America (USOCA). (Staff and members of the Editorial Board of *CM* were among those who first conceived of USOCA.) In October 1983, even more than previously, the long-range aggressive policy of the Reagan administration became a living reality to us, fed by daily reports of new attacks by the CIA and its protégés. We saw directly the effects of these attacks in terms of human lives and literal destruction of economic resources and facilities. We saw how swiftly the Reagan administration could move toward the edge of the precipice of direct military intervention—even if only to pull back temporarily.

This issue of *Contemporary Marxism* is an attempt to make available to U.S. readers firsthand accounts of that situation—and to convey to an American public that time and time again has expressed its opposition to U.S. intervention in Central America the realities of U.S. aggression, as well as the vitality and originality of the Nicaraguan Revolution. But this volume is also the product of a longer-range analysis of the editors of *Contemporary Marxism*. We believe that progressive activists, and indeed in a sense all U.S. citizens in the current conjuncture, have a historic responsibility to defend the accomplishments of the Nicaraguan Revolution, as well as a long-range interest in doing so.

As the first serious challenge to U.S. hegemony over the Western Hemisphere since the Cuban Revolution 25 years ago, the revolutionary government in Nicaragua is a living example of the possibility of ousting a U.S.-backed dictatorship and establishing a society that serves the majority of its population. Any setback to the Nicaraguan Revolution would mean a serious setback for progressive forces throughout the hemisphere.

For the people of the United States, the prospect of a direct U.S. attack against the Nicaraguan Revolution would have very direct effects, because it would necessarily involve a massive and costly U.S. military intervention; nothing less would have any possibility of success. The logic of such an intervention by the U.S. government implies a draining of the economy at the expense of the American people, a reinforcement of the power that is imposing austerity upon the American people, and repression on a massive scale against those who actively oppose the intervention. In addition, it raises the specter of a broader confrontation between the U.S. and the socialist bloc.

To permit the Reagan administration to make Nicaragua and Central America generally a theater of East-West conflict, then, is to allow the "line to be drawn" in a way that ultimately threatens progressives throughout the Americas. Conversely, to defend the gains made by the Nicaraguan Revolution and the right of the peoples of Central America to self-determination is to defend the right of the people of the United States and the entire hemisphere to an equitable social order, and against the violent thrashing of a dying but still lethal empire.

San Francisco
January 31, 1984

NOTES

NOTE: In addition to consulting published sources, we have conducted extensive interviews with well-informed observers of U.S. policy, which proved essential for the development of the analysis presented here.

1. *New York Times* (July 17, 1983).
2. *New York Times* (July 22, 1983).
3. *San Francisco Chronicle* (July 14, 1983); and other press reports.
4. *New York Times* (July 20, 1983).
5. Interviews; *San Francisco Examiner* (July 24, 1983).
6. Interviews; Council on Hemispheric Affairs press release (January 10, 1984).

7. See Seymour Hersh, *The Price of Power: Kissinger in the Nixon White House* (New York: Summit Books, 1983), p. 619.

8. *New York Times* (July 19, 1983).

9. Council on Hemispheric Affairs press release (January 10, 1984).

10. *San Francisco Chronicle* (November 25, 1983); and documentation below, in this volume.

11. *New York Times* (October 22, 1983); *Barricada* (October 18, 1983).

12. *San Francisco Examiner* (November 14, 1983).

13. *London Times* (October 30, 1983); *New York Times* (November 11, 1983).

14. *New York Times* (November 23, 1983).

15. Kissinger Commission Report (Report of the National Bipartisan Commission on Central America), manuscript version, January 1984, p. 4 (hereafter referred to as KCR).

16. KCR, p. 91.

17. KCR, p. 114.

18. KCR, p. 110.

19. KCR, p. 102.

20. KCR, p. 53.

21. Council on Hemispheric Affairs press release (January 11, 1984).

22. *Washington Post National Weekly Edition* (November 21, 1983).

23. *Washington Post National Weekly Edition* (January 30, 1984).

24. Interviews; *Washington Post National Weekly Edition* (January 23, 1984); *Time* (January 23, 1984); and numerous other news reports.

25. *New York Times* (January 12, 1984, and January 15, 1984).

26. *New York Times* (April 2, 1981), cited in Susanne Jonas, "The New Cold War and the Nicaraguan Revolution: The Case of U.S. 'Aid' to Nicaragua," in Marlene Dixon and Susanne Jonas (eds.), *Revolution and Intervention in Central America* (San Francisco: Synthesis Publications, 1983), p. 232.

27. Jonas, op. cit., p. 231; Richard Ullman, "At War With Nicaragua," *Foreign Affairs* (Fall 1983), p. 48.

28. Ullman, loc. cit.

29. Ibid., p. 40; and direct documentation below, in this volume.

30. KCR, p. 126.

31. KCR, p. 27.

32. See, for example, Roger Fontaine's recommendations summarized in *Miami Herald* (August 24, 1980).

33. KCR, p. 115.

34. KCR, p. 114.

35. KCR, p. 119; see also *New York Times* (January 12, 1984).

36. KCR, pp. 110-11.

37. This account is summarized from Jonas, op. cit.

38. See *New York Times* (April 6, 1983).

39. "Central America: Anatomy of a Conflict" (published by Carnegie Endowment for International Peace); summary of report in *In These Times* (January 25-31, 1984).

40. Poll cited in *Guardian* (February 1, 1984).

The Suez Syndrome: U.S. Imperialism in Decline

Marlene Dixon and Ed McCaughan

This paper was delivered at the XV Latin American Congress of Sociology in Managua, Nicaragua, in October 1983, on behalf of the Institute for the Study of Labor and Economic Crisis in San Francisco. Marlene Dixon is the Director of the Institute.

To (British Prime Minister) Eden, the Suez crisis was a challenge to Europe, and to British influence, in the whole non-European world. . . . It symbolized those acts of restraint which, had they been applied in time in the 1930s, would have prevented a war which, apart from being a tragedy in itself, had brought Britain to a state of powerlessness where she could not defend her most vital interests without American permission.

> F.S. Northedge
> *British Foreign Policy: The*
> *Process of Readjustment 1945-1961*

History has dark lessons for us concerning the last convulsive throes of falling empires. The habits of empire, when empire begins to fail, seem to produce a fatal refusal to admit that one is losing the game and a suicidal recklessness provoked by power entering senility. While the United States is far from impotent in its present decline, neither does it have statesmen at its helm, and so the government of the United States should be considered a clear and present danger to peace, sanity, and the ability to support rational solutions to the world's manifold and explosive dangers. Militarism is clearly at the center of Reagan's so-called "revolution."

> Marlene Dixon,
> "World Capitalist Crisis and the Rise of
> the Right," *Contemporary Marxism*

Introduction

We gather here at a time when warships of the United States patrol the seas in an undeclared war against a tiny nation but recently delivered from exploitation and oppression that those very same warships symbolize to the world. As citizens of the United States, present at this gathering, it is not enough to simply state that we oppose the policies of our government, at home and abroad. We must also understand why we are here, what has brought us to this time and place and to these conditions.

Above all, we must recognize that the United States of America has been an imperialist, colonial power since its founding as a British colony based upon the expropriation of indigenous Amerind peoples. The full blossom of U.S. imperialism after the War of Independence emerged from the annexation of the American Indian nations west of the original colonies to the Pacific Ocean, concluding with the annexation of Mexican territories (the U.S. Southwest today, comprising Texas, New Mexico, Arizona, Utah, Colorado, Nevada, and California). Beginning at the end of the 19th century, the Spanish American War, a full-blown expression of U.S. expansionism and modern imperialism, resulted in the annexation of Puerto Rico and the Philippines, and the neocolonial domination (i.e., economic, indirect control of a foreign territory and its government) of Cuba, and shortly most of the Caribbean and Central America.

These early annexations were sold to the American people (and a large isolationist popular movement) as wars to "free" countries from the yoke of European colonialism. This mystification became the main ideological basis of all subsequent U.S. imperialist wars and interventions. After World War II this ideology was transmogrified to present U.S. wars and interventions as a policy of stopping the spread of tyrannical "communism" and protecting the "free world." In fact, the true basis of U.S. imperialism was the Monroe Doctrine, claiming all of the Western Hemisphere as within a U.S. "sphere of influence," replaced after World War II with the Truman Doctrine, which claimed the whole of the capitalist world, Japan, Southeast Asia, Africa, the Middle East, and Western Europe, as within a U.S. "sphere of influence."

The ideology of the U.S. as the "protector of liberty" is a state ideology, taught in the public school system, in the universities, state and private, and reflected in all of the major organs of the U.S. mass media. A particularly virulent ideological mystification for U.S. neo-imperialism (i.e., the practice of extending control or domination of nations by means and actions of other client nations) was expressed in the developmental theory of the Alliance for Progress era. This theory rationalized imperialist penetration of the Third World with the argument that "underdeveloped" nations merely needed a sufficient infusion of capital in order to reach take-off, or the stage of development that would then allow them to repeat the same economic evolution of capitalist growth that occurred in Europe and the United States. There are no better examples of the bankruptcy of "developmentalism" than the present condition of both Brazil and Chile. It is for these reasons that understanding the reality of the American Empire today is important to us as North Americans, for as a people we have been kept ignorant by state and mass media indoctrination about the nature of our own nation, its government, and its policies.

From the U.S. military intervention in Greece in the 1940s through the current U.S. aggressions in Central America and the Middle East, the record of U.S. foreign policy has been one of shameless hypocrisy. In the guise of defending freedom and democracy against an international "communist conspiracy," one duplicitous U.S. government after another has supported the world's most brutal dictators as the guarantors of "business as usual" for corporate interests. Truman transformed this lie into "Doctrine" with his declaration that the U.S. would intervene anywhere in the world to support "free peoples (read capitalist/bourgeois societies) who are resisting (read repressing) attempted subjugations by armed minorities (read movements in defense of popular sovereignty)."

In the more than 200 U.S. armed interventions throughout the world since 1946, the policy of the United States has been consistently to support client bourgeoisies (or military establishments) who would defer to U.S. interests and give free access to U.S. transnational corporations. Keeping the "free world" safe from communism meant the protection of capitalism and the small number of bourgeois and petty bourgeois classes willing to subordinate themselves and their countries to U.S. domination, both political and corporate. Yet the contradiction of U.S. neo-imperialism is simply this: capitalism is repressive, exploitative, and greedy; imperialism is repressive, exploitative, and greedy — the result? The systematic destruction of native economies and looting of the nations' resources. This results in massive social inequities which in turn provoke resistance from popular forces, which can only be met with repression by regimes that are expected by their masters in the U.S. government and in U.S. transnational corporations to maintain the capitalist status quo; the weaker the country, the more virulent the foreign and domestic exploitation, the more repressive the government is required to be to stay in power. In this sense, we may term U.S. foreign policy as *fascist* in that it demands the defense of its capital interests by insisting that its "agents" (dictators like Somoza, Pinochet, and Marcos) impose naked, terrorist bourgeois rule to suppress working class and peasant struggle. Yet, in the cycle of exploitation and repression, resistance unfolds nonetheless toward reform or revolution, the overthrow of U.S. client governments by popular socialist movements.

Charts 1 and 2 illustrate U.S. intervention on behalf of repressive client regimes, and the ultimate failure of most of these policies as one country after another has broken the yoke of U.S. domination.

These charts allow us to contemplate the decline of an American Empire relatively young in historical terms and illustrate the seriousness of the generalized crisis facing the capitalist world-system. It was only 160 years ago that the Monroe Doctrine declared the entire North and South

Chart 1. Keeping the World Safe for "Free Enterprise": Major U.S. Overt and Covert Military Interventions, 1945-1975*

Country	Year	U.S. Intervention	Current Situation
China	1945-49	Expeditionary force occupied parts of China with U.S. Air Force support to suppress the liberation of the Chinese people.	China is powerful component of socialist sector of the world-system.
Greece	1946-49	U.S. and Britain intervened to crush communist partisans and establish repressive rule of Colonels, securing Greece as key U.S. military base.	Socialist government threatens U.S. control.
Korea	1950-53	Truman sent two divisions of US ground troops to aid S. Korean forces attempting to take over N. Korea. U.S. also engineered U.S. resolution to authorize invasion of N. Korea in violation of U.N. Charter.	Socialist government rules N. Korea, while 40,000 U.S. troops sustain S. Korean capitalist dictatorship.
Iran	1953	U.S. backed coup overthrowing progressive Mossadegh government. U.S. gained access to oil and reinstated Pahlavi as Shah to rule Iran as a subimperialist client regime.	Islamic Republic ruled by right-wing nationalist Ayatollah Khomeini, who continues to repress Left, but has removed Iran from U.S. orbit.
Guatemala	1954	U.S. supplied arms, planes, and pilots to over-throw progressive nationalist Jacobo Arbenz government and installed first of a string of brutal military dictatorships.	U.S.-backed military dictatorship in control—facing growing armed popular movement.

Lebanon	1958	Eisenhower sent 10,000 troops to support pro-Western government of Chamoun and to crush pro-Nasser nationalist Lebanese opposition.	Reagan has sent 3,200 Marines and U.S. flotilla to support right-wing Phalange government against popular Moslem forces.
Cuba	1961	Failed Bay of Pigs landing by exiled mercenaries in CIA plan to overthrow new revolutionary government and re-establish Cuba as U.S. neocolony for sugar corporations, tourism, trade, and Mafia.	Cuban Revolution has survived repeated attempts by U.S. to destabilize it.
Dominican Republic	1965	40,000 U.S. Marines suppressed mass rebellion whose aim was to restore a democratically elected government. Balaguer dictatorship imposed.	Failure of dictatorship has given rise to reformist social democratic government still hamstrung by U.S. capitalist domination.
Vietnam	1965-73	Massive U.S. military intervention to stop national liberation movement, including 3 million tons of bombs dropped, widespread chemical herbicides, and CIA assassination program which alone killed 40,000 civilians.	A united, socialist Vietnam triumphed over U.S. aggression.
Chile	1973	CIA backed overthrow of Allende and established Pinochet's bloody military dictatorship, with an estimated 40,000 killed.	Popular protests threaten to topple the 10-year tyranny of Pinochet.
Angola	1975	U.S. authorized $14 million to finance attempt to overthrow Angolan government.	MPLA's socialist government remains in power.

* For references, see page 17.

American continents a U.S. sphere of influence. It was only 135 years ago that the Mexican American War secured the entire expanse of what is now the Southwestern United States for the American Union. It was less than 125 years ago that the American Civil War marked the triumph of industrial capitalism in the U.S. and America's emergence as an up-and-coming semi-peripheral power in the world-system. And it was only 85 years ago that the U.S. embarked on its first major imperialist offensive with the Spanish American War, a war which, in the words of Felix Greene, won for the new American Empire:

> . . .the outright takeover of the Philippines and Puerto Rico; the virtual takeover of Cuba; a sphere of influence over all of Central America; strategic domination of the Caribbean; and the opening of all South America to United States' investments—an area which, until then, had been predominantly under British and French influence. The war against Spain was just the beginning, but with it the United States was fully launched upon her imperialist course (Greene, 1981: 80).

Chart 2. Success Rate of 11 Major U.S. Counterinsurgency Interventions Over the Past Four Decades*

Failures:	5 have been complete failures: China, Cuba, Vietnam, and Angola, which are now all socialist, and Iran which, while far from socialist, is no longer under U.S. control.
Disappointments:	3 have given rise to governments increasingly unwilling or unable to protect U.S. interests: Greece, Lebanon, and the Dominican Republic.
Draws:	3 dictatorships remain in power, but only as a result of massive U.S. aid: South Korea, Guatemala, and Chile.

* For references, see page 17.

The Contradictions of U.S. Imperialist Policies

Early U.S. interventions, which resulted in either the direct annexation of territories or neocolonial domination, were often carried out at the expense of declining colonial powers like Spain. These interventions were shrouded in the false illusion of wars of liberation and independence. Nothing could have been further from the truth, but the lie of American imperialism intervening on behalf of freedom and democracy was established in this early period and only grew in its level of hypocrisy as the United States emerged within the world-system as a core capitalist power.

Both World War I and World War II, but particularly the latter, greatly accelerated the rise of the United States to hegemony within the world-system. The near-total destruction of Europe—and of Europe's empires—cleared the way for the United States to secure its supremacy worldwide. But this is a history filled with ironies, as each step closer to imperial hegemony also produced new contradictions and the seeds of the empire's demise. The Marshall Plan, for example, which generated enormous profits for American corporations, also laid the bases for Europe's eventual competitive advantage over the United States: European industrial plants were rebuilt with modern technology while American plants gradually slid into obsolescence. Likewise, as we've seen from the charts above, the very imperialist repression required to secure and maintain America's transnational capitalist empire, particularly after World War II, generated resistance and rebellion.

The postwar era also marked the partitioning of the world between capitalist and socialist camps, as the U.S. came to define its major challenger in the world-system as the Soviet Union. In its efforts to isolate revolutionary movements and young socialist states, the U.S. consistently forced them to turn toward the Soviet Union, and in this sense the brutality of American imperialism no doubt forced a greater unity on the competing socialist bloc than would otherwise have been possible.

Thus in a historically very brief period of time, the United States moved from a colonial possession of Britain, to a young bourgeois democratic revolution, to a rapidly industrializing semi-peripheral nation, to the supreme capitalist core power, and eventually to the declining imperial power we wish to discuss today. This is a history in which the nations and peoples of Latin America have played, and continue to play, a central role.

Latin America:
The Decline of Empire in America's Back Yard

So let us return now to our original question: Gathered here in Managua, how do we understand the current aggressions of the world's most powerful military machine against a Central American nation smaller than almost any of the 50 States in the American Union? We understand that the entire revolutionary process in Central America seriously threatens U.S. influence, and therefore transnational corporate interests, in what have long been perceived as the most secure territories of the American Empire.

It was two decades after the triumph of the Cuban Revolution before any new crack appeared in U.S. hegemony over the Americas. But today the entire Central American region is in revolutionary upheaval, threatening to break free of the neocolonial sphere originally staked out in the Monroe Doctrine. Despite an increasingly Vietnam-like intervention, the U.S. has been unable to overthrow the Sandinista Revolution in Nicaragua or to crush the revolutionary movements in El Salvador and Guatemala. Now there is a growing possibility that El Salvador will soon join Cuba and Nicaragua as an entire network of sovereign, socialist states. Supported by the one world power willing to support them, the Soviet Union, this bloc of young socialist states would greatly strengthen the potential of the socialist sector of the world-economy and would represent the first viable alternative to fascism, counterinsurgency, and neocolonial domination in Latin America. The likelihood that these developments will continue to unfold quite rapidly is far greater than could have been imagined 20 years ago.

If this is true, then we can also see a not-too-distant future in which Mexico, the largest, wealthiest, and most developed nation of the region, remains the only buffer between the United States and an entire zone of popular revolution. Yet, in reality, Mexico represents not a stable buffer, but the penultimate revolution. Wracked by economic crisis, half of Mexico's workforce is underemployed; the country owes over $80 billion to the transnational banks, and it barely avoided default on its loans in 1982—a situation which called into question the future of the entire world financial system.

Further, beyond Mexico and Central America, the waves of revolutionary movement have spread south to Colombia, Peru, Bolivia, Chile, Argentina, and even Brazil. For more than a decade, the peoples of much of South America have appeared effectively silenced by the series of U.S.-backed military coups imposed to crush the powerful workers' movements of the '60s and '70s. Today there are growing guerrilla movements in Peru and Colombia, communists in the government of Bolivia, mounting protests against austerity in Brazil, a renewed labor movement in Argentina, and a mass movement which threatens to topple the CIA-created Pinochet regime in Chile.

Throughout Latin America, we are indeed witnessing the demise of empire, the breakup of America's self-proclaimed sphere of influence. For the United States, the loss of Central America alone, not to mention the other key nations of South America and eventually even Mexico, would be comparable to Britain's loss of India and the African colonies. We are no longer talking about the loss of a single, relatively isolated island in the Caribbean. We are now talking about the potential loss of control over nearly $10 billion in direct investment by U.S.-based corporations in Mexico and Central America. We are talking about more than 1,400 at least partially U.S.-owned businesses in Central America. Over half of the 500 top U.S.-based manufacturing companies have Mexican manufacturing operations. Mexico and Guatemala have oil reserves now conceivably even surpassing Saudi Arabia in their long-term potential (Baird and McCaughan, 1979; and The Resource Center, 1982.) The Panama Canal continues to be a strategic element in control of world commerce.

Ronald Reagan may believe his own ideological rhetoric about the "Soviet threat" in Central America, but the men behind him—the executives of Citicorp, Exxon, Bank of America, and General Motors—view Central America in terms of dollars and cents. In their minds, Reagan's job is not to save the Central American people from the evils of communism but to save their long-cherished and lucrative base of operations from the Central American people. It is not an issue of East vs. West; it is an issue of popular sovereignty vs. the ability of the transnationals to continue their uninhibited looting of an entire continent. And this is the issue which, in fact, has informed all of U.S. foreign policy for the past four decades.

To be sure, this is not the first time that the ability of transnational corporations to control investments, resources, and markets has been challenged by Latin American revolutions or popular movements. In the past, as we have seen, the U.S. government, as a representative of U.S.-based transnational capital, has more often than not successfully intervened to stop such challenges. Today, however, the contradictions posed by declining hegemony make it increasingly difficult for the U.S. to control developments even in the Western Hemisphere.

Let us now take Mexico and Brazil as two cases in point. Mexico now has a foreign debt of some $80 billion; Brazil owes an estimated $90 billion. Neither country is able to pay, a fact which quite literally threatens the entire capitalist financial structure with collapse, given the depth of the current generalized economic crisis. The IMF thus has intervened in both countries, demanding imposition of austerity policies as a condition for further credit, as it has done many times before in many other countries. But the IMF's ability to impose austerity cannot be so readily taken for granted as it was a few years ago. U.S. banks, which are the principal suppliers of credit, have little option but to pump yet more money into Brazil in order not to lose everything. The magazine *Business Week* has said that to avoid pushing Brazil into default, the IMF may well have to disburse more money, despite Brazil's failures to comply with agreements. Should that happen, *Business Week* warns, "Mexico, Argentina, Peru and other debtors in equally desperate straits will demand that the Fund ease austerity measures imposed on them as a condition for getting similar bailouts" (*Business Week*, 1983:27). Thus, in the context of the current crisis of capitalism, while the banks certainly wield great power, the threat of default gives countries like Brazil and Mexico—if they are willing to use it in a united and decisive manner—an enormously powerful weapon with which to force concessions out of the banks and core nations.

The example of Brazil's foreign debt underscores still another aspect of declining U.S. hegemony and inter-imperialist rivalry in the region: The United States' traditional European allies no longer fall into line as they once did. Despite pleas from the U.S. Treasury, Federal Reserve Board, and the IMF, many Central European banks are unwilling to extend Brazil any new credits (*Business Week*, 1983: 28). European-based capital, and therefore European governments, have their own cards to play. This has been true not only in the case of the Brazilian debt, but more generally in regards to overall U.S. policy in Central America. Twenty years ago, the U.S. had a considerably easier time getting its allies to respect its sanctions against the Cuban Revolution than it now has gaining support for its intervention in Nicaragua and El Salvador.

Behind this example also lies the fact that in an era of transnational capital, while there are still tremendous advantages to having a powerful U.S. government to act as the world's policeman, corporations no longer rely exclusively on one nation-state to mediate their interests globally. Transnational capital now operates through a system of nation-states with which it shares a dual power relationship (Dixon, 1982: 129-46).

In the case of Central America, the transnational ruling class, regardless of its national base, has a convergence of interests in opposing socialist revolution. Yet, within that convergence of interests there are also differences. U.S.-based transnational capital, given its long historic involvement in Latin America, likely has more at stake in preserving the status quo than does European-based capital, which perhaps can more easily see the possibility of a lucrative role in a Central America that does not depend on the perpetuation of client dictatorships. Thus transnational capital hedges its bets in Central America and appears to back Reagan's attempts to militarily control the region while simultaneously supporting European Social Democracy's attempts to influence the political outcome of the conflict. Such eroded influence in what for so long were considered by U.S. policymakers as subservient banana republics is surely sufficient to strike fear in the heart of the imperial center, and even more so when we consider the broader world context in which the Central American crisis has developed.

World Capitalist Crisis and the Limits of U.S. Power

Today, 160 years after the Monroe Doctrine and 40 years since the U.S. emerged from World War II as the hegemonic power in the world-system, the ability of the U.S. government to unilaterally impose its will is increasingly constrained not only in Latin America but throughout the world. The limitations facing the U.S. Empire stem from four factors:

1) The world crisis in capitalist accumulation, which has resulted in the steady decline in competitive strength of the U.S. national economy; furthermore, the U.S.-based transnational banking system is heavily compromised by the debts of the less-developed countries (LDC's) and the danger of massive defaults;

2) Alterations in the relative positions of core states within the context of inter-imperialist rivalries, a situation that has produced a competitive failure of U.S. manufacturing and export strength;

3) The spread of economically competing socialism, as new revolutions in Asia, Africa, and Latin America have strengthened the socialist sector of the world-economy; and

4) Domestic opposition to intervention, as the United States emerged from Vietnam drained and defeated, with the majority of U.S. people united in opposition to more Vietnams; furthermore, the looting of the domestic economy, which was a result of the Vietnam intervention with the resulting domestic crisis of profitability, has led to the imposition of austerity capitalism upon the industrial working class and the massive erosion of the service sector of the government. In this way, the implosion of empire has indeed resulted in the imposition of IMF austerity measures upon the people of the U.S., a fate heretofore reserved for the masses of the LDC's. The "implosion" of empire and its consequences have led to a popular concern with the fate of the economy and strong anti-war, anti-intervention sentiments.

The decline of U.S. imperial power and growing domestic opposition after Vietnam meant that the U.S. government no longer had the power to set the terms of its relations with other countries unilaterally. U.S. options were more limited, and the U.S. as a world power was no longer able to force its will unrestrainedly on other nations through instant and direct military intervention, as it had been able to do in literally hundreds of instances up through the 1965 Dominican Republic intervention and the Vietnam War itself. This situation gave rise to a new imperialist tactic, neo-imperialism: the practice of extending control or domination over nations by means and actions of other client nations. Thus, particularly beginning in the mid-'60s, the U.S. attempted to develop a group of regional subimperial powers, that is, nations subject to a larger power and which act in the interests of that power to subordinate lesser powers. Concretely, the U.S. attempted to develop subimperial client regimes in three regions of the empire: the Middle East (Israel, Saudi Arabia, and Iran), Africa (South Africa), and Latin America (Brazil).

Tremendous economic and particularly military aid were poured into these nations to guarantee their ability to carry out the dirty work no longer politically feasible for the U.S. to implement directly. Not only did domestic opposition in the U.S. make direct intervention untenable, but the reality of super-power rivalry in a nuclear age encouraged the U.S. to avoid direct confrontation with the Soviet Union—at least, this was the case up through the Gerald Ford administration.

The experiment with neo-imperialism, however, has been a dismal failure. Iran has since removed itself from the U.S. orbit, and Brazil and Saudi Arabia are increasingly undependable as they confront their own internal and international contradictions. South Africa is of limited value because its brutal, unashamed racism has so isolated the apartheid regime internationally. That leaves Israel as the principal remaining subimperialist client, carrying out its function not only in the Middle East but even in Central America, where it provides arms, training, and/or technical assistance to the repressive Guatemalan, Honduran, and Salvadoran dictatorships and to the counterrevolution in Nicaragua. Thus since Vietnam the United States has been increasingly unable to contain revolution, either by direct intervention or through subimperialist powers.

The Suez Syndrome

If on the one hand declining U.S. hegemony and increasingly international isolation have weakened the U.S. government's ability to unilaterally impose its will, they have also produced a U.S. government which increasingly threatens world peace as it declines from the apex of imperialist power to unbridled militarism. With Reagan's recent actions in Central America and the Middle East, one is reminded of the Suez Canal Crisis and the mad, last-ditch effort of another declining power to preserve its shrinking influence. As we said in the opening quotation from *Contemporary Marxism:*

History has dark lessons for us concerning the last convulsive throes of falling empires. The habits of empire, when empire begins to fail, seem to produce a fatal refusal to admit that one is losing the game and a suicidal recklessness provoked by power entering senility (Dixon, 1981-82: 2).

In the 1950s, Egyptian President Gamal-al-Nasser's growing prestige as a Third World leader and his nationalization of the Suez Canal threatened Britain's already diminished influence in the Arab world. Allying with France, which feared Nasser's support of the Algerian revolution, and using Israel's invasion of Egypt as a pretext, Britain intervened in Egypt, threatening the world with a new war. Internationally, Britain hoped events in Hungary would serve as a distraction, and domestically, efforts were made to stir up war fever with racist, antiforeigner propaganda. The Suez intervention was generally justified by England as drawing the line against fascism in Egypt, a ludicrous attempt to equate Nasser's nationalism with fascism in order to mask the reality of a naked imperialist adventure.

Britain's intervention, however, was a dismal failure. Even the U.S. opposed Britain's actions, as the new world power sought to increase its own influence in the Middle East by establishing relations with Arab regimes. Opposition became more consolidated inside England as well, with Parliament seriously divided. Britain was finally forced to declare a cease-fire, having failed to re-establish its control over the Canal.

Thus, the suicidal character of falling empires stems from a regression to earlier forms of direct military intervention, almost as if it were symbolically essential to invoke images of past glory. Yet, these inevitably doomed militarist adventures serve only to prove finally and irrevocably that power will not rise phoenix-like from the ruins. It is this last, convulsive invocation of power that we term the "Suez Syndrome," after Eden's catastrophe at Suez.

Similar to Britain's failure in the Suez Crisis, the relative weakness of the current U.S. situation, in spite of Reagan's loud barks and toothless bites, reflects the dependence which a military power has on the economic power of its principals. The world runs on wealth, not guns. As economic supremacy is eroded, all the gunboats and "carrier battle groups" in the world will not re-establish what has been lost. What the Suez Syndrome, the crazed thrashing of a senile power, *can* do is launch a nuclear war, by accident, design, or stupidity, which could spell catastrophe for all life as we know it on the entire planet.

Nonetheless, Reagan seems incapable of learning from history. Instead, this demagogue of American conservatism seems determined to create his own Suez. On one side of the globe he has surrounded Central America with gunboats and armed Honduras to the teeth for a possible provocative invasion of Nicaragua. On the other side of the world he has U.S. Marines and warships shelling Beirut and pushing the Soviets to the very edge of war by firing on Syrian positions, all because America's subimperialist ally, Israel, can no longer politically maintain the occupation of Lebanon, and Reagan has completely alienated the Arab world.

As Reagan and his administration pursue their policy of military adventurism, they do so without the consent of the American people. Reagan acts only because he exploits the near-monarchical powers which are invested in a President of the United States, urged on by hard-line right-wingers such as former National Security Adviser William Clark, and completely unhampered by a gutless U.S. Congress. Yet such is the madness of his most recent Suez Syndrome actions that some voices of concern are being heard even from among the ruling elites themselves. Like the industrialists and bankers who supported Hitler, wrongly believing they could control him while his dictatorship pulled Germany out of depression, significant transnational corporate representatives are now beginning to be frightened by their own creature, and are appealing to Reagan for moderation. Witness Robert McNamara's recent statements calling for prudence in any response to the Soviets.

This does not mean that the transnationals have abandoned Reagan; Shultz is still Secretary of State, even if his power over foreign policy has been at least temporarily eclipsed by archconservatives Clark and Kirkpatrick. The transnationals are still hedging their bets with Reagan, waiting to see what he can do. After all, he is still the Ronald Reagan whose domestic policies allowed deregulation, fewer controls on monopolies, the facilitation of mergers, bail-outs, and increased military spending. So who knows, they no doubt reason, perhaps Reagan will save Central America for the Empire after all, perhaps he will reassert U.S. influence in the Middle East. If not, there are agents other than Ronald Reagan to whom the transnationals can turn.

Ronald Reagan's Suez. . .Where?

In the meantime, however, we have a declining empire in the hands of a provincial, self-important spokesman of American conservatism who is perfectly capable of taking the world to nuclear war to fulfill his megalomanic dream of historic fame and power as the ultimate savior of the American Empire. Where might Ronald Reagan's Suez occur? There are two quite likely possibilities: 1) the Middle East, where Reagan threatens to engage Syria in a war, and 2) Central America, where Reagan has been pumping for a war with Nicaragua for many months. A foreign enemy is needed to support a policy of militarism. Reagan's search for a "Falklands" sure-fire vote-getting issue leads him to attack Nicaragua and Syria, hoping they will prove to be convenient paper tigers, as was Argentina to Thatcher; unfortunately this leads him into risking confrontation with the Soviet Union, hardly a paper tiger. In only a few short weeks, he has detained Soviet ships in the Caribbean, carried out the most irresponsible provocation with the Korean airliner incident, and fired upon Syrian forces in the Middle East.

Increasingly isolated internationally and facing growing opposition to his war policies at home, Reagan now attempts to turn the Korean airliner tragedy into a platform for his militarism. What was very likely a spy mission set up to provoke the Soviets has become part of Reagan's futile efforts to justify war against any and all opposition to the maintenance of U.S. influence and thus any threat to the operations of U.S.-based transnational corporate power. And all the while attacking the Soviets, Reagan suddenly appears as the "peace maker," issuing statements about arms reduction in a context in which the Soviets can hardly be expected to believe the sincerity of such phony gestures.

Thus far the Soviets have acted with admirable restraint, in the face of the most provocative and taunting adventurism. Indeed, it is quite plausible that what allows Reagan a provocative and often hysterical anti-Sovietism is Washington's conviction that the Soviet Union will not, in fact, allow itself to be provoked into military retaliation. Does it never occur to the cretinous reactionaries around Reagan that they have opposite numbers in the Soviet apparat? Nonetheless, the entire process of arms control, peaceful coexistence, and reduction and eventual elimination of nuclear weapons is strangled and set back by the present reactionary administration. In the midst of all the hypocritical hysteria over the destruction of a Korean aircraft trespassing on highly sensitive airspace, we must remind ourselves, and others, that it is the Soviet Union that is keeping the peace, not the United States. Furthermore, we must remind ourselves that nuclear war is indeed a very real possibility. As Sidney Lens recently wrote (Lens, 1983: 202):

> On at least seventeen occasions the United States came to the brink of nuclear war. Five times we came close by accident. Nine times we threatened or planned a limited nuclear strike — twice during the Korean conflict, three times during the Vietnam War, during the civil war in Laos, the 1958 Lebanon crisis and the 1961 Berlin crisis, and in 1955 to hold the islands of Quemoy and Matsu for the Nationalist Chinese. Three times we were eyeball to eyeball with the Russians: in 1946, when Truman said he would order nuclear attacks on Soviet territory if they didn't get out of Azerbaijan; in 1962, during the Cuban missile crisis; and in 1973, during the Yom Kippur war, when the United States declared a Defense Condition 2 alert in the Mediterranean — one step from war — after the Russians sent warheads to Egypt because the Israelis were not adhering to a cease-fire agreement.

If the world's final war is to be prevented, the world community of nations must isolate Reagan internationally, as they did Great Britain during the Suez Crisis, condemn his war policies, and defend the sovereignty of the peoples against whom he has unleashed history's deadliest war machine. At the present time, progressives must see that the hope for world peace lies in the Soviet Union's ability to remain firm and unprovokable. At the present conjuncture, with Washington pursuing reckless militarist policies (and Reagan obsessed with re-election fever), the truly moderate force we must hope for would be (and has been) the Soviet Union's refusal to be provoked into nuclear, or even conventional military confrontation with the United States. However, while it is our hope that the Soviet leadership can maintain its present restraint in the face of Reagan's provocations, we must also recognize that unforeseen changes may occur within the Soviet leadership or in response to Soviet public opinion. There may be changes necessitating an alteration of Soviet foreign policy with respect to the United States and Reagan's interventionist actions, particularly in regard to the Middle East or to Cuba and Central America. A U.S. Suez Syndrome indeed threatens not only the peace, but the very survival of the world.

Conclusion

In the process of its decline, the empire of the United States has turned inward on itself—on its own people—and we live in a new era. This is the era of the implosion of empire, in which the people of the U.S. will begin to experience what has been the fate of the colony and the neocolony. As we wrote earlier in the foreword to *Revolution and Intervention in Central America* (Dixon and Jonas, 1983: i-ii):

> There were those Liberals in the United States who thought that a Republican Administration would be more moderate in foreign policy than the Democrats. The Liberals were wrong, they did not perceive that the forces of reaction in the United States were growing with malignant intelligence, that the collapse and impotence of the Democrats and of New Deal liberalism put no brake, no restraint, upon what is transparently a government of the right wing of the domestic corporate ruling class. Yet, it does not rule alone, that is also clear. In the United States we have at last a government that is direct rule by capital, a United Front of capital no longer hampered by the populism of a failing Democratic Party.

> So it has come to pass that the outward face of the United States, the face of the imperialists, the face of CIA, Special Forces, the face of transnational capital, that face has now turned inward to confront the masses of the people in the United States. It is the *implosion* of Empire, it is the very beginning of an era in which the people of the United States will begin to see the democratic veils stripped away from the face of American power, they will begin to experience what has been the fate of the colony. It seems to me that the people of the United States have fulfilled a prophecy: First they came for the communists, but I was not a communist so I did not protest; then they came for the Jews, but I was not a Jew so I did not protest; then they came for the Catholics, but I was not a Catholic so I did not protest; and then they came for me, and there was no one left to protest.

With the worldwide economic crisis, with the efforts of transnational corporations to restore their profit levels at any price, with the frantic attempts to restore U.S. hegemony in the world, it is not only the peoples of other nations who have been made to suffer but also the people of the United States itself. In the U.S., unemployment stands at the highest rate in decades, the standard of living sinks, two million people are homeless, wages are cut, and workers are forced to accept increasingly miserable conditions on the job. The repression and terror in Central America are accompanied by rising repression in the U.S.; there is a war against domestic labor as well as the international war of the U.S. against workers' movements. As the Cold War, America's first offensive against "international communism," was accompanied by McCarthyism and the destruction of the CPUSA, as the war in Vietnam was accompanied by COINTELPRO, domestic surveillance, and repression of the Left, so, too, is Reagan's new militarism accompanied by renewed efforts to control domestic unrest. Thus Reagan's unqualified support of the CIA and FBI and the administration's systematic erosion of basic civil liberties. Indeed, the democratic veils have begun to be stripped away from the Janus-headed face of U.S. power.

Clearly, we live in an era of tremendous contradiction, an era of great hope and danger. There are spaces provided by the demise of America's Empire which, if we are bold and intelligent, can be used to advance our shared cause of peace and sovereignty. At the same time there are great dangers of holocaust and devastation, and we must avoid all provocation without compromising our ultimate goals.

The people of the United States carry a heavy burden during this period. We must mobilize public opinion—which already opposes Reagan's militarism—into effective action against intervention; we must stand firm in our belief that the defense of the Central American revolutions is the defense of a just and reasonable future for us all. There is much to do, too few to do it, and certainly no time for sectarianism within the solidarity movement to stand in the way of all new efforts to organize against intervention. The U.S. government, as a representative of transnational capital, has defended the world's most brutal and subservient right-wing dictators. A U.S. government that was responsive to and generally represented the will of the American people would be a defender of freedom and popular sovereignty, and such a government must be our ultimate aim.

For Latin America, the present period will require united, decisive actions by all nations that retain any semblance of independence from Washington. Reagan must be isolated and Latin America must be united in its defense of Nicaragua and the popular movements throughout the Americas, especially in El Salvador. Those nations which put such faith in their own ability to play both sides of the fence with U.S. imperialism should rethink the lessons that our common history has provided. Finally, the debtor nations of the world must act together, using the potential weapon of default, to challenge once and for all the stranglehold of transnational capitalist power wielded so ruthlessly by the banks and funding agencies.

The Empire which has so long enslaved the peoples of the Americas is indeed losing its grip. If we are wise, the future can be ours, a future in which, as Carlos Fonseca Amador once said, "The dawn is no longer a temptation."

REFERENCES

Baird, Peter and Ed McCaughan
    1979   Beyond the Border: Mexico and the U.S. Today. New York: NACLA.
Business Week
    1983   (June 6), pp. 27-28.
Dixon, Marlene
    1982   "Dual Power: The Rise of the Transnational Corporation and the Nation-State:
            Conceptual Explanations to Meet Popular Demand," Contemporary Marxism 5,
            pp. 129-46.
    1981-82 "World Capitalist Crisis and the Rise of the Right," Contemporary Marxism 4,
            pp. 1-10.
Dixon, Marlene and Susanne Jonas (eds.)
    1983   Revolution and Intervention in Central America. San Francisco: Synthesis
            Publications.
Greene, Felix
    1971   The Enemy: What Every American Should Know About Imperialism. New York:
            Vintage Books.
Lens, Sidney
    1983   "A Law of Nations: World Government Reconsidered," The Nation (Sep-
            tember 17), p. 201-05.
Northedge, F.S.
    1962   British Foreign Policy: The Process of Readjustment, 1945-1961. London: George
            Allen and Unwin, Ltd.
Resource Center, The
    1982   Dollars and Dictators.

*Information for Charts 1 and 2 was gathered from the following sources: Douglas F. Dowd, *The Twisted Dream: Capitalist Development in the United States Since 1776* (Cambridge, Mass.: Winthrop Publishers, Inc., 1977); Andre Fontaine, *History of the Cold War: From the Korean War to the Present* (New York: Vintage Books, 1970); Felix Greene, *The Enemy: What Every American Should Know About Imperialism* (New York: Vintage Books, 1971); F.S. Northedge, *British Foreign Policy: The Process of Readjustment, 1945-1961* (London: George Allen and Unwin, Ltd., Ruskin House, 1962); *Plain Speaking* (San Francisco, January 16-31, 1982)

PART I

Reagan's Escalating War: From Economic Strangulation to CIA Attack

A Chronology of U.S. Efforts to Overthrow the Nicaraguan Government

Reprinted and updated from U.S. Out of Central America (USOCA) "Prepare Now: After Grenada, Nicaragua May Be Next" (San Francisco: USOCA, November 12, 1983).

When Reagan finally decided to invade Grenada, many of us had already forgotten that CIA plots to overthrow the Grenadian government had been revealed months earlier in major U.S. news media. Should the U.S. government, or its military clients operating out of Honduras, invade Nicaragua, we have little excuse for surprise or shock. Since the Sandinistas came to power in July 1979, actions have been taken by the U.S. almost every month to destabilize, terrorize, intimidate, isolate, and overthrow the government of this sovereign nation. Following is a partial chronology of these efforts—a stark reminder to all of us that Ronald Reagan is not one to hesitate in embarking on dangerous, militarist adventures.

1979-80
The $8.9 million credit allocated to Somoza by the Import-Export Bank is reduced to $40,000. The Bank suspends guarantees for financing Nicaraguan imports, especially affecting the purchase of spare parts.

February 1981
The U.S. State Department releases a "white paper" depicting Nicaragua as the epicenter for arms traffic to Salvadoran insurgents.

The payment of $15 million as part of a $75 million credit is suspended by the U.S.

March 1981
Parade magazine discloses that ex-Somoza Guardsmen are being trained in the U.S. for paramilitary attacks on Nicaragua.

$10 million credit for wheat purchases within the PL 480 program is suspended.

April 1981
Indefinite suspension of all future bilateral assistance is announced due to supposed arms traffic to El Salvador; $11.4 million credit for rural development and educational and health care programs is suspended.

June 1981
In apparent response to widespread rejection of U.S. charges against Nicaragua contained in February "white paper," Secretary of State Haig raises new charge that Nicaragua has received Soviet tanks. Press criticism of "white paper" allegations stops.

August 1981
Honduras grants permission to the U.S. to build a military base in the Gulf of Fonseca, a body of water shared by Nicaragua, Honduras, and El Salvador.

September 1981
Joint U.S.-Honduran military maneuvers are held.

October 1981
U.S. naval maneuvers off coast of Nicaragua.

November 1981
Reagan administration intensifies charges and threats against Nicaragua. Secretary of State Haig tells members of Congress that Nicaragua is becoming a powerful totalitarian state which threatens U.S interests; refuses to rule out military action against Nicaragua.

Regular Honduran troops attack the Nicaraguan border post at Guasaule on two separate occasions, using machine guns and mortars.

December 1981
President Reagan authorizes a $19 million CIA-directed plan for paramilitary and terrorist operations against Nicaragua. In apparent initial implementation of this plan, terrorist attacks, code-named "Red Christmas," are launched in Nicaragua's remote northeast border area. Other immediate targets of attack are Nicaragua's only oil refinery and cement plant.

U.S. representative to the World Bank vetoes a $500,000 project proposal for the development of agricultural cooperatives.

Bomb explodes on AeroNica plane.

1982
U.S. threatens to cut meat imports from Nicaragua if it buys Cuban purebred studs.

January 1982
After meetings with U.S. Under Secretary of State James Buckley in San José, Costa Rica, the foreign ministers of Costa Rica, El Salvador, and Honduras announce the "surprise" formation of the "Central American Democratic Community." Nicaragua and Panama, among others, are excluded from the meeting.

CIA plot to blow up a Nicaraguan refinery and a cement factory and to assassinate Comandante Leticia Herrera is revealed.

February 1982
U.S. pressure on World Bank leads it to take unilateral actions against

Nicaragua, suspending the credit program and requesting an economic stabilization program.

Increased intelligence activity by planes and ships against Nicaragua; Defense Secretary Caspar Weinberger secretly negotiates with Honduras and Colombia to establish U.S. bases.

Steadman Fagoth, leader of Miskito Indians, goes to Washington, D.C., for the State Department; blames Sandinistas for massacre of Indians using photos that in fact date from 1978 while Somoza was still in power and were taken by the Red Cross.

Terrorist bombing at Managua Airport.

March 1982
The U.S. government launches a major public relations effort to demonstrate the threat posed by Nicaragua. The effort fails to demonstrate that Nicaraguan military dispositions are anything more than defensive.

U.S. announces presence of 72 U.S. military personnel in Honduras and Honduran General Gustavo Alvarez authorizes the transit of U.S. troops through Honduran territory.

March-June 1982
106 *contra* attacks in Nicaragua, including sabotage of bridges, warehouses, and crops; sniper fire against Sandinista soldiers.

May 1982
U.S. press reports reveal that CIA-backed counterrevolutionaries in Honduras are being directed by U.S. Ambassador to Honduras John Negroponte.

July 1982
Paramilitary attacks on Nicaragua increase dramatically.

Joint U.S.-Honduran military maneuvers are held near Nicaragua's remote northeast border. U.S. planes move equipment and a battalion of Honduran troops to a new permanent base in the border area.

September 1982
Lt. Col. John Buchanan, USMC (Ret.), briefs a House subcommittee on the critical border tension between Honduras and Nicaragua. In a detailed analysis of Nicaragua's military capability, Buchanan describes Nicaragua's "military buildup" as defensive in nature. He also warns of a possible Honduran invasion of Nicaragua in December. Buchanan states that his assessment of Nicaraguan military leads him to conclude that the capabilities of the Sandinistas have been deliberately exaggerated by the Reagan administration. "One can only conclude that the Reagan administration is distorting the facts in order to justify covert operations aimed at overthrowing the Sandinistas and an unprecedented military buildup in Honduras," says Buchanan.

October 1982
Standard Fruit Company reneges on its commitment to market Nicaragua's banana exports.

November 1982

Newsweek magazine reveals extensive details of the U.S. paramilitary war on Nicaragua. U.S. officials confirm that the operation is intended to "keep Managua off balance and apply pressure."

December 1982

U.S. President Reagan designs his Latin American trip to include visits with the leaders of all three countries neighboring Nicaragua. Nicaraguan leader Sergio Ramírez points out that U.S. diplomats continue to refuse to see high-level Sandinista officials. The U.S. has still not responded to Nicaragua's last diplomatic note of August 1982 urging peace talks. The U.S. also continues to oppose peace talks between Nicaragua and Honduras.

Boland amendment passes House 411-0. This forbids the use of "military equipment, military training or advice, or other support for military activities... for the purpose of overthrowing the Government of Nicaragua or provoking a military exchange between Nicaragua and Honduras."

January 1983

Terrorist attacks against Nicaraguan civilian population increase; on January 16, 60 ex-Guardsmen armed with rifles, mortars, and grenade launchers attack 200 coffee pickers at Namasli, 24 kilometers from Honduras.

Two days before initiation of Big Pine maneuvers, 120 ex-Guardsmen launch amphibious attack on Bismuna, only 6 miles from Honduran border, and near the site of planned U.S.-Honduras parachute drop.

February 1983

1,600 U.S. troops and 4,000 Honduran troops participate in Big Pine maneuvers. C-130 transports move $5.2 million worth of equipment to Mocoron, 25 miles from Nicaragua's Atlantic Coast border. U.S. press reports subsequently reveal that these arms were transferred by Honduran Army to ex-Guardsmen.

Ex-Guardsmen ambush and kill 17 members of Sandinista Youth Militia contingent, who are protecting coffee pickers near Matagalpa; 50,000 Nicaraguans attend memorial service in Managua two days later.

March 1983

Major invasion of Nicaragua begins by 1,200 ex-Guardsmen who have infiltrated from Honduras in "Task Forces" of 200-300 men. Initial press reports quote exaggerated claims from counterrevolutionary Radio September 15. Heavy casualties suffered by invaders as Sandinista Army disperses their forces. A French physician studying mountain leprosy (cutaneous leishmaniasis) is killed when scattered Guardsmen attack Rancho Grande. Minister of Defense Humberto Ortega says that ex-Guardsmen are not a serious threat, but that the real danger is the attempt to provoke war with Honduras. Nicaragua reports several episodes of artillery fire by Honduran Army against border posts.

Nicaragua denounces invasion as U.S.-supported in U.N. Security Council.

U.S. Representative Jeane Kirkpatrick says that fighting is an internal Nicaraguan problem; 55 nations support Nicaragua's position; only El Salvador and Honduras side with the U.S.

April 1983

An April 6 *New York Times* article discusses leaked National Security Planning Group document from April 1982 detailing Central America policy projections. Provisions include: efforts to counteract Social Democratic and Mexican opposition to U.S. policy; progaganda and economic pressures against Cuba; continuation of covert activities against Nicaragua; attempts to stir "factional strife" among Salvadoran Left; and avoidance of congressionally mandated negotiations.

In the wake of the March invasion, U.S. major media expose in detail U.S. role in covert war. April 4 *Time* magazine places top direction of operation with CIA and U.S. Army in Panama, who relay instructions to Honduran high command via U.S. Ambassador John Negroponte. They in turn direct FDN general staff composed of former National Guard officers. According to April 18 *Time,* U.S. aid to FDN includes "supplying training, arms and intelligence on troop movements in Nicaragua's northern provinces gathered by spy plane."

Jack Anderson reveals U.S.-Israeli development plan along Costa Rica's northern border with Nicaragua, which includes road-building and the establishment of new settlements. Costa Rican opposition alleges that project is part of plan to destabilize Nicaragua.

House Intelligence Committee calls for end to covert aid to ex-National Guardsmen. Numerous congressmen declare that covert aid is in clear violation of Boland amendment.

President Reagan addresses joint session of Congress; he declares that "The national security of the Americas is at stake in Central America." Nicaragua, Cuba, and the Soviet Union are accused of exporting revolution. President denies U.S. is attempting to overthrow the Sandinistas and draws standing ovation for saying, "There is no thought for sending U.S. combat troops to Central America."

In Democratic rebuttal of Reagan's speech, Senator Dodd states, "The Administration fundamentally misunderstands the causes of the conflict in Central America...this Administration has turned to massive military buildups...its policy is ever-increasing military assistance...it only leads to a dark tunnel of endless intervention."

Ex-Guardsmen launch new attack from Honduras two days after speech, killing in cold blood 13 civilians, including two nurses and a West German physician, at a roadblock. West German internationalists in Nicaragua occupy their embassy, asking that their government protest U.S. support of ex-Guardsmen.

May 1983

April 29 Harris poll released, showing U.S. public to be against

U.S. policy by two to one. Harris describes the results as "a solid rejection" of a policy which is perceived as militarist and lacking any possibility of success.

U.S. reduces quota of sugar bought from Nicaragua by 90%.

House subcommittee votes 9-5 to prohibit covert aid against Nicaragua; simultaneously approves $80 million in overt aid to "friendly countries" for arms interdiction. Senate votes to continue covert aid until October 1983, with provision requesting Presidential consultation.

Armed attacks from Costa Rica are begun. Eden Pastora's group ARDE murders 11 *campesinos* near San Carlos; other families are threatened with death if they refuse to join or assist ARDE. A ferry boat donated by West Germany is destroyed in the Rio San Juan. Three West Germans traveling on river to photograph ruined boat are attacked; one is killed and two are kidnapped. ARDE announces capture of two "East German military advisers."

Administration announces plans to send 100 Green Berets to Honduras to train 2,000 Salvadoran troops. U.S. will also man new radar station near Tegucigalpa.

Lt. General Wallace Nutting, head of U.S. Southern Command in Panama, says that an open-ended increase in U.S. involvement is needed to "stop Marxist expansion."

June 1983
Three U.S. diplomats are implicated in plan to assassinate Nicaraguan Foreign Affairs Minister Fr. Miguel d'Escoto.

July 1983
U.S. sends 19 ships with 16,456 troops and dozens of fighter jets to the coasts of Nicaragua; also sends 4,000 U.S. ground troops for Honduras—operation is called Big Pine II.

Reagan appoints Henry Kissinger to head a Commission on Central America.

House of Representatives votes down covert aid by passing the Boland-Zablocki bill.

September 1983
The International Airport in Managua is bombed, as is the home of Foreign Minister Miguel d'Escoto.

The port of Benjamín Zeledón on the Atlantic Coast is bombed, destroying 400,000 gallons of diesel fuel as well as the oil supply for the Department of Zelaya.

Oil unloading facilities at Puerto Sandino are destroyed in a CIA-directed *contra* attack.

Destruction of public buildings, homes, and trucks at El Espino.

A border post near Honduras is destroyed by mortar shells fired by

Honduran army which was providing cover for *contra* forces.

200 *contras* attack Nicaraguan customs installation at Peñas Blancas on the Costa Rican border after bombing a Nicaraguan army post nearby; Costa Rican authorities pull back leaving area clear for the mercenaries.

October 1983

Attack on port of Corinto destroys 3.2 million gallons of gasoline and oil, and hundreds of tons of food and medicine.

Attack on oil pipelines at Puerto Sandino, which leads to ESSO refusing to ship oil to Nicaragua.

Daniel Ortega, Coordinator of the Government of National Reconstruction of Nicaragua, declares a state of emergency.

Attack by ex-National Guardsmen on town of Pantasma, killing 47 people and causing $2 million in damages.

House again votes down covert aid; vote now passes to the Senate.

The administrator of the Nicaraguan Medical Supply Center denounces that the presence of North American naval ships off the coasts of Nicaragua is stopping the arrival of medicine to the country. As a result of the refusal to grant loans to Nicaragua by international lending organizations, the Ministry of Health has a deficit of $10 million for medical equipment and supplies.

November 1983

U.S invades Grenada with 6,000 troops and occupies the country.

Over 50 incursions by Honduran planes into Nicaraguan airspace to provoke antiaircraft reaction.

Nicaraguan fishing boat burned; crew kidnapped.

Propaganda intensifies in Honduras about Nicaraguan invasion of Honduras.

Many stories circulate about impending invasion, troop buildup on Honduran border of *contras,* troop buildup of Hondurans and Guatemalans on Salvadoran border.

Senate approves covert aid; sent to Conference Committee, composed of members of the House and Senate Intelligence Committees.

5,000 U.S. troops begin amphibious landing exercises in Honduras.

The Central American Defense Council studies legality of joint military action against Nicaragua and recommends direct U.S. participation in case of an "extreme crisis."

Edén Pastora travels to U.S. to appeal for more aid for the *contras.*

U.S. denies visa to Tomás Borge.

Damages caused by U.S.-financed attacks against Nicaragua amount to $2 billion; 300 rural schools are forced to close; 53 teachers killed; 12 health stations destroyed.

Through November 1983, the counterrevolution claims lives of nearly 800 Nicaraguans; 715 more wounded, 37 disappeared, 433 kidnapped.

Nicaraguan government holds meetings with hierarchy of Catholic Church in effort to reduce their opposition.

U.S. under secretary of Defense meets with military leaders of CONDECA nations.

CIA admits *contras* will not be able to defeat the Sandinista government.

Reagan pocket vetoes certification process of human rights in El Salvador.

December 1983

U.S. and Honduras announce Big Pine III maneuvers to take place in 1984; current maneuvers end in March 1984.

Kissinger Commission visits Mexico and Venezuela; debate reported among commission members over conditioning aid to El Salvador upon an end to right-wing death squad violence.

Nicaragua offers amnesty to people who left the country and to Miskito Indians arrested with the *contras.*

Bishop Salvador Schlaefer joins group of Miskito Indians going to Honduras, resulting in another media event for the propaganda war against Nicaragua.

January 1984

Kissinger Commission releases report calling for $8 billion in aid to Central America, and for continued aid to the *contras;* leaves open the possibility of direct U.S. intervention in Nicaragua. Fails, however, to build bipartisan consensus, and debate continues over military aid and U.S. policy.

Reagan requests additional $250 million in military aid to El Salvador for 1984; seeks $350 million for 1985.

Nicaraguan government announces plans for elections that are scheduled for 1985.

Contra attacks continue by air and sea against agricultural areas, main ports, and fishing boats.

U.S. helicopter violates Nicaraguan airspace and is shot down; pilot is killed; according to *Time* magazine (1/23/84), the helicopter crew was assigned to enlarge a *contra* air base in Honduras, a staging area for *contra* air raids into Nicaragua.

Sources:

Nicaraguan Perspectives 3 (Winter 1982); 5 (Winter 1983); 6 (Summer 1983); *CounterSpy* 6, 3, (May-June 1982); *Central America Alert* 3, 5, and 6; *Barricada International* (June 6, 1983); *La Voz de Nicaragua* (November, December 1983).

The Economic Strangulation of Nicaragua

This is the transcript (translated from Spanish and edited) of a briefing given by officials of the Ministry of Foreign Trade to a delegation organized by U.S. Out of Central America (USOCA) in June 1983. This briefing explains Nicaragua's traditional dependence on trade with the U.S., and the general situation of unequal exchange between Nicaragua and the advanced industrial countries. These factors are the background for the current economic vise being applied against Nicaragua by the United States through acts of economic aggression (cutting off the sugar quota, forcing Nicaragua to divert precious foreign exchange earnings to defense, etc.), also detailed here.

During the period of Somoza's rule, Nicaragua's economy was fundamentally one that fit into the international division of labor by means of its exported goods—chiefly cotton, coffee, bananas, and such minerals as gold and silver. In the case of the mineral products, the transnational corporations were directly involved, basically those representing North American capital. The Somoza group, having political hegemony, also took advantage of the country's natural wealth, appropriating for itself the profits from those exports.

Within this process, certain financial groups consolidated, assuming their place in the chain of intermediaries, both internal and external, in this productive process. So what we have is the formation of a structure, an economic group that appropriated for itself the profits generated by Nicaragua's exports.

Besides the Somoza group, there were two other groups—one which revolved around the Banco de América, and the other associated with the Banco Nicaragüense. It is important to note the existence of these three groups. Before the triumph of the revolution, there was a lot said about the contradictions among the bourgeoisie, and in the last phase of the war, in the two or three years preceding the triumph, the contradictions among those groups had become quite considerable, given the fact that Somoza's group wanted to assure itself the major part of the profits from surplus produced by the country, including the profits from export surplus. These economic groups, with the Somoza group in hegemony, secured for themselves the benefits of the country's role in the international economy—as well as from their relationship with the transnational corporations operating in Nicaragua.

At the same time, these groups, through their financial power and their monopolistic control over the domestic trade apparatus, were then able to build up a chain of internal trade to handle the purchase of cotton, coffee, etc. This forced small producers to sell at very low prices in relation to the going rates on the international market—the difference was largely appropriated by the three financial groupings. This, then, served to reinforce and perpetuate the power of those three financial groups, while at the same time contributing to political domination by the consolidation of a small oligarchy.

That is why we say that foreign trade during the Somoza era was designed to maintain the exploitation of the majority of the population.

Thus, foreign trade is not a neutral apparatus, but a means by which the ruling class consolidates both economic and political power. Furthermore, the profits gained by these ruling sectors in the Somoza era, the foreign currency earned through exports, was spent on a high level of luxury consumption. We have since witnessed how things have changed in that regard.

Furthermore, dollars were sent out of the country, invested in foreign bank accounts bearing the names of people associated with these financial groups; they even invested in enterprises abroad, so that in fact, under Somoza, the foreign exchange earnings generated by the labor of our agricultural producers were not applied towards the economic and social development of Nicaragua.

It is therefore important to address the question of how foreign trade changed under the Popular Sandinista Revolution. Today, in contrast to the past, Nicaragua's foreign trade is designed to correspond to the logic of the majority of the population.

How has this been accomplished? What is the proof of this?

To begin with, there now exists a Ministry of Foreign Trade, as well as enterprises of foreign trade that did not exist before. In the past, anyone could export or import if they wished; and clearly, under these conditions of unrestricted import or export, those who controlled economic power were the ones who could participate in foreign trade, since they managed the channels through which to buy and sell.

Thus, the creation of the Ministry of Foreign Trade and its enterprises signified that the Sandinista government now has the authority to direct, plan, and organize imports and exports with the goal of benefiting the majority of the country's people. Despite this, not all of our foreign trade has been nationalized. The Ministry of Foreign Trade controls approximately 70% of the exports, but there are certain exports managed by other sectors of the state, such as gold and marine products, making a total of approximately 80% of the export trade under state control.

The Ministry of Foreign Trade has its own structure, while in addition there exist seven enterprises in foreign trade that are accountable to the Ministry. They operate with a certain degree of autonomy: the enterprise that exports cotton is ENAL (Empresa Nicaragüense de Algodon); an enterprise exporting coffee, sugar, and bananas; the enterprise that exports meat—ENCAR; EPRES, which exports nontraditional products, such as peanuts, mangoes, ginger, rum, most fruits, and certain manufactured products. There is ENIA, the enterprise which handles the importation of materials for agricultural production, such as agri-chemicals, fertilizers, and organo-phosphates; and the enterprise that imports certain lines of products such as machinery, wire, and steel, milk (as a raw material), and communications products, such as the telephone booths you have seen in several places.

The formation of the Ministry, and especially of the enterprises under its jurisdiction, has helped to break the extensive commercial network that existed in the past. These enterprises buy directly from the producers and sell directly to the international market. In this way, the earnings from foreign trade remain within the national economy. This is a very difficult and complicated task, because in Nicaragua 75% of the coffee comes from small producers; 77% of the cotton comes from small producers; and 90% are small producers in the case of sesame seed.

At the same time, the nationalization of the banks favors the financing of all these small producers throughout the country. It is important to understand that in the case of cotton, for example, we have a crop that is completely dependent on financing, whereby prior to its harvest a payment has to be made to the farmer before production can be realized. It follows that both a nationalized bank and the enterprises in foreign trade are very important in the development of a national productive sector. Further, the enterprises of foreign trade, the nationalized bank, and a program of agrarian reform in the process of forming cooperatives for the small producers—these three components are decisive levers in the economic and social transformation of the country.

Now then, what are the goals that have been set in the foreign trade sector?

On a political level, there's the need to achieve national autonomy for the area of foreign trade. Achieving national autonomy means diversifying our channels of trade, given that these channels are fundamentally oriented towards the U.S. Perhaps it would be helpful to familiarize you with certain statistics that demonstrate the way in which we have diversified these channels in both the areas of imports and exports. (See Charts A and B.)

Two tasks, these two goals, are proposed. We refer, first of all, to diversification of the market. These statistics show a drastic reduction in exports to the Central American Common Market, as a percentage of Nicaragua's trade overall. In 1977, 21% of our exports were directed towards the Central American Common Market. This percentage has fallen drastically, by no means due to policy on the part of Nicaragua. The political problems that you are familiar with, in countries such as El Salvador, Guatemala, Honduras, and throughout Central America, and the economic problems

Chart A: Exports*

Markets	1977	1978	1981	1982
Central American Common Market	21.0%	22.6%	13.9%	12.8%
Association for Latin American Integration	2.6	0.5	2.1	3.6
European Economic Community	28.4	27.9	19.4	23.6
U.S.	22.7	23.2	25.8	24.2
COMECON	1.0	0.2	7.6	6.2

*Figures represent exports as a percentage of Nicaragua's total foreign trade. Source: Nicaraguan Ministry of Foreign Trade

Chart B: Imports*

Markets	1977	1981	1982
Central American Common Market	23.1%	21.1%	15.1%
Association for Latin American Integration	14.4	26.0	27.2
European Economic Community	14.1	11.4	14.1
U.S.	30.8	26.3	19.0
COMECON	0.7	3.3	11.5

*Figures represent imports as a percentage of Nicaragua's total foreign trade. Source: Nicaraguan Ministry of Foreign Trade

in these countries, have caused significant reductions in their purchasing levels. On the other hand, frankly speaking, the level of production in manufactured goods has fallen in Nicaragua. The problems of foreign exchange have made the purchase of raw materials difficult: it is imperative to understand that the Central American Common Market and its industrialization depend upon the technology, raw materials, and inputs originating in the U.S. And the only way we can purchase these things from the U.S., if we are able to do so at all, is on a cash basis. While Nicaragua has enjoyed generous lines of credit from other countries, these very often do not satisfy the need for raw materials in our manufacturing industries.

It is a similar situation with respect to imports, but with one difference. As you can probably well appreciate, during 1981 we were importing heavily from the Central American Common Market—21% of our imports came from the CACM as opposed to 13% of our exports to the CACM. We had an enormous deficit. This forced us, in 1982, to reduce all luxury consumption which had its source in the Central American Common Market, with the objective of reducing our deficit with the Central American countries. It is also worthwhile to point out that in 1982 the re-activization of a series of industries began—industries which had still been disabled in 1980 and 1981. It took us two years before we could re-activate certain industries to produce for us what we were forced to import from Central America in 1980-1981.

The second important market for Nicaragua has been Latin America—Mexico and South America, or what was previously referred to as the Latin American Association of Free Trade. As you can see, the rise in imports is quite remarkable: this is explained chiefly by the increase in imports from Mexico and to some degree Venezuela, due to the fact that Nicaragua buys all of its oil products from those two countries.

We have made an effort to increase exports in order to compensate the imbalance in trade. We managed, in 1981-1982, to export several thousand tons of sugar to Mexico, since we foresaw the U.S. policy of blockading this product. But the desire to export to Mexico and other Latin American countries is no easy task. Mexico produces the same things Nicaragua does, which means we have to seek alternative goods to produce—and this is where diversification of our export product has relevance.

With regard to the European Economic Community, those export goods that suffered reductions in production levels due to the war are now recovering, making possible a recovery of the import and export trade with Europe. Immediately following the revolution, there was a sharp decline in trade, but that tendency is being reversed, and we have found a consistently positive political disposition towards trade with Nicaragua on the part of the Europeans.

We will leave consideration of the U.S. until last, since there are a few special comments we would like to make, things which you yourselves are capable of observing.

With the countries of COMECON, with the socialist countries, there has been a substantial increase in trade. There is a significant rise in imports because lines of credit have been opened up for us in the areas of machinery, equipment, and replacement parts. Consequently, we have made an effort to increase our export levels with the socialist countries in order to balance the trading levels with them.

One of the things which has facilitated a growth in our exports is that, with many countries such as Mexico and the socialist countries, we have signed medium-term trade agreements, and this, in turn, makes it possible for us to plan both our exports and the use of those resources. Now, with regard to the United States: imports from the U.S. have been reduced greatly. There are various reasons for this: First, that it is a planned policy, in anticipation of a blockade situation, such as was used against Chile and Cuba. Second, a strictly economic reason, which we mentioned before, is that it is very difficult for the country to purchase cash [dollars] in the way we previously did. The enormous scarcity of foreign exchange in Nicaragua prohibits us from buying from the U.S. in the way we did in the past. Now, an important point related to this is the fact that our industries, in both the public and private sectors, have depended upon buying from the U.S., given the technological productive structure of our country; we are much more accustomed to the type of machinery and replacement parts that come from the U.S.

On the other hand, there hasn't been a significant decrease in exports [to the U.S.]. But we do expect a decrease next year. Our figures show that we will have a significant drop due to the reduction in sugar sales, which were crucial in our export trade with the U.S. But in addition to sugar, about 85 to 90% of meat produced is exported to the U.S. Historically, beef production in this country was established to supply the North American market. Likewise with sea products—80% of the lobster and shrimp is exported to the United States.

[The context for all of this is that] prior to the revolution, 100% of the exports of sugar, meat, bananas, and sea products went to the U.S.

We'd like to make a comment about the banana exports. 100% of the bananas are still going to the U.S., despite the sudden departure of the United Fruit Company and its extensive efforts to block our bananas from the American market. As you might know, the banana companies make worldwide earnings in the marketing of the product, not in its production. In general, they are no longer involved in production, but control the marketing. When United Fruit got out of Nicaragua last year, it began to use every means it could to block us from directly marketing our bananas in the U.S.; the company mounted a propaganda campaign claiming that the Nicaraguan banana was a bad product. Furthermore, the three executives of a company that was helping Nicaragua market bananas had a bad accident—the three were run over by a truck. We're not accusing anyone, but there must be something rather strange going on.

At any rate, given the importance of the export of our products to the U.S., you can understand the seriousness of the policy adopted by the U.S. government to reduce the quota of sugar imported directly from Nicaragua. In other areas, our fishing boats were pirated to Honduras, and there was a general decline in the planting of crops immediately following the revolution, because the planting season coincided with the period of insurrection. As far as the industrial sector, we already mentioned the problems of raw materials and the shortage of replacement parts.

I would like to add, regarding the drop in exports. In 1981-1982, some of the products that had traditionally been exported began to be kept for internal consumption—basic consumer products. For example, milk, which previously was an export product, is now produced for internal distribution.

Along with the internal problems in production and export, we have external problems to deal with. The increased costs of imports, especially in 1980, are not due solely to the causes we mentioned earlier, but are also affected by the drastic increase in the price of oil towards the end of 1979.

These figures bear heavily on Nicaragua, given the seriousness of the situation. In 1979 Nicaragua spent $65 million on oil imports; in 1980, $148 million; and in 1981, $172 million—for more or less the same volume of oil. If you compare this figure with what Nicaragua received for its exports, you can see that between 30% and 35% of those earnings had to be spent on oil. This should explain why it became necessary last year to ration the use of fuel. That is an effect of the international economy. Lately the price has dropped from $34 to $29 a barrel, so we expect to be able to breathe a little easier.

However, it is important to point out that this year, as a result of the conflicts in the country, it may be necessary to spend the same total amount on imports, despite the aforementioned drop in prices, since we are forced to channel a lot of the resources which would normally go towards other ends into our defense in the zones of conflict. The allocation of these resources allows the people, the forces defending the borders, to mobilize themselves—and the need for mobilization has increased.

Another factor affecting us is that, as you well know, during 1981, and through 1982, there was a severe recession in industry throughout the world, including the U.S., causing considerable inflation (just recently beginning to drop), and high interest rates. This too has affected us.

There are two other external factors that affect Nicaragua internally, and these are: the increased interest rates since 1980, which went as high as 20% and 21%, and the increased rate of inflation throughout the industrialized world. On the other hand, it was precisely during those years that we saw a tendency towards a decrease in the prices of Nicaragua's export products. What we have had, then, is a situation of double jeopardy. Our buying power for importing has been reduced, while obtaining credit has become more expensive and more difficult and it is less available.

Let us give but one example of the decrease in buying power of our exported goods. In 1972 Nicaragua could buy a tractor with 319 quintals of cotton, but in 1981, it cost 461 quintals. (One quintal equals 2.2 tons.)

The point of this is that Nicaragua must export more quintals of cotton, more coffee, in order to buy the same amount it did in 1972. This is an indication that the inflation in the United States and the industrial countries has occurred at a higher rate; that is, the inflation has grown while the price of their imports has dropped. It is a dramatic example of what in technical terms is called a deterioration in the terms of trade. In another case, in 1972 Nicaragua could buy 13 barrels of oil with one quintal of coffee; in 1981, that one quintal of coffee bought only three barrels. The same is true with other products that Nicaragua is obliged to import.

A final point to mention, in answer to one of the questions you had, concerns Nicaragua's foreign debt. Our debt to foreign private banks, which is paid at international interest rates, forces us to pay out 85% of our total export earnings to service the debt. That leaves us less than $100 million with which to make indispensable purchases. It is important to clarify that most of what we are paying nowadays is interest, since the principal has been renegotiated into medium- and long-term agreements.

Economic Effects
of Imperialist Aggression

This article appeared in Barricada, *Section "Lunes Socio-Económico," June 27, 1983.*

"We have been obliged to mobilize resources to confront aggression in all its aspects, which has meant diverting financial, productive, and human resources to defense tasks and, as a consequence, dealing with greater difficulties in the development of our economic programs." The Coordinator of the Government Junta of National Reconstruction (JGRN), Comandante of the Revolution Daniel Ortega, reported this to the Council of State May 4, 1983. The following article is dedicated to analyzing military aggression and some of the immediate consequences for our economy.

This undeclared war—which, overseas, absurdly enough, has been called "silent" or "secret"—has caused many deaths among technicians, peasants, and workers; considerable material losses; and significant delays in the country's development plans. It is also necessary to add that popular defense mobilizations, the necessity of maintaining numerous armed citizens and workers on the war fronts, affects work in production and in the government. Among the principal economic problems we single out are:

• The abandonment of cultivation, particularly of grain in the countryside.

• The destruction of vehicles, tractors, trucks, and road construction equipment.

• Delay in the construction of roads and dwellings, especially in the countryside.

• Blowing up of bridges.

• Burning of forests on a large scale.

• Destruction of Child Development Centers (CDI's), schools, health centers, etc.

This destruction and sabotage translates into a reduction of production and a delay in the development plans that the revolution would like to carry out in our society, particularly among the rural population.

The answer of the revolution has been blunt; self-defense cooperatives in the countryside, revolutionary vigilance in the cities to avoid sabotage and to control speculation. In this way, many attempted actions against the well-being of our people have been prevented.

The government has implemented emergency plans for sowing grain, for constructing roads, and deepening the process of agrarian reform in the war zones. In this way, with the concerted action of the people and its government, it has been possible to face up to the greatest problems.

Nevertheless, the day-to-day situation in the capital, in the other cities, and in the countryside is characterized by scarcity of some products and services. And in fact, the war requires that priority be given to defense tasks, to provisions and health care for the fighters at the battle fronts who are defending our sovereignty. To a certain extent, these priorities lead to a decreased supply of products in the cities.

If to those factors we add the reduction in imported products due to the shortage of foreign exchange, we can see that, in the last analysis, there is a direct relation between imperialist aggression and many of the day-to-day difficulties that we have to confront with ever greater organization and consciousness of their causes.

I. In 1982, More Than $60.0 Million Lost Due to the War*

Between May 1982 and May 1983, an initial (and certainly incomplete) inventory tells us that the war caused losses totaling $61.2 million, divided as shown in the chart below.

Destruction of Material	14.6
Damage to Production	36.2
Idle Capital**	10.4
Total	61.2

*The dollar values in this article are based on the commercial exchange rate of 10 córdobas to 1 dollar—Eds.
**"Idle capital" is partial and refers only to the export of wood and gold that could not take place.
Source: Government Junta of National Reconstruction

This figure of $61.2 million represents 2-3% of the gross domestic product of the country. Even this does not reflect actual losses because it does not account for that which was *not* produced due to the mobilization of workers, technicians, and professionals for defense tasks, and it also does not account for the allocation of resources for defense purposes, such as those needed to guarantee the food and health of the fighters mobilized in the war zones.

In 1982, Reagan delivered $19 million through the CIA to finance counterrevolutionary activity (it is thought that total CIA expenses already exceed $30 million), increasing the military expenses imposed on the revolutionary government to meet the aggression.

II. Delays and Sabotage of Production

Before the sabotage in June 1983 of lanes of the Rio Blanco-Siuna highway, which cost the country $2 million, the Ministry of Construction reported total losses of $4.5 million distributed as follows:

- More than $2.5 million due to delay in maintenance of existing road networks. This means that in some zones of the country the service roads have deteriorated, and as a result, it is more difficult to transport the harvest.

- $.95 million on the road from Waslala-Siuna, of which $.35 million correspond to the destruction of the roadway last year.

- $.93 million due to delay in the improvement of the airstrips in Puerto Cabezas and Rosita.

It was not possible to install drinking water facilities in Ocotal.

In the energy field, plans for the development of the COPALAR project had to be temporarily suspended. Some plans for small-scale dams by the INE (Nicaraguan Institute of Energy) were also paralyzed by the impossibility of working in zones where the counterrevolutionary forces are active.

III. Aggression Against Education and Health

Comandante Ortega, in his presentation before the Council of State, indicated that in this sector, "in spite of the advances made, the situation still is difficult, confronting problems that for structural reasons will be solved in the medium or long term." In addition to the structural problems that the revolution is solving, it is also necessary to solve obstacles thrown up by the aggression.

In 1982, the Ministry of Health (MINSA) had to interrupt the antipolio campaign and had to close 15 health stations in Regions I, V, and VI due to the conditions imposed by the war situation. In this period, MINSA reports the death of 12 doctors, among them two internationalists, killed along with the civilian population in cowardly attacks by the [counterrevolutionary] bands.

In the field of education, the situation has been even more difficult. In Regions I and VI, and in Special Zones II and III, 310 Popular Education Centers were closed; two elementary schools were destroyed in Region VI, and 37 rural teachers and 8 professors were killed between May 1982 and May 1983.

IV. Attacks Against Production

In the productive sector, the most affected areas have been agriculture and forestry and to a lesser extent, mining and fishing. In the course of last year, 40,000 hectares of pines were burned, which represents a loss of $20.0 million. On this occasion, the counterrevolutionaries kidnapped brigades of workers, stole their work equipment, and burned their offices and dispensaries. The drop in the supply of wood is not unrelated to this situation. Since the triumph of the revolution, the production of wood has never reached 50% of what it was before, and with the implementation of the plan of the Northeast Forest Company, it was thought that we could exceed the earlier levels and satisfy national demand. Obviously the military activities in the area of the project are going to complicate the attainment of the hoped-for goals. This has consequences in the construction sector, and affects all the carpenters who have difficulty obtaining lumber.

The Agricultural Sector

In its most recent estimate, the Ministry of Agricultural Development and Agrarian Reform (MIDINRA) reports losses of $25.0 million distributed as shown in the chart below.

War Losses in Agriculture*

Region	Agriculture	Livestock	Equipment/ Machinery	Infra- structure	Total
I	$9.81	$1.23	$.84	$8.65	$20.53
II	-	-	-	-	-
III	-	-	-	-	-
IV	-	-	-	.02	.02
V	.23	.03	-	-	.26
VI	2.98	.04	.10	.33	3.45
Z.E.I	.01	.01	.02	-	.04
Z.E.II	.01	-	.04	-	.05
Z.E.III	.50	-	.01	.03	.54
TOTAL	$13.54	$1.31	$1.01	$9.03	$24.89

*Figures are expressed in millions of dollars.
Source: Ministry of Agricultural Development and Agrarian Reform

The most affected region has been Region I (Nueva Segovia, Madriz, Estelí). Within Region I, the Laureano Mairena enterprise suffered losses of almost $7.2 million, of which more than 60% are due to the destruction of buildings and infrastructure for making cigarettes.

The most affected areas have been the Area of People's Property (APP) and the peasant cooperatives. The latter have had losses of more than $10.0 million alone in Region I. And we haven't mentioned the 8 peasants killed and the 40 kidnapped by the beasts [counterrevolutionaries—Eds.].

In Region VI (Matagalpa-Jinotega), attacks have been directed essentially at the peasant sector where the counterrevolution has caused more than 106 deaths and has produced a total of $34.5 million in damages, mostly in the Yalí and Wiwilí zones.

Nevertheless, it is necessary to clarify that the economic effects of those losses are very small in comparison with the decline in production caused by the terrorist action of the bands. These actions force the peasants to retreat to areas closer to the cities for protection, and do not permit the arrival of equipment and technicians at the necessary time, resulting in a decline in the peasant production of grain. The implementation of self-defense cooperatives has begun to counter this situation.

V. Mobilization of the Armed People, Assassination of Technicians, Workers, and Professionals

The economic costs cannot be evaluated solely in terms of material damage caused by the war, because there are also the *compañeros* killed in criminal ambushes while doing their duty, the *compañeros* mobilized in the Reserve Battalions and the militias who have to abandon their work to go and defend the country.

Comandante Ortega, in the discussion cited, stated that between May 1982 and May 1983 alone, 7,616 *compañeros* were mobilized into the Infantry Reserve Battalions, and 3,215 into the Popular Sandinista Militias.

The Comandante added: "157 *compañeros* were killed and fell in combat, of which 58 were technicians, 23 professionals, 2 internationalist doctors, and 73 workers, drivers, peasants, and others."

VI. Faced With Aggression, the Revolution Answers: More Organization

The impressive participation of the people through its organizations, the militias, the Sandinista Defense Committees (CDS's), the Voluntary Police, revolutionary vigilance, and the defense organs of the revolution (Popular Sandinista Army, State Security and the police) has limited the effects of aggression. Thanks to them, all the attempts of imperialism to develop urban terrorism have been frustrated, and the principal economic objectives of the war zones are effectively protected. Thanks to them, an increasingly firm battle against speculation is also beginning to be waged.

Today, the shortage of exchange, the impact of aggression and the cut-off of supplies (also produced in large part by the aggression) require a redoubling of organization and a closing of ranks to form a common front against the enemy, whose military actions are accompanied by hoaxes, speculation, attempts at sabotage, etc., and whose objective is to damage and defame the revolution.

To conclude, let us recall the words of Comandante Daniel Ortega, who said: "In order to confront this terrorist escalation, the Ministry of the Interior has depended more deeply and profoundly on the working people. Thanks to the work of the Ministry of the Interior and thanks to this effort of the people, all the enemy's attempts to develop terrorism in the cities have been completely neutralized; it has been possible to strike innumerable blows at the counterrevolutionary military units, by means of the Sandinista Popular Army or the forces of the Ministry of the Interior itself. The principal economic objectives have been protected, and important blows prevented even in the areas where large units of counterrevolutionaries are operating; the negative effects of the propaganda campaigns have been reduced and we have been able to discover the plans of the enemy beforehand."

To maintain and consolidate those achievements, to prepare daily to meet new aggression, and to defeat that aggression is the order of the day in Nicaragua.

Food Supply: Nicaragua's Daily Challenge

This article is reprinted from Envío *(September 1983), a publication of the Instituto Histórico Centroamericano (Central American Historical Institute) of Managua, Nicaragua.* Envío *is published in English and Spanish.*

"Sorry, we're all out" is a phrase one often hears these days in Managua and throughout Nicaragua. Some days it's eggs, or bread, or milk; at other times it's laundry soap, or chicken, or cheese. In July there were lines to buy meat and bread. By August these shortages had been dealt with, but corn was lacking. Rumors circulate about shortages; they are sometimes true, sometimes not, but it is always difficult to disprove a rumor.

Food supply is a daily challenge for the new Nicaragua, a challenge which is reflected in both the successes and the failures of the planned reconstruction process.

The complexity and scope of the problem have obliged us to limit this article to basic food products and laundry soap, as these most affect the majority of the population.

Hoarding, Lines, Fears

In addition to the acute food supply problem provoked by either temporary or partial shortages, the situation is aggravated by hoarding. Hoarding takes place at all levels, from the wholesalers and small merchants who hoard to increase their profits or to destabilize the government, to individual families who are simply responding to the real fear of not being able to buy enough food for one's self or for one's family.

This psychological factor of fear cannot be separated from the context of the difficult situation in Nicaragua today. One need only remember the CIA-sponsored maneuvers in Chile during the Allende government — which created artificial food shortages and, hence, widespread panic — to realize that the CIA could use food shortages in Nicaragua as part of its "covert" war. [Emphasis added — Eds.]

In addition, sectors of the international press never tire of offering specific examples of shortages in Nicaragua to suggest that living conditions under the "planned economy" of the Sandinistas are worse than during the Somoza regime. The May 1983 issue of the German magazine *Stern,* for example, carried a photo of shoppers lined up in front of a Managua supermarket. The magazine failed to mention that the picture was taken before the store opened in the morning. A *New York Times* article of August 16 mentioned lines to buy beans, yet in fact there is no bean shortage.

Certainly, there have been lines, but recently these have diminished. One of the contributing factors is the system of rationing for sugar, rice, oil, and laundry soap. Problems still exist, and the lines have not disappeared completely, particularly in Managua, where the situation is worse because of the city's unstructured and overpopulated situation. It is also true that Managuans were always first and best served for years and hence developed eating habits not seen in the rest of the country.

Lines are not a phenomenon outside of Managua, but shortages do exist. People in El Limón and San Juan de Limay have told us, "Day after day, we only eat rice and beans."

The repercussions of the food supply problems are serious. These problems call into question the capacity of the revolutionary government to assure supplies for the entire population within the context of a mixed economy. Shortages have led to increased governmental controls on the market, in order to ensure a supply of basic products for the whole population. These controls meet strong resistance from truck drivers, wholesalers, retailers, and small vendors, whose only worry under the previous regime was their own profit margin. Out of this confrontation arises the nearly uncontrollable problem of the black market. This is both a political and social problem, which results from the economic structure of a poor country only beginning to consolidate its new economic structure.

The Food Supply Problem

Shortages result when demand exceeds supply. Yet, in general, in Nicaragua's domestic market, the imbalances do not arise from a reduction in domestic production. With the exception of certain products, such as corn, beef, milk, and cottonseed (the raw material used in making cooking oil), the production of all other basic products is higher than before the revolution. The Center for Research on the Agrarian Reform (CIERA) notes that:

> The phenomenon of shortages is related to two distinct problems. On the one hand, there is the question of the efficiency of the food production system and of the flow of inputs and products throughout the food production chain. Several problems converge here which prevent food from reaching consumers on a regular basis, or in sufficient quantity and at prices that are within their reach. On the other hand, shortages must be understood as a symptom of the revolutionary transformation of income and consumption structures. The development of more equitable structures generates a higher level of demand and consumption, which places pressure upon supplies and creates conditions tending towards shortages.

In the First Seminar on Food Strategy, held in Managua in January 1983, the inefficiency of the present system was recognized in the areas of collecting, transporting, and distributing food supplies, because these are divided between various ministries. It was suggested that the National Food Program (PAN) be strengthened in order to fulfill its coordinating function.

But the problem of the increase in demand cannot be solved so easily. Demand has increased along with the population (there are 200,000 more Nicaraguans now than three years ago) and because of the reorganization of the domestic market, which now gives the majority of the population greater access to basic goods. Various factors have contributed to an increase in the purchasing power of those Nicaraguans who were formerly isolated by distance or class. These changes revolve around the redistribution of income, which has been affected by actual increases in income or by fixed price controls. The end result is that the standard of living of the poor has increased. Diet, particularly in the rural areas, is also much better now. For example, the consumption of eggs, bread, chicken, pasteurized milk, sugar, and cooking oil is much higher than four years ago.

The Principal Causes of Shortages

A Dependent Economy and the Lack of Foreign Exchange

The food system depends almost totally on imported products, equipment, and machinery. The shortage of foreign exchange caused by both a balance of trade deficit and the inherited debt prevents the purchase of capital goods necessary to increase productive capacity (such as irrigation or threshing equipment). This also affects the purchase of spare parts for processing machinery, of vehicles for transporting food, and even of bottles for milk and oil. In general, the lack of foreign exchange creates bottlenecks throughout the food system. The same foreign exchange shortage also implies drastic reductions in food imports, so that there is not a sufficient supply of powdered milk, vegetable oil, wheat, corn, or vegetables.

The dependent economy has been deeply affected by the U.S. economic blockade, including the areas of food imports and exports. The canceling of the wheat credit in March 1981, Standard Fruit's cancellation of its banana marketing contract in September 1982, and the 90% reduction in the sugar quota in May 1983 are but a few examples of a chain of destabilizing economic aggressions. These, combined with U.S. pressure upon international financial organizations such as the World Bank, have also limited Nicaragua's access to foreign credit.

Problems of Control

After the triumph, the government created the Ministry of Internal Commerce (MICOIN) to guarantee the population's access to basic goods. But direct control over supplies is difficult in a mixed economy in which state and private interests compete. Currently, through Nicaraguan Basic Foods Enterprise (ENABAS), MICOIN controls 50% of the distribution of beans, 30% of the corn, 80% of the rice, 90% of the sorghum, and 100% of the oil, laundry soap, salt, and sugar. With control over 40%

of the total volume of basic goods distribution, ENABAS has established an important position in the domestic market, especially by developing secure distribution channels: 2,647 popular stores, 11 supermarkets and employees' stores in more than 500 workplaces. But the other 60% of distribution is still dominated by a traditional network of some 37,000 retailers located mostly in the cities.

The coexistence of the two networks has created a type of double market that lends itself to various forms of speculation. This speculation inhibits an equitable policy of pricing or distribution to protect the majority of Nicaraguans. The supermarkets located in the middle class neighborhoods are better supplied than the ENABAS stores in the poorer neighborhoods. Up until August of this year, the supermarkets were able to buy directly from wholesalers or from the factories. The supermarkets were also guilty of selling the rationed products only on the condition that the shopper bought other goods.

Managua's Eastern Market with its 8,000 vendors is considered the weakest point in the price control policy, although abuses also exist in the newer markets. For example, small merchants take advantage of the state's subsidized sales in order to resell these basic products at a higher price. These speculative maneuvers affect the social structure of consumption by raising the prices of goods to the detriment of the poorer classes, who do not have the means to buy at the higher prices. But these same people united in mass organizations have kept the problem of speculation from becoming more serious than it already is.

The Problem of Gaining Control of Production

The problems of price control begin with ENABAS's inability to capture a sufficient proportion of the agricultural production. ENABAS buys up 45.7% of basic grain production, but does not exercise effective control over products such as beef, pork, chicken, eggs, milk, and vegetables. Here we will examine two products that illustrate the complexity of planning and gaining control of the production. Corn is the product in shortest supply at the moment, and laundry soap is the only industrial product controlled by MICOIN.

Corn: The most pressing food supply problem at the moment is that of corn. The last two harvests have not met production goals, and recovery on a short-term basis is not possible. As a result, nearly all the corn consumed in Nicaragua from now until the next harvest in early 1984 will have to be imported. For the months of August to December, 70,000 tons of corn imports are planned.

One has to take into account the importance of corn in the Nicaraguan diet to understand the impact of this shortage. For the average Nicaraguan, a day without tortillas is like a day without bread for a European or a day without rice for an Oriental. The Nicaraguan diet has many corn-based meals and drinks: different types of tortillas, *tamales,* and *chichas,* which are "cottage industry" products, made in the home to be sold from house to house. Thus, many small intermediaries earn their "daily tortilla" from corn. MICOIN has no other alternative but to import in order to maintain the supply level. But this is a stopgap measure which emphasizes the urgent need to restructure the whole production cycle of this basic grain.

Domestic corn production is largely in the hands of small and medium sized producers. Because of past difficulties in meeting their own consumption needs, and the prices offered by ENABAS, these producers prefer to keep the grain for their own needs or to sell it on the black market. State producers of corn cannot make up for the amount of private corn production that is not captured by ENABAS. In addition, the lands traditionally used for corn cultivation have reached the limits of their fertility, and there are often unforeseen problems with climate, such as last year's floods, which destroyed a large part of the irrigation equipment. Another factor is that any agrarian reform implies short-term reductions in output, until the new owners of the redistributed land gain the necessary experience, and an adequate infrastructure is created for a more rational system of production and distribution.

At the present time, ENABAS captures only 17.9% of the corn harvest. The price offered by ENABAS encourages both private and state producers to sell their harvest as corn on the cob on the black market instead of selling it to ENABAS as grain.

Laundry Soap: The problems of laundry soap supply are similar to those of cooking oil, insofar as both products depend upon the same ingredient: cottonseed. Cottonseed production is slowly returning to pre-revolutionary levels. For example, 117,000 tons of cottonseed were produced in 1982-83, which was only 53% of 1977-78 production. This drop in production is clearly visible in the 1982 imports of cooking oil, which were 18 times greater than in 1978.

Laundry soap production, however, has increased rapidly, rising from 30.8 million pounds in 1976 to 62.5 million pounds in 1982, and is expected to reach 72.6 million pounds in 1984. But laundry soap production is highly dependent upon imports, which are in turn highly dependent upon foreign exchange. The shortage of foreign exchange challenges the government to reduce imports while improving production and distribution.

In early 1983, ENABAS took control of soap distribution in order to compensate for the reduction in imports. With the rationing of laundry soap, each person receives four bars a month. This has led to concern, as some people felt the ration to be inadequate. To aggravate the picture, laundry detergent disappeared from the markets for a period of time. The INIZA company in Grenada that produces detergent is privately owned, and this hindered MICOIN's task of dealing with hoarding.

In order to import all the needed soap inputs—suet, perfume, and coconut oil (which, since the burning of the coconut processing plant in Bluefields last year, must also be imported)—an extra $4 million will be needed for next year, according to MICOIN. Thus the government must decide whether it will spend the money to continue soap production at full capacity, or act to restrain the excessive use of laundry soap. Nicaragua has the highest per capita usage of laundry soap in Central America.

Among the measures taken to confront the problem is the construction of warehouses, which at the moment do not exist. But there are external problems as well. Recently, the arrival of a boat carrying raw materials for soap was delayed for 80 hours because the boat had to navigate around the U.S. war fleet. The delay brought soap production to a standstill, but the problem was not publicly announced, to avoid hoarding of soap. The problems created by short-term delays have been overcome by the rationing system and a small reserve supply.

Hoarding

Hoarding takes place at all stages of marketing, and above all with those products that can easily be stored (such as rice, corn, cooking oil, sugar, and powdered milk). At the consumer level, hoarding can also be a psychological response, and this reaction can be one of the most potent weapons in the hands of the opponents of the revolution. According to the MICOIN vice-minister in charge of supply, one week of shortages for any given product implies eight weeks of work to rebuild consumer confidence and thus be able to re-establish a sufficient supply. Just one rumor can start a vicious circle for any given product, as the rumor of an impending shortage can lead many, especially those who are better off, to buy more than they normally need, leading to shortages that make the rumor a self-fulfilling prophecy.

But if hoarding only took place at the consumer level, it would not cause major supply problems. The serious problems caused by hoarding occur at the production and distribution stages.

With respect to distribution, intermediaries and distributors at all levels, both private and public, engage in hoarding. Other problems are caused when certain products do not reach the secure channels established by ENABAS, but are concentrated in the hands of wholesalers and merchants, who then raise their prices.

Bottlenecks and Transportation

A bottleneck is defined as the incapacity of one stage of the production and distribution system to handle all the output of the previous link in the chain. Bottlenecks arise from the lack of infrastructure and of an adequate marketing system. They also reflect the lack of an efficient investment policy. Up until now, state investment has been concentrated at the level of primary production. While basic grains production will double by 1990, investments to increase storage capacity are only increasing by 50%. Thus investments must guarantee the capacity of each step in the postproduction process, i.e., processing, storage, transportation, etc., to keep pace with increased production.

This problem is exacerbated by the irrational ebbs and flows of an uncoordinated and extremely diversified transportation network. Around

30% of basic grain losses suffered by ENABAS are due to this problem. The transportation bottleneck is tightened by the U.S. economic blockade, especially in terms of spare parts necessary to repair the trucks. The lack of a secure transportation network is one of the principal supply problems for remote areas. Another factor is the lack of refrigerated trucks needed to carry milk, chicken, eggs, and fish over long distances.

Problems of Institutional Organization

The Seminar on Food Strategy addressed the lack of unified planning and of strategy, the lack of inter-institutional coordination, and the inconsistencies found in policy criteria and in the agro-industrial development method. Also discussed were the planning problems caused by imprecise data and the lack of both technical resources and personnel in the field of statistics.

Examples of these problems abound. There have been mistakes made in calculating harvest shortfalls as well as in estimating importation deficits. There have also been cases in which imported raw materials or food arrived late, provoking problems in the domestic market. There have also been bureaucratic problems in the system of assigning foreign exchange and/or authorizing imports.

Solutions to the Food Shortage Problem

What can be done? Julio López, Vice-Minister of MICOIN, suggests that food supply problems are like a window through which everyone can glimpse the most obvious weaknesses of the economic system. To use another metaphor, food shortages are like the tip of an iceberg—the real problems in trying to restructure the economic system are seen in the one area that affects the most people. Solutions to such a multifaceted problem are difficult to find—a situation made even harder by the present threats and blockades.

Short-Term Solutions

On the short-term level, there are no real solutions. Since the lack of foreign exchange is the major limitation, it is difficult to foresee a period in the near future when Nicaragua will be able to resolve completely the food shortage problem. Nicaragua can no longer make up for shortages by importing as easily as before, so the country depends to some degree upon donations and favorable credit lines to buy food and agro-industrial machinery.

On the other hand, some of the symptoms of the food supply problem can be addressed by improving the marketing and distribution of food. The government subsidizes the cost of six basic products in order to keep prices within the reach of the majority. These subsidies cost the government $67.4 million (based on a commercial exchange rate of 10 cordobas to 1 dollar—Eds.) in 1982. The government also controls the price of the other basic goods. These price controls are not entirely effective, however, as producers will sell to merchants who give them the best price. As a result, these products are found only in the private markets, rather than the government-controlled markets.

As a short-term action designed to address the problem of lines and to create a more equitable distribution, ration cards were introduced to regulate the purchases of sugar (since January 1982), rice (January 1983), cooking oil, and laundry soap (April 1983). With these cards, each person can buy 5 pounds per month of sugar, 4 pounds of rice, 1 liter of cooking oil, and 4 bars of laundry soap. There have been instances in which the cards have created problems of favoritism; these are almost impossible for the state organizations to control.

To make all these measures widely understood, various institutions have published educational material: leaflets, studies, special newspaper articles, etc. The theme of food supply is also frequently discussed in the weekly "Face the People" program, in which government ministers and leaders of popular organizations meet with and answer questions from the people in different neighborhoods. There is also discussion at the *barrio* level in the block committees. While all this contributes to a clear understanding of the problem, it does not resolve the food shortages.

Currently, many efforts are being made to improve the organization and coordination of the different state institutions involved, of the commercial sector, and of the consumers themselves, in order to increase control from below. But all this takes time.

It is important to note that the capacity for control, either "from above" (i.e., the state) or through popular mobilization, is quite limited. A small ministry such as MICOIN, which has some 30 inspectors for all of Managua, cannot hope to monitor the 30,000 merchants or the 11,000 vendors in the capital. There is also a lack of qualified persons to undertake the task of explaining the dimensions of the food supply problem to people at the grassroots level. Thus, in the short term, not much change can be expected.

Medium- and Long-Term Solutions

As we have seen, the problem of food supply begins at the level of production and is amplified by the irrationalities of the marketing and distribution systems. Thus medium- and long-term solutions must be sought in all those spheres.

Production: The general lines of the government's food policy are guided by a philosophy of agricultural and food development based on the goals of food self-sufficiency and security, independent development, and a mixed economy.

The point of departure for the government strategy is the priority given to basic consumption and to the goal of reaching as quickly as possible the levels of consumption recommended by international health organizations. These nutritional requirements should be met by national production to avoid the vulnerability that comes from food dependency.

Some concrete means of realizing this overall goal are:

• The application of advanced technology to the process of basic food production that has hitherto been reserved for the agro-export sector.

• The reordering of land use so that a large part of basic food production can take place in the rich Pacific lands, which, since the 1950s, have been used almost exclusively for agro-export production;

• The provision of foreign exchange to purchase irrigation equipment for large tracts of land;

• A better use of land, to be encouraged by providing incentives for multiple annual harvests and for crop rotation.

The active participation of *campesinos* in the development of food strategy at the level of production must be increased by:

• Facilitating the distribution of financial, human, and material resources;

• Promoting the formation of cooperatives among small and medium sized producers.

In order to address the problems related to Nicaragua's food dependency, it is necessary to continue with the series of programs and projects being implemented by the government, such as:

• Promoting the agro-industrialization of natural resources, in order to process domestically produced raw materials and save foreign exchange on imports;

• Seeking new financial and commercial relations with countries that offer favorable credit lines without conditions;

• Seeking commercial agreements that provide guaranteed markets for exports.

Marketing and Distribution: All those involved in the question agree that this sensitive and unproductive sector must be reorganized. But the concrete means of achieving this goal are not clear. To suggest the path that policies in this area are going to take, we present here some of the suggestions made by representatives of the mass organizations and the state institutions in the Seminar on Food Strategy:

• Capturing production: The state and private producers who are cooperating with the process should be assigned a larger share of corn and bean production, since ENABAS is not receiving sufficient quantities of these products. This would neutralize the tendency of *campesinos* to sell their harvest in private channels where prices are higher.

• Wholesale marketing: The large quantities of basic foods held by private wholesalers should be limited; this practice fosters speculation. There should be marketing control policies to control the profit margins of the large wholesalers, or these activities should be turned over to state agencies.

• Retail marketing: The number of small ENABAS stores should be increased and the "general stores" should be organized in associations. The state should probably have some participation in the sector in order to guarantee that price controls are met.

• Transportation: The scarce transportation resources should be redistributed to serve not only agro-export needs but also domestic consumption needs.

Conclusions

The problem of food shortages in Nicaragua will not disappear overnight. Nicaragua is an underdeveloped country with all the current problems inherent in underdevelopment, as well as those inherited from a 45-year dictatorship. In addition, the country suffers from the effects of the counter-revolutionary forces both inside and outside of the country, and natural disasters like the floods followed by drought of last year.

Despite these real problems, and the current food shortages, visitors to Nicaragua are impressed by the physical condition of the people. One sees few cases of malnutrition—although this condition does exist, for the most part in the countryside, where the lack of education often compounds the food supply problem.

This is not to say that the Nicaraguan diet is good. The diet of the majority of the population is characterized by nutritional imbalances. For example, an enormous quantity of cooking oil and sugar is consumed, and, in general, the diet is based upon carbohydrates, with insufficient levels of proteins and vitamins. There is a need for grassroots education on proper nutrition, outlining the foods that must be eaten daily to preserve good health. But the eating habits and tastes of a country's population have deep roots in the nation's history and culture, and new habits take years to teach.

The picture we have drawn is not very encouraging, but tremendous efforts are being made to improve the situation. The government is working to end the temporary food shortages and is committed to developing good security for the future. But the problems are enormous and the limitations are real. All the best food programs and projects in the world are not enough to eliminate shortages if the initiative comes only from above. Food supply is a problem that concerns everyone and the help of everyone is needed to resolve it.

Counterrevolutionary Activities Against Nicaragua

Lenin Cerna
Comandante Guerrillero y de Brigada

This is the transcript (translated to English) of a speech delivered by Lenin Cerna, head of State Security in Nicaragua, to the Anti-Imperialist Tribunal of Our America, held in Managua in October 1983, and attended by Contemporary Marxism *Editor Marlene Dixon.*

On behalf of our National Directorate and our heroic people, we welcome the comrade delegates, the comrades of the chair, and the special guests of the Anti-Imperialist Tribunal of Our America (TANA), a bastion of dignity and of struggle for humanity, against imperialism.

To speak of the activities of the Central Intelligence Agency against the Nicaraguan Revolution would take a long time, just as speaking about the aggression of North American imperialism against our people would take a long time.

This long history, which has elicited a formidable response from our people, is today very intense because of the level of aggression and the level of cruelty of the CIA—and also because of the response of our people, who have not let themselves be intimidated, no matter how many crimes [the Reagan] administration has planned against our people.

This phase, starting at the end of 1980 and the beginning of 1981, has reached a scale that only the CIA could implement. It began with "simple" advice to ultrareactionary organizations in the heart of our country, with the creation of other organizations necessary to fulfill the diverse plans that the CIA was going to implement against our revolution—this was the beginning. Cooperativist organizations began to emerge in our midst, organizations that appeared, extraordinarily, after the triumph of our revolution, in contrast with their former absence—humanitarian and charitable organizations which began to develop financial programs of aid to the small businessman and small proprietor. This activity received a strong impetus and also was linked to the extraordinary rise of diverse forms of religious protest initiated at the end of 1980 and the beginning of 1981. These were the first signs of public activity that our revolution could prove to be directed by that great master of terrorism and manipulation—the CIA.

From there began the travels and the program of aid to Nicaraguan "refugees," supposedly persecuted and effectively outlawed by the people of Nicaragua: the [Somocista] ex-National Guards who had committed genocide against our population—pilots, forces trained by special troops, whose principal and basic advisers were the North Americans. Later these programs, after being exposed, were moved to Miami and to other points in the United States, some of them very well known within that well-informed circle in Miami. Hundreds of ex-National Guards arrived there, and from there were transferred to other points in Latin America, where they underwent training courses in terrorism and sabotage techniques, which they would later implement as the plans of U.S. imperialism were developing.

Within Nicaragua, there was activity in the sphere of religious manipulation, as well as an activity well known by all, the exploitation of the Revolution's supply problems—problems of providing vital necessities for the population.

The CIA began to finance diverse programs as pointed out. Each one was part of a perfectly organized plan. Towards the end of 1982 loans and financing arrived for those sectors traditionally affected by the revolutionary process—when I say "traditionally" I am not referring to antiquity, but to those carefully chosen people and areas of commerce within the normal life of our country that were tied in one way or another to the system created by Somoza. In this way more than 60,000 people in Managua in different ways came to depend on the loans and financing provided through various channels as part of the CIA's plan.

By late 1982 or early 1983, this approach had been applied to other problematic areas facing the revolution. Interestingly, a possibility for financing always appeared, provided that people organized themselves into cooperatives or into programs closely tied to people who were directly connected with functionaries of the CIA in Nicaragua, known and denounced by our revolution.

Thus the fact that this revolution has won the prestige and respect of the peoples of the world for its open character has been precisely one of the elements utilized by the CIA to develop profoundly divisive activity in the religious and economic spheres.

As I was saying, we cannot speak of only one way in which the CIA intervenes against Nicaragua. We must speak about a series of operations that are intended to destroy the Sandinista Revolution. A series of operations in which the financing and organizing of the group of former National Guards are a part. A series of operations in which the lack of access to food supplies, the problem of transport, the problem of health are part. We could not speak of this if we did not know that these operations have been and are being directed by people connected with other well-known functionaries of the CIA.

Thus it is not strange for us, as it can't be strange for you, for example, that the CIA official, Richard Smith, who paid attention to the reactionary parties here, would play an outstanding role in [developing] the Somocista Guards in Honduras. It is not strange that a functionary who attended to the trade union sector here is precisely a functionary involved with dissident elements [operating] in Costa Rica.

In the advance of [its] plans, as one of the small steps in the area of active operations, the Company blew up an Aeronica plane on the ground as it was getting ready to leave Mexico for Nicaragua.

Subsequently, in an operation also very characteristic of the Company, in Tegucigalpa, Honduras, an airline passenger who never boarded planted a time bomb on a plane that exploded at Augusto César Sandino Airport in Managua, killing workers in the terminal.

Immediately afterwards, the blowing up of the Rio Negro bridges stands out, as well as the attempt to blow up the Ocotal bridge, supposedly (according to certain statements by prisoners) with the goal of impeding the flow of arms to El Salvador.

Parallel to this, complete counterrevolutionary units are equipped with weapons of a regular army—and we could say with an advantage over a regular army—weapons appropriate for the type of war they need to carry out. Weapons that, actually, were unknown at the level at which regular armies operate in Central America.

We also know about the effort to unite the diverse groups of the counterrevolution—an effort which, despite the difficulties because of the very characteristics of the *contras,* [the CIA] subsidizes and provides resources and even contacts and contracts for training some of them in other parts of Latin America.

At the same time, in this symphony of death against our people, we have the increasing use of greater and more costly resources, such as the airplanes used in various activities against us, first for espionage and ultimately in the bombings—the most notorious and largest being the Augusto César Sandino Airport, where a plane of those mercenaries was shot down by our people.

They also use aviation to supply counterrevolutionary units in various parts of the country. They are beginning to use speedboats, well known by all of you and known by us even before the revolutionary triumph, as one of the activities of the CIA, used against other people, and denounced on several occasions.

Then too, we here are starting to have experience with the C-4 explosive; we knew of the cruelty of the CIA; we knew the cruelty of North American imperialism; and we are starting to feel it vividly through this new stage. The famous planes used by the Company in Vietnam, in Laos, in Cambodia, used against Cuba and against other countries, have been used in Nicaragua at a very high rate since the beginning of March of this year. There is an incredible amount of this activity, which has been steadily increasing, which stands out in the dates that follow. For example, on September 6, 1983, in the proximity of the Pasacaballos bridge, skin diving equipment was found that permits those using it to remain underwater for 9 hours. Equipment was found that recycles air in such a way that bubbles cannot surface. The C-4 is always characteristic in the employment of these criminal undertakings.

On September 8, two days later, the same groups destroyed the buoys where the boats in Puerto Sandino are moored. You will see that we've collected a series of items [as evidence—Eds.]. If you observe the cover, at a simple glance, you will notice that the adhesive material of this knapsack is the same as that of the explosives; it is the same as on this delay mechanism, all of which were seized at different times, on different dates, and in different locations.

Thus the story of this begins at the end of 1982 when the CIA offered a contract (that is the term they use—contract) to a known Argentine criminal, Osvaldo Villegas, to carry out operations against targets vital to the Nicaraguan economy on the coasts, as well as other noncoastal targets— operations which are designed to paralyze the economy of the country.

At the end of 1982, the U.S. Central Intelligence Agency realized that for all the technology they might have, for all their millions of dollars, history is against them, because the plans developed since 1981 had not been successful. Thus the famous leaders, made "leaders" through their propaganda campaigns, boosted up by the North American leaders, who present them as champions of freedom, etc., in fact had no solid basis in the theater of war against the people of Nicaragua. And so the new plans for the destruction of the Nicaraguan economy appeared, designed to create, as a byproduct, discontent among the people that would produce future possibilities for destabilization.

Villegas, who moves about extensively in Honduras and Costa Rica, [with] 18 Argentine advisers, turned up in Panama and Miami, searching for teams for this type of operations. He even contracted a group of mercenary Cuban *gusanos* [exiles—Eds.] and Argentines, for training in these activities and the execution of these plans.

At the beginning of 1983, several courses were given, directed by those advisers, in the Gulf of Fonseca and in other parts of Honduras. Some results were achieved from this training operation, which they called "Operation Buzos," [Buzos means "diver," but is also slang for "thief"—Eds.] but they did not satisfy the North Americans, who prepared their own courses on the island of Roatán in the Atlantic Ocean off Honduras, very close to Puerto Castilla, where there is a fleet of U.S. ships. They prepared various courses and trained some Nicaraguans, of whom we have one under arrest. The training was primarily based on objectives of destroying the following targets: Corinto, the Pasacaballos bridge, the fuel tanks in the areas of Ports Sandino and Corinto, and (through sabotage) commercial or noncommercial ships that approach Nicaragua.

For all this, the training took time. But according to information we have subsequently obtained, the North Americans decided to employ Argentines, Cuban *gusanos,* and other mercenaries (among them Panamanians) to carry out these operations.

These operations began late, in the month of September, although they had been programmed to start in July, by the time of the fourth anniversary of the Popular Sandinista Revolution. But in less than a month — September 6, September 23, October 1, 9, and 14, they destroyed important points of our economy and retired to their bases in Honduras and Costa Rica with absolute impunity, in spite of the denunciations made at the time and on each occasion. Even knowing the locations where these groups are found, where the means with which they carried out the activity are found; we have pointed out over and over again the points from which the planes leave to supply the counterrevolutionary units that bomb the targets, as in the case of Corinto; and all has been unfruitful [in stopping it], for reasons that you know.

So I cited for you the different dates, among which is September 8, when they bombed the Sandino Airport, the same day that they destroyed the buoys and the conductor pipe for the supply of petroleum — I have a piece of that tube.

On September 6, we found precisely these [C-4 explosives] with this equipment.

On September 13, one of these groups infiltrated a cooperative of fishermen and blew up boats and fishing equipment of the people in the area. On September 23, a plane coming from Costa Rica bombed a center of alcohol production which supplies the medical necessities of the country. On October 1, forces coming from Costa Rica destroyed fuel tanks that supply the mines of Bonanzas and Rosita. On October 9, they destroyed the fuel tanks in the port of Corinto, utilizing a speed boat of the kind used for training in Roatán and here in the Gulf of Fonseca. On October 14, they returned to destroy the buoys and the conductor pipe. I want to explain that this pipe is submerged 5 or 6 kilometers from the coast. Due to the limitations in our naval forces it is very difficult for us to take action against this type of incursion.

These have been the most relevant of the activities of the CIA against our country, in addition to actions which, we know, have been directed toward the infiltration [into Nicaragua — Eds.] of commandos for the destruction of electric plants, fuel bases, assassination of our leaders, assassination of peasant leaders. In short, these are actions for the destruction of the training schools for the building of roads to develop our country; destruction of the schools through which the revolution has made an extraordinary effort to pull our country, our people, out of darkness; the murder of teachers and health brigade members who are in the mountains, trying to improve the conditions of our peasants.

Finally, these are forms of activity which we have been denouncing to the world, that our small country has been facing against all the power which U.S. imperialism can marshal; these are actions that only the cooperation of honest men, worthy of this humanity, can somehow help our people to confront.

We know that we count on the backing of the peoples of the world, but we also know that this backing is not enough. We are able to say to you, comrades, delegates, that our people, who have fought heroically in very difficult conditions, who have had to face this criminal Company, have not lost a single gram nor a single ounce of their determination to continue standing up with pride. Therefore we are here before you, to demonstrate once again our spirit to our enemies.

In concluding, a few days ago an airplane was shot down by our militia. According to one of those arrested when the plane crashed, these planes come from Phoenix, Arizona. A few days ago, after that plane was shot down, two fugitives remained who had succeeded in escaping capture by our people for the moment. These fugitives were captured by the militia 48 hours ago. In accordance with the policy of our revolution, we are going to bring them here so that you can convey our spirit and the impressions of these two prisoners. I believe that the most important case is the last one, who had succeeded in evading the popular militia, but finally was captured. I also think that the occasion is important to rub our truth against the lies, the immorality of the CIA and their tools. These organisms paid for and directed a campaign saying that these fugitives were dead, in order to help rescue them. And we want to say that, in the spirit of our people and their indignation, there is no doubt as to what should be done with these pirates. But we have a disciplined people, a people respectful of the orders of our National Directorate and, for that reason, we maintain our position firmly with respect to any element that might be captured. I believe that the most important thing is for you to talk with these prisoners and find out directly the truth of what we have said—the truth which some functionaries of the countries that we have pointed out as their guardians have persisted in denying. [Cerna then demonstrated some equipment captured from the *contras*—Eds.]

In the beginning of 1981 the C-4 explosive started to appear here. We never had access to these things in the time of Somoza. This is the explosive charge which holds approximately 6 kilograms of the C-4, making it able to blow up at any hour. This is the equipment that I was referring to, which can be, as they say, "recycled." We didn't know that. This is the equipment used by the "teams," as they say over there, destined for these underwater activities. This was also found—this is very interesting because it is a buoy with a device that enables the boat to emit a screen of black smoke when it makes a retreat.

Thus, comrade delegates, comrades of the chair, we have tried to synthesize an activity very difficult to synthesize, if it were not for the knowledge that we all have of this criminal organization. It is enough to know that it is called the CIA, and that we are confronting it. We are sure that, with your denunciation, with your cooperation and that of the truly free men of the world, we can also defeat it.

Thank you very much.

The CIA Takes Direct Charge: The Attack on Corinto

Nancy Stein

Nancy Stein is on the Staff of the Institute for the Study of Labor and Economic Crisis.

During the course of 1983, the Reagan administration significantly escalated its attacks against the Nicaraguan government, with the CIA assuming direct command of the operations of the counterrevolutionaries located on the borders of Nicaragua.

Since 1981, when the CIA first began to funnel money to them, the counterrevolutionaries have carried out murderous attacks on border towns, shelling buildings and machinery, destroying border posts and crops, and terrorizing and killing people working in the harvests, as a way of economically disrupting the country.

Beginning in March 1983, the *contras,* increasingly supplied by the CIA with airplanes, have stepped up bombing raids. However, the real objective of the *contras,* to seize and hold territory and declare a new government, has never even been remotely approached (*NYT* 10/16/83). As a result of the ineffectiveness of the *contras,* on their own or even backed by the Honduran Army, the CIA has now taken direct charge of the sabotage operations against Nicaragua, launching coordinated attacks from Costa Rica, Honduras, and the Atlantic Coast.

Economic Sabotage

The CIA reportedly decided over the summer of 1983 that attacks aimed directly against industrial and transportation targets inside Nicaragua would be a faster and more effective way of hurting the popular government than previous efforts by the *contras* (*NYT* 10/16/83). Thus began a brutal policy of directly targeting the economic infrastructure of Nicaragua—for example, oil supplies, pipelines, food stocks—in order to cripple the economy and bring the government to its knees. This policy represented a qualitative leap in the campaign of economic destabilization that was designed to create shortages and exacerbate tensions and dissatisfaction within the country, particularly among the middle class and members of the opposition groups. Now, the U.S. took aim at the heart of the Nicaraguan economy.

The strategy of economic sabotage resulted in the following actions:

- September 8: The International Airport in Managua was bombed.
- September 8: The port of Benjamín Zeledón on the Atlantic Coast was bombed, destroying 400,000 gallons of diesel fuel as well as the oil supply for the Department of Zelaya (*NYT* 10/13/83).
- September 9: Oil unloading facilities at Puerto Sandino were destroyed (*NYT* 10/11/83).
- October 10: The attack on the port of Corinto—the most devastating attack—described below.
- October 14: CIA-trained saboteurs again blew up major oil pipelines at Puerto Sandino, an action designed to cut off Nicaragua's oil supply. In response to this, the transnational corporation ESSO announced it would no longer transport Mexican oil to Nicaragua.

CIA Provides Planes for Destruction

The planes used in these attacks have come from the CIA. According to an exposé in the *New York Times,* CIA-owned planes used in the Vietnam War have found their way into the hands of various *contra* groups. While the CIA has tried to conceal the ownership and movement of the planes, public documents have made it possible to trace back the sales of aircraft to companies connected to the CIA. In addition, former intelligence and military personel, as well as current CIA agents, are supplying equipment, training, and support to the *contras*. With this assistance, the *contras* now have an air force of their own, independent of the Honduran military, and are capable of waging more serious attacks on the people of Nicaragua (*NYT* 11/8/83).

The Attack on Corinto

In the most destructive action to date, on the night of October 10, the *contras,* directed by the CIA, attacked the port of Corinto, destroying tanks containing 3.2 million gallons of gasoline, oil, and diesel fuel, and hundreds of tons of food and medicine. The attack caused fires that forced the 25,000 residents of Corinto to be temporarily evacuated and destroyed the port facilities. Initial estimates were that the attack would cost $5-10 million and the destruction of fuel amounted to *over 1% of the country's annual fuel consumption.*

Comandante Henry Ruíz, member of the National Directorate of the FSLN, inspecting the damage in Corinto after the bombing, stated clearly:

> This is the aggression of the U.S. It is not a new stage of the counterrevolutionary war, nor an undeclared war. It is a dirty war with the dirtiest of objectives. . . .The aggressive escalation of imperialism began with air attacks and it put in perspective

the role of the CIA in the counterrevolution in carrying out their plans. The CIA and the Reagan administration are responsible for carrying out the plans—the attack on Corinto is an open act of aggression by the U.S. against Nicaragua (*Barricada* 10/13/83).

On October 14, Comandante Daniel Ortega, Coordinator of the Government of National Reconstruction, was forced to declare a state of emergency and later announced a program of rationing of various materials, particularly oil and gas, as a result of the attacks by the CIA. Also in response to these attacks, the government has had to reallocate resources so that health, education, housing, and other programs have had to be disrupted in order to respond to the escalation of U.S. aggression.

Testimony From the *Contras:* CIA Takes Direct Charge

Nicaraguan newspapers contain further evidence of the CIA taking charge of the operations against Nicaragua, in the testimony of captured counterrevolutionaries. The former members of Somoza's National Guard who constitute the Honduran-based *contra* movement testified that the CIA did not find them reliable due to the extent of corruption and distrust within their own ranks. In the case of one former National Guard, Pedro Ortiz, the CIA had him arrested and imprisoned in Honduras because he tried to set up his own army and was disrupting their plans (*Barricada International* 10/24/83).

Another report described the state of the Nicaraguan Democratic Force (FDN), saying that its level of chaos and incompetence was so great that the "CIA had to assume absolute control of the operations against Nicaragua"(*Barricada International* 10/24/83).

A captured counterrevolutionary, who was Somoza's personal pilot, explained that the CIA did not trust "the FDN's ability to carry out special actions....Neither the direction nor the execution of major actions are entrusted to the (former national) guards."

The sabotage of the ports of Sandino, Corinto, Benjamín Zeledón, and Cabezas was directly the work of the CIA according to this testimony. The pilot said that *contras* were being trained to sabotage the ports of Sandino and Corinto, although the actual attack was allegedly carried out by "truly specialized CIA commandos" because the *contras* were not competent enough (*Barricada International* 10/24/83).

The attack on Corinto had been planned since at least July 1983. At that time, U.S. officials acknowledged to the press that the CIA had been asking for detailed maps of three Nicaraguan ports, including the port of Corinto, as part of a covert plan to mine the harbors to prevent Soviet ships from docking there, to develop contingency plans for landing troops, or for other purposes, such as bombing the ports, which is what took place at Corinto just a few months later (*San Francisco Examiner* 7/17/83). At the same time, the CIA stepped up efforts to train *contras* in Honduras, in sabotage techniques and commando tactics. One Somocista Guardsman captured by the Nicaraguan government in October testified that he was trained by the CIA on the Honduran island of Roatán in the handling of underwater explosives and weapons (*Barricada International* 10/24/83). The U.S. had also provided explosives to Argentine-trained sabotage teams designed to blow up facilities at various ports (*San Francisco Examiner* 7/17/83).

Ripping Off the Facade of Negotiations

Before the escalation of attacks on strategic economic targets in Nicaragua, there was still some question about the issue of negotiations and the role of the Kissinger Commission in Central America. The major attacks on Corinto and Sandino occurred in the same week when the Kissinger Commission was about to visit Nicaragua. The message was clear. If the U.S. were committed to a diplomatic solution, the CIA would not have been trying to cripple the Nicaraguan government. In the light of the Kissinger Commission Report of January 1984, it seems clear that the Reagan administration has no desire to coexist with the Nicaraguan government in its present form, and that the CIA-directed economic sabotage was part of an overall strategy of escalation and aggression.

Terror in Pantasma

Rod Bush and Richard Schauffler

Rod Bush and Richard Schauffler, of the Institute for the Study of Labor and Economic Crisis, were members of a delegation to Nicaragua organized by U.S. Out of Central America (USOCA) in October 1983.

On Tuesday, October 18, 1983, the village of Pantasma in northern Nicaragua was viciously attacked by the CIA-backed *contras,* based in Honduras, who murdered 47 people and left $2 million in damages to the town's economic infrastructure. For 13 hours the band of counterrevolutionaries, some 250 in all, plundered the village, killing, looting, kidnapping, burning. Like My Lai, this was one more brutal atrocity in a long line of atrocities by U.S. or U.S.-backed forces, committed in the name of "God, freedom, and democracy." And as in the case of My Lai, such tactics only indicate that the *contras* are a force whose will to fight is extremely tenuous because of the increasing demoralization within their ranks; and further, that such actions are not a sign of a confident force sure of victory, but of a desperate army attempting to claim a victory and inflict damage at any cost.

In dramatic contrast to the *contra* army, driven to insane cruelty by the contradiction of their mission—to destroy their own people—the citizens of Pantasma showed remarkable resolve:

> Not one tear, not one lament, not one flower will there be in this valley for the death of our fellow peasants, teachers, and soldiers, our massacred people. The tears will now be the arms we will take up to destroy every one of the criminal Somocistas.

The first North Americans to witness in detail the full horror of Pantasma were members of a delegation organized by a national U.S. organization, USOCA (U.S. Out of Central America). We were on a week-long delegation and stayed an additional day to go to Pantasma and see firsthand what had occurred. Throughout the trip we had ample opportunity to witness the remarkable courage with which the Nicaraguans confronted their difficulties. Everyone we met emphasized that they wanted us to witness their reality, to understand their struggle and the depth of their commitment. Most important, they wanted us to take what we had witnessed and convey it to the American people.

After a three-hour drive to Jinotega, our bus left paved roads with armed guards, climbed a ridge, and traveled down into the green valley of the Rio Pantasma. We could see Honduras in the distance. One key bridge was out, and our bus forged the river to get across. We talked to the people of Pantasma from early afternoon until late at night. As the story of Pantasma unfolded, what moved us as much as the horrors and atrocities was the determination of the people to persevere, to defend the achievements of their revolution, and to rebuild what had been destroyed.

The cooperatives at Pantasma had been models of agricultural production, in the very heart of the coffee region. *There was absolutely nothing of military significance in Pantasma!* The *contras* destroyed every tractor, every truck, a lumber mill, a school, a health center, the development bank, the office of adult education, and much of the new housing in the cooperatives. The attack was designed as part of the current CIA strategy to destroy the economic infrastructure of the country. It was also aimed at terrorizing the peasants just prior to the beginning of the coffee harvest. Coffee is Nicaragua's second most important export crop, and this year's harvest must succeed in order to earn desperately needed foreign exchange.

Buildings were still smoldering as we walked through the village; on the walls the slogans written by the *contras* with the blood of their victims were still visible. We learned that the attack began at 5:30 a.m., and that the largely unarmed civilian population of Pantasma, because of their geographical isolation, had to defend themselves for 10 hours before reinforcements arrived and drove the *contras* out of the area.

Apolonia López Díaz told us:

> They came and seized us in our houses and took us hostage. They made us lie down on the floor; with a bayonet, they picked up my baby by her shirt and lifted her up. They said we were all militia and sons of bitches. They told us they were going to kill everyone in the cooperative because they didn't want to see people organized; they said we didn't belong on this land. We were told to leave the area or we would be murdered and our homes destroyed. You see how they attacked us. What they did has no name.

When the assault began there were three militiamen and one policeman on duty. Nonetheless, the *contras* were held at bay for hours by the fierce resistance mounted by civilians with rifles and handguns, who were trapped in the buildings where they worked. For others without arms, resistance took the form of placing their bodies between the *contras* and the facilities they sought to destroy, and refusing to allow them to be attacked. In this way the grain silos and a seed warehouse were saved.

Others defended themselves with words, attacking the ideological assumptions that sought to justify the *contras* as a political force in Nicaragua. One of the chief *contras* slogans is "God, Homeland, Liberty, or Death." Yet when they lined up a group of unarmed women to kill them, one woman challenged:

> Why are you going to assassinate us? We are all Nicaraguans, a consecrated people. Jesus Christ is not inflicting this on us—it is you who have taken the word of God to assassinate us and humiliate us humble women. Jesus Christ died for the truth, and for the truth we will also die.

This courageous statement was a direct challenge to the ideological justification drummed into every *contra* recruit, the justification for their existence as a political force: if not for "God and Country" then for whom— this killing of unarmed people? Especially those *contras* from social backgrounds similar to that of the residents of Pantasma were vulnerable to this argument from unarmed people. On the other hand the brutality of the *contras* is directly traceable to their creation as a mercenary army by the CIA, under the political leadership of the Somocista National Guard. The combined tutelage of the murderously efficient CIA technocrats and the Somocistas deforms the *contras* as human beings—thus their characterization by the Nicaraguan people as "beasts."

The people of Pantasma stood up to defend what their revolution had accomplished. Carlos Vaquero, FSLN Political Secretary for the region, explained:

> With the revolution, everything changed for them. They used to live up in the hills and plant with a hand spike. Now the best land, the flat land is theirs. The tractors we saw destroyed back there were used to prepare the soil. The cooperative had actually fulfilled 100% of their production plan, and they were happy about it. This cooperative had become a model for the area. After work the adults went to school because none of them learned to read and write under Somoza. Over there we also had a preschool, now it is ashes. Today we are preparing to clean up. We will rebuild in the same location the houses of the widows of this cooperative. There are 16 widows and 57 children without fathers here. We are their fathers, their uncles, their brothers—we are everything.

The spirit of the people and their determination not to be driven backward into illiteracy and exploitation echo throughout Pantasma. This spirit is in direct contrast to the destructiveness of the *contras,* who would destroy all that has meant a better life for the people of Pantasma—the schools, the cooperatives, the development bank, trucks, tractors, and so on. This indicates a profoundly backwards and reactionary outlook, which would literally restore the people of Pantasma—and all of Nicaragua—to the conditions of hopeless poverty and powerlessness that existed under Somoza.

Mercedes Pérez García, whose slain husband was president of one of the cooperatives here, concluded our visit by telling us: "I believe that we are committed to continue the struggle, to fight as our compañeros fought, to pick up the guns they left when they fell—and to help increase production, which was their hope."

PART 2

The Regional Context

CONDECA:
Another Face
of U.S. Intervention

This article was prepared by staff members of the Institute for the Study of Labor and Economic Crisis.

U.S. efforts to revive the Central American Defense Council (CONDECA), a vestige of U.S. intervention from the 1960s, may well provide Reagan with the cover for his next military aggression in Central America. As a military force, i.e., as a regional alliance among the pro-U.S. military establishments, CONDECA is not a viable proxy for U.S. intervention, because there is no army in Central America strong enough to be diverted from the task of putting down its own domestic insurgency to participate in any significant way in another country. As a "regional organization" asking for "U.S. assistance" (i.e., intervention), however, it could perform a function similar to that of the Organization of Eastern Caribbean States in Grenada.

CONDECA is a "regional organization" for "mutual assistance" among the military establishments of the most repressive, right-wing governments in Central America. It was initially created in 1964, at the initiative of, and under the supervision of, the Pentagon and the Central Intelligence Agency (*Guatemala,* edited by Susanne Jonas and David Tobis, 1974). The "founder and overlord" of CONDECA, according to Robert White, former U.S. ambassador to El Salvador, was the U.S. Southern Command, based in the Panama Canal Zone (*NYT* 11/11/83).

CONDECA's objective was to coordinate the efforts of the Central American armies in combating the resistance movements through joint counterinsurgency training and actions, and centralized intelligence operations. It is significant that Nicaraguan dictator Somoza was the Central American linchpin of CONDECA until his overthrow in 1979.

CONDECA provided a useful function for the U.S. government—it allowed the U.S. to increase its political control of the region without having to intervene directly. Roque Dalton, a Salvadoran revolutionary poet and leader, killed in 1975, once said that the main strength of imperialism in Central America was its ability to use local structures to protect its interests and to avoid direct U.S. intervention (*Guatemala* 1974).

Today, there exists no real "regional community" in Central America, since many of the economic and political institutions of U.S.-directed "regional cooperation" have been virtually destroyed as a result of conflicts among the Central American governments and of changing conditions in the region overall. Even CONDECA itself had been practically dormant, particularly since the overthrow of Somoza, despite U.S. efforts to keep it alive.

Since October 1983, however, the Reagan administration, through top Pentagon officials, has increased efforts to reactivate CONDECA, quite likely as a prelude to a direct U.S. intervention in Central America, and to deal with Nicaragua or El Salvador on a regional level. According to the *New York Times,* reports of a secret October meeting by CONDECA reveal that CONDECA is studying the legality of a joint military action against Nicaragua. It also recommended that the U.S. provide logistical support and aid, and "in case of extreme crisis, direct participation" (*NYT* 11/11/83).

Two secret meetings of CONDECA were held by the defense ministers of El Salvador, Guatemala, and Honduras, with observers from Panama and Costa Rica, under U.S. General Paul Gorman, the head of the U.S. Southern Command. Gen. Gorman has been identified as an important force in policymaking on Central America and a key architect of the naval and military maneuvers that took place off the coast of Nicaragua and are taking place in Honduras. His role is to build up the military dimension of the policy (*NYT* 8/19/83).

The current CONDECA treaty provides for assistance to any Central American country that is threatened by aggression or "by any other fact or situation." In the secret meeting in October, the group discussed further under what circumstances this treaty could be applied, focusing on Nicaragua as a target (*NYT* 11/11/83). The precedent for intervening was set in 1972, when Guatemala and Nicaragua aided the Salvadoran military in putting down a coup attempt, including bombing areas within El Salvador. Today, El Salvador could also be the next target for CONDECA.

But in what sense could CONDECA intervene? One indicator is the position of the Guatemalan Army, by far the strongest in the region. When Gen. Mejía Víctores took power in August 1983, he appeared to be very willing to involve Guatemala in the regional conflict on Reagan's behalf, and declared full support for Reagan's policy in Central America. On the eve of the coup he actually met with the head of the Southern Command and the defense ministers of Honduras and El Salvador. Later, Mejía hosted leaders of the Salvadoran, Honduran, and Panamanian Armies, as well as the head of the Southern Command, to initiate the revival of CONDECA. Guatemala is the headquarters of CONDECA, and Mejía was designated the president of the alliance.

Recently, however, Guatemalan leaders have shown a diminishing interest in participating in CONDECA, since they are fighting a guerrilla war within their own borders. Six years after the CIA-sponsored coup in 1954, the resistance began in Guatemala and since that time has plagued the right-wing dictators continuously. Army officers have reported that they need all of their men to keep the countryside under control, and in fact have never had troops to fight an external war. As one minister of the Guatemalan government put it, "We have our own problems here and have to put our house in order before we pretend to be able to help our neighbors" (*NYT* 11/23/83).

On December 20, Mejía also affirmed that Guatemala would not participate in military maneuvers in Central America, contrary to reports that Guatemalan armed forces would be part of the Big Pine III maneuvers in Honduras later in 1984. At the same time, Foreign Minister Fernando Andrade made statements denouncing pressure by the U.S. to take on a more active role in Central America.

However, even though Guatemalan officials are saying that they can't afford to be drawn into a regional conflict, it is possible that during one of the CONDECA meetings last fall, the military chiefs of Guatemala, El Salvador, and Honduras may have drafted a contingency plan for future cooperation among their armed forces, to come to each other's assistance. There have been persistent reports of Guatemalan troops on the Salvadoran border, and given divisions that exist within the Guatemalan Army, the possibility cannot be discounted that these troops would move in if needed (COHA Press Release 1/9/84; *ENFOPRENSA* 12/16/83).

The recent statements may also be an attempt by Guatemala to pressure the U.S. to renew economic and military aid and lift the ban that Congress imposed in 1977 because of human rights violations (*ENFOPRENSA* 12/30/83). But there is hardly any need for pressure from the Guatemalans in this regard, since the Reagan administration has urged the restoration of military aid for some time. Most recently, the Kissinger Commission Report recommended restoring military aid to Guatemala—possibly in the hope that the Guatemalan Army would then be able to control both internal insurgency problems and respond to regional conflict with such aid.

Even if Guatemala does not play a direct role in military intervention in the region, it is a key actor nonetheless. Mejía is opposing the initiatives of the Contadora Group for peace in the region, and Guatemala is being used by Israel as a base for weapons manufacturing. Israel is planning to produce arms in Guatemala to equip the armies of the CONDECA nations with comparable weaponry (*Informador Guerrillero* 10/2/83). Israel has been functioning as a U.S. surrogate by providing military aid to the Guatemalan military, which the U.S. has been prohibited from doing since 1977. Israeli assistance is designed for counterinsurgency operations, and the CONDECA nations are likely markets for these weapons.

But the real danger represented by the revival of CONDECA lies not so much in its reality as a material military force as in the *political* use that the Reagan administration could make of it in intervening in El Salvador or in attempting to overthrow the revolutionary Nicaraguan government. Reports from many reliable sources, in the U.S. and international press, and contained in the report of the CONDECA meeting, project a scenario whereby the Somocista *contras* would invade Nicaragua from Honduras, hold a chunk of territory in northern Nicaragua, establish a "provisional government" in the area, and then appeal to CONDECA to send troops to defend that "provisional government"—with U.S. forces in Honduras and U.S. ships offshore providing logistical support and intervening directly if necessary (*London Times* 10/30/83; *San Francisco Examiner* 11/12/83). As one Pentagon source has stated, "Although (this scenario) does not explicitly provide for American troops, it could easily," in the same manner that the Organization of Eastern Caribbean States "requested" U.S. help in Grenada—i.e., providing a regional cover (and excuse) for an actual U.S. invasion (*San Francisco Examiner* 11/2/83). CONDECA would function as part of the scenario to draw in the United States. In other words, any intervention by CONDECA, political or military, is essentially a U.S. intervention.

Honduras as a U.S. Base Against Nicaragua

Centro de Información de Honduras (CENIH)

This document was written by the Centro de Información de Honduras (Honduras Information Center), in May 1983. It was translated by CENIH, with minor subsequent editing for U.S. publication.

I.

With the Sandinista victory in Nicaragua in July 1979, the United States lost its political and economic control over that country. Because of its geographical position, Honduras, a poor yet relatively stable country, was chosen by the Carter administration to be of key importance in its policy of retaining political and economic control over the rest of Central America, and destroying the example of Nicaragua.[1]

The Carter administration set out to create a "non-military option" in Honduras. Honduras would be an example of democracy, backed by a strong armed forces. For those seeking change in Central America, Honduras would be seen as an alternative to the Nicaraguan process, as the bulwark against communism, and as a barrier between Nicaragua and the guerrilla forces in El Salvador and Guatemala. During the Carter administration, the Nicaraguan experience exposed the contradiction of employing a policy based on human rights while endeavoring to retain economic and political control. The Reagan administration swept this contradiction away, giving priority to economic and political control and to the defeat of communism over human rights considerations, and began programs of military and economic (Reaganomics) aid to its friends in Central America to achieve these goals

Nearly four years later, as a result of these policies, Honduras and Nicaragua are on the verge of war—one that can only spread into a regional conflict. Poverty and repression are increasing within Honduras, which inevitably means that Honduras will suffer the civil war and violence of her neighbors.

II.

[By 1981,] Honduras was to return to constitutional government, backed by a strong armed forces. The policy of returning to constitutional order coincided with the aspirations of the majority of Hondurans. The military government had lost its credibility and the base upon which it had come to power (to resolve the chaotic social disorder over the question of land and agrarian reform). The reformist platform which had been the base for the 1972 coup no longer existed. The economy was in crisis, and the military were blatantly corrupt (expensive government!). In an area and country where coups and dictatorships are the rule, not the exception (in Honduras there has been military rule from 1963 to 1980, with the exception of 1971-72), the balance of power was always going to be in favor of the military. This was made clear from the start: before the elections, the military High Command called the presidential candidates of the two main parties and laid down the conditions upon which they would allow the elections to proceed. There would be no investigation into corruption, and all ministerial appointments would have to be approved by the High Command.* Clearly, to remain in office, the future President would have to make some alliance with the High Command.

In the November 1981 elections, the people voted overwhelmingly against the National Party, with its traditional alliance with the armed forces, and for the Liberal Party with a tradition of reforms. The Liberal President, Dr. Roberto Suazo Córdova, took office in January 1982. Theoretically, with an absolute majority in the National Assembly, he could have been reformist in ideology. However, the Suazo Córdova group within the Liberal Party itself is not reformist and has fraudulently denied any say to the reformist wing, the Liberal Alliance of the People (ALIPO). The choices for Minister of Finance, Minister of Labor, and for the head of the armed forces clearly indicated that the new government's ideology would be that of "national security."

Suazo Córdova appointed Gustavo Alvarez—a man well known for his national security ideology and his fierce anticommunism—as head of the armed forces, and thus, the new Liberal government made precisely the alliance the people had rejected in voting against the National Party. The North American ambassador and the business community had also made it clear what economic policies had to be followed in order to revive Honduras's disastrous economy. Darío Humberto Montes (a former adviser in legal matters to private business) was made Minister of Labor, and Gustavo Alfaro, former secretary to the Council of Private Enterprise (COHEP), was apppointed Minister of Finance. The die was cast. National security ideology and Reaganomics prevailed, although these had failed previously in Argentina, Uruguay, and Chile. From that moment onward,

---

* The armed forces (through the Constitution) have complete control over all security: the right to make their own internal promotions and demotions; and the President must consult the head of the armed forces before making any decision on military matters.

at every point the power of the military would increase, and that of the civilian government decrease: opposition would be systematically eliminated, poverty would increase, and there would be no reforms in favor of the majority.

III.

The subordination of the constitutional government to the armed forces has been obvious over the past year and a half:

- Four clandestine cemeteries were discovered, and although the government promised a full inquiry, nothing was ever done.
- Alvarez was made a General by Suazo Córdova, who had to amend the Constitution to do this. Consequently, Alvarez assumed nearly absolute control of the armed forces.
- Disappearances, clandestine prisons, torture, extrajuridical killings were publicly denounced. The National Assembly refused to set up a Human Rights Commission to investigate. The judiciary is obviously intimidated.
- The armed forces proposed the antiterrorist law (which violates the Constitution), and the National Assembly approved it in a single day.
- Col. Torres Arias accused General Alvarez of internal repression, and responsibility for the disappearances, and claimed that a special unit under a Capt. Alexander Hernández operates the clandestine prisons and torture. The National Assembly refused to set up a commission to investigate the allegations and accused Torres Arias of treason.
- The existence of ex-Somocista National Guard training camps was denounced. Again no investigation, only a flat denial of their existence by the government.
- Salvadoran refugees are harassed by Honduran soldiers; the Salvadoran Army is allowed to enter Honduras and the camps and take back refugees. The government did nothing. Nicaraguan refugees, on the other hand, are given better treatment and more freedom.
- Honduran troops entered El Salvador to support the Salvadoran Army against the guerrillas. The government denies this ever took place.
- A demonstration over wages by the Front of Popular Unity-June 25th (FUP-25, see below) was violently broken up, and its leaders imprisoned and tortured: a few token protests were made in the National Assembly.
- Three airstrips in Honduras were to be extended by the U.S. so that in an emergency these could be used by the U.S. The government said that this was not true as the National Assembly would have to approve the project first. The project went ahead, and bids for the first airstrip extension were sought by advertisements in the Honduran papers—with responses to be sent to the U.S. military.
- A radar station has been set up, and manned by U.S. personnel.

The permission of the National Assembly is not needed.
- The possibility of training Salvadoran troops in Honduras (by U.S. advisers) was first denied, since the National Assembly would need to debate this first. Then the Vice President of the National Assembly said that their permission is not needed, for this would be no different from normal student, or trade union exchanges, and would therefore only need an agreement between the armed forces involved.

All the people who have disappeared are said to be training to be guerrillas in neighboring communist countries, according to the military, and Suazo Córdova himself has begun to say the same thing. Obviously there is almost no legal opposition in the country. The National and Liberal Parties are in agreement, and thus, these parties present no opposition within the National Assembly, while they spend their energies on internal party disputes. The Party of Innovation and Unity (PINU, with three deputies) offers nothing and is not heard. Only the lone Christian Democrat, Efraín Díaz Arrivillaga opposes legislation, offers alternatives, and tries to set up investigatory commissions.

Neither the government, nor obviously the armed forces, consider that trade unions and *campesino* (peasant) organizations should be consulted in the decisions that are made. The President on a number of occasions has referred to them as disruptive antipatriotic sectors.

There is no alternative means of information. The radio stations and the four daily newspapers (with the occasional exception of *El Tiempo*) offer no alternative interpretation of events and indulge in crude anticommunist, anti-Nicaraguan propaganda. Often the newspapers will not take paid advertisements on human rights abuses, let alone report on them.

The traditional left-wing parties (the pro-Moscow Communist Party of Honduras, the pro-Peking Marxist-Leninist Communist Party, and the Socialist Party (PASO) offer no organized opposition, and their leadership left Honduras during the wave of repression in June through August of 1981. The strength of these parties remains only in the trade union and *campesino* organizations in which their members are active. The Popular Revolutionary Union (URP), a break-away group from the Communist Party, has little strength because its leadership have either been murdered or are classified as having disappeared during that same period.

Neither the trade unions nor the *campesino* organizations organized in the Honduran Workers Union (CTH) with its affiliation to AFL-CIO/ORIT [Inter-American Regional Organization of Workers, the Latin American regional trade-union organization dominated by the AFL-CIO—Eds.], nor those organized in the General Workers Union (CGT) affiliated to Christian Democratic Ideology (CLAT) have offered any opposition to the present direction of events within Honduras. The only opposition comes from the trade unions organized in the Unitarian Federation of Honduran Workers (FUTH) and the *campesino* organizations in the Honduran Front of Campesino National Unity (FUNACAMH), both with left-wing orientations, which together with other popular organizations have formed the FUP-25. Formed in July 1982, this front of worker, *campesino*, student, teacher, Christian, and urban organizations is working to repeal the antiterrorist law, to defend human rights and workers' rights, and to oppose U.S. intervention in Central America.

The FUP-25 demonstration in October 1982 was violently broken up by the security forces, and many leaders were taken prisoner and tortured. All were subsequently released. It was a clear act of intimidation by the security forces as the demonstration was over the right to be paid the 13th month and 8th day [pay bonuses to workers—Eds.].

FUP-25's strength comes from the individual organizations that make it up, and it is not as yet a force in itself as a front. The teachers' organizations within FUP-25 have been subject to some crude tactics intended by the authorities to destroy them. A break-away alternative group held separate elections. This minority group was then recognized by the government (Ministry of Education), the armed forces, and the judiciary as the true representatives. This tactic has failed; the struggle continues. A similar tactic was tried with the Union of Workers from the Sula Agricultural and Cattle Company (SITRACOAG). The leadership was challenged by a group of workers formed into a "democratic front," but this latter group failed to win. Subsequently, the actual leadership was gunned down by military personnel on loan to the company. Four people were murdered in this attack on March 29, 1983.

Aside from FUP-25, the Commission for the Defense of Human Rights in Honduras (Dr. Ramón Custodio López) is challenging the present regime, as is the newly formed Committee of the Relatives of the Disappeared (COFADEH). Both of these are fearlessly challenging the military-liberal alliance and its democratic pretense, and stand out in a country where fear abounds.

The armed, left-wing Popular Revolutionary Forces (FPR) and Los Cinchonceros, or the Popular Movement of Liberation (MPL), are small clandestine organizations that have carried out bombings, hijackings, etc.

IV.

The guidelines for the government's economic policies were laid down by U.S. Ambassador Negroponte, before the Liberal Party took office. More or less the same guidelines were given by a business group led by Facusse (in a document known as the Facusse Memorandum) and by the Honduran Council of Private Enterprise (COHEP). In broad terms the guidelines were:

- preference for private business
- incentives for private foreign investment
- reduction in state corporations
- cutbacks in social programs and public spending
- increased indirect taxes

- removal of price controls
- acceptance of IMF conditions guaranteeing future loans

More or less, this has been the policy. Such "remedies" have failed to resolve the economic crises in other countries, and have only increased the level of poverty and the country's indebtedness. Thus, while confidence has been restored (to some extent), and loans have been received, the standard of living for the majority has dropped. In a population of some 3,500,000, 20,000 people lost their jobs in 1982 and the number of people unemployed is 250,000 (25% of the economically active population), while 400,000 are underemployed. In the countryside, 60% of the families (240,000) do not have enough income or produce enough food for an adequate diet. In addition, 70% of the work force in the countryside has only seasonal work and 57% are unemployed. The Ministry of Health calculates that 25 children (under 5) die daily from some form of malnutrition, or diarrhea (Honduran Center of Documentation, CEDOH; Coordinator in Support of the Struggle of the Honduran People, COALPHO). The government's economic plan for 1983-86 is a continuation of these policies. Despite its rejection by the Honduran school of economists, and the obvious effects of these policies for the majority of the people, when the plan was put before the National Assembly, only Efraín Díaz voted against it.

Although the government's statistics indicate a massive granting of land titles, the Agrarian Reform is completely inadequate. In fact, the government has been catching up on a backlog produced by the inefficiency of the past eight years, and these titles represent little or no new redistribution or granting of land. Thus, in some areas in the countryside (Santa Barbara, and Olancho) tensions are mounting and the authorities have used the antiterrorist law against those who have taken land. Currently it is estimated that there are about 200 *campesinos* in jail for taking land.

V.

Until recently, the traditional Catholic Church's conservative hierarchy has been in agreement with the authorities. During 1981, they did almost nothing about the military harassment of Father Fausto Milla (who had to leave Honduras), and about the two Caritas workers that were killed while working with Salvadoran refugees. The Church hierarchy gave complete support and legitimacy to the new government. It refused to allow the French priest, Father Boulang, to remain and work in Honduras (he had worked for at least seven years in Olancho) when it was clear that the military authorities wanted him out. However, from this position of total agreement, the hierarchy has become more aware of the Honduran reality, and the Pastoral Letter of October 1982, offered a clear understanding of the situation. In it the economy, violence, politics, and the possibility of war were discussed in terms that clearly expressed concern and a desire to defend the rights of the Honduran people. Its condemnation of the civil defense committees which had recently been formed was clear and total.

It is therefore not surprising that the military-liberal alliance has begun to distance itself from the Catholic Church. Thus, in January 1983, there was no official *Te Deum*, and neither Alvarez nor Suazo Córdova attended the ceremony for the feast of Our Lady of Suyapa, the patroness of Honduras and the armed forces. Indeed, as in other parts of Latin America, the authorities have turned to the evangelical sects for support, and as in other countries, their increase is notable (see "La penetracion protestante en Honduras," CEDOH, April 1983). The Summer Institute for Linguistic Studies, which in recent years has been expelled from Mexico, Peru, and Panama for its CIA connections, has published a bible in garifuna and is working with these indigenous communities in the Department of Yoro. The Catholic Latin American Bible was condemned as subversive by a recently arrived pastor, Mario Fumero.

However the clearest indication of the break with the Catholic Church, and the authorities' preference for those evangelical sects which support their ideology,* is seen in the setting up of the Association for the Progress of Honduras (APROH), formed by prominent military, political and business people in order to strengthen Honduran democracy.

The President, Suazo Córdova, at the ceremony granting legal status to the newly formed organization and to its president, General Alvarez, commented that he was pleased to see that the organization contained only the better elements in Honduras and that the trade unions and *campesino* organizations were not included, for these, often, had opposite aims.**

APROH is linked to an international group, the Confederation of Associations for the Unity of the American Societies (CAUSA). CAUSA is one of the organizations set up by the Unification Church in the United States (better known as the Moonies) and is a political, anticommunist organization with enormous funds available. CAUSA's president is the South Korean Bo Hi Pak who is a frequent visitor to Suazo Córdova and to Alvarez. The Moonies and CAUSA are in the process of setting up in Honduras. The Catholic hierarchy condemned the Unification Church and CAUSA and forbade its members to take part in either (Pastoral Letter, 4/11/83).

VI.

The evidence of the buildup of the Honduran armed forces, its training and logistical support for the ex-Somocista National Guard and the Salvadoran Army in accordance with the U.S. administration's policy is well documented. The Honduran armed forces have taken part in two joint maneuvers with North American logistical support and advisers (Halcon Vista and Big Pine).

* The comparison of these developments with the sect-related Ríos Montt regime (1982-83) is striking—Eds.

** APROH has issued the first public call for a U.S. military solution against the government of Nicaragua, stating that "the only alternative is a military alternative, Grenada style"—Eds. (*San Francisco Examiner* 11/8/83).

In June 1982, Honduran troops crossed into El Salvador; they have also given logistical support. Since the Reagan administration took office, the Honduran armed forces have protected, trained, and given logistical support to the Nicaraguan counterrevolution. Without this, the current waves of attacks against Nicaragua could not be sustained. The build-up of the Honduran armed forces can be simply put in the increase in military aid from the U.S.: In fiscal year 1980, the military aid was $3 million; in 1981, it was $5.5 million; and in 1982, it was $32.3 million. Given the ideology of the Honduran High Command, and that of the Reagan administration (as well as its intentions), it is hardly surprising that Honduras and Nicaragua are on the verge of war, and that, according to Robert White, former U.S. ambassador to El Salvador, after a visit to Honduras at the beginning of April 1983, "Many of the Honduran military want war" (cited in *La Tribuna* 4/11/83).

The Liberal President Suazo Córdova moves constantly around the country using rhetoric that is anticommunist, anti-Nicaraguan, and which appeals to the religiosity of the people. He holds himself up as a model and example of Catholicism, and uses the religiosity of the people to justify national security ideology and repression. His government is democratic, opposed to the communism of Nicaragua and of the guerrillas of El Salvador. There are neither political prisoners nor people who have disappeared in Honduras. There are no camps of ex-Somocista National Guards; the government is not supporting the counterrevolution in Nicaragua (there is a civil war in Nicaragua); we do not intervene in another country's internal affairs. Strikes are unpatriotic and subversive. The taking of land will be met with force. The armed forces are loyal and obedient to the constitutional government. All reports to the contrary are part of an international communist smear campaign against the democratic institutions of Honduras: Honduras, which is desirous of peace in the region, yet must defend its democracy, its sovereignty against communist infiltration. Any criticism within Honduras, any groups denouncing repression, disappearances, or Honduras's loss of neutrality are condemned as subversive and said to be made by unpatriotic people who simply spread the lies and assist the international campaign of disinformation currently being mounted against Honduras's democracy and the constitutional government.

With God and Suazo Córdova all the problems of Honduras will be solved. All is under control and the Honduran people are in safe hands.

VIII. Conclusions

1. At best, Honduras is governed by a military-liberal alliance, which makes democratic government in Honduras a sham. Its political and economic policies are dictated by the Reagan administration which does not consider the actual needs and wishes of the Honduran people, but rather its own imperative of retaining complete political and economic control over the Central American region.

As a result, Honduras is no longer neutral: it is supporting the continuation of the dictatorship in Guatemala, a repressive, right-wing government (oligarchy) in El Salvador, and the counterrevolution in Nicaragua. Through Honduras, the U.S. has regionalized the tensions and the conflicts. In order to achieve this, Honduras has experienced internal repression on a scale not known before as all legal opposition to Honduras's role and its political and economic policies is eliminated either through intimidation and voluntary exile, or through disappearances and political assassination. In a country unused to such repression, fear is present. Only a few have the courage and conviction to speak out.

2. Although the abuses of human rights are privately deplored by many upper-middle class Hondurans, they do not wish to see the changes that have taken place in Nicaragua. They are anticommunist (and therefore anti-Nicaragua). They wish to preserve the status quo, but deplore the price: repression. If they are aware that this is the price, they often do not connect maintaining the status quo with repression. Their attitude is revealed in the example of a November 1982 *Newsweek* article. The article revealed U.S. Ambassador Negroponte's and the Hondurans' involvement in equipping, training, and protecting the Nicaraguan counterrevolutionaries, ex-National Guardsmen. The middle class was concerned that events could be getting out of hand, and that Honduras could be getting involved in something that would be the beginnings of violence and civil war for them and that would threaten their way of life. They were not concerned about the poverty and the injustice inside Honduras. There was no condemnation of the [Reagan] administration's policy for the region as such.

3. Disappearances, the elimination of legal opposition (such as the attempts against the teachers' unions) will be on the increase as Honduras moves nearer to war, and/or becomes more involved in the events in Nicaragua and El Salvador.

May 1983

Sources

The primary sources for this article are: the Honduran Center of Documentation (Centro de Documentación de Honduras, CEDOH); the Honduran Committee for the Defense of Human Rights (Comité para la Defensa de los Derechos Humanos en Honduras, CODEH); the Coordinator in Support of the Struggle of the Honduran People (Coordinadora en Apoyo a la Lucha del Pueblo Hondureño, COALPHO, México); Víctor Meza, *Evolución de la Crisis en Honduras;* Reports by the Honduran Institute for Socioeconomic Research (Instituto de Investigaciones Socio-Económicas de Honduras, INSEH, México); and daily newspapers.

A Permanent U.S. "Maneuver"

Instituto de Investigaciones Socio-Económicas de Honduras

This monograph was published in Spanish by the Instituto de Investigaciones Socio-Económicas de Honduras (Honduran Institute for Socioeconomic Research) in Mexico, in the August 1983 issue of the INSEH series "Information and Documentation Analysis."

Introduction

Honduras, along with the other Central American countries, gained its political independence from Spain in 1821. The inability of the dominant sectors of Honduran society to build a political and economic project resulted in the establishment of an enclave economy, the maximum expression of domination, and the existence of a neocolonial state.

England was able to establish its influence in Honduras during several decades of the last century through the orientation of production toward the necessities of the English textile bourgeoisie, through the exploitation of mineral resources and the trade in the islands of Oahia and Mosquitia, and through a loan for the construction of a railway system. There was also interest in the construction of a canal and a railway that would link both oceans. England, however, was not the only country interested in Honduras and Central America; the United States defined its interest and objectives in the Monroe Doctrine (1823). These interests grew, forcing England to accept the Clayton-Bulwer Treaty [1850] that obligated it to share the Central American "booty," then slowly replacing it as English colonial capitalism weakened.

American capitalism attained economic and political primacy in Honduras at the beginning of the 1880s; the crushing control of American capital was seen first through investments in mining and later in the banana companies.

Economic domination was accompanied by political hegemony that generated civil wars and produced chiefs of state and a dominant class whose primary function was to manage society to serve American capital. In order to assure American political and economic predominance, the U.S. would send in the Marines as many times as they believed necessary, on the pretext of protecting life and property of Americans living in Honduras.

The weakness of the local dominant sectors, their own class consciousness, and the existence of a permanent American presence impeded the formation of a modern capitalist state in all its extensions. This would last until the beginning of the 1950s under the direction of the American military, which for 3 years led the First Battalion (Military Assistance Agreement of May 1954). So from its birth, the "modern" Honduran Army remained under the control of the United States; military training and its ideological base were controlled by the American military. The same can be said for war-related supplies, organization, and tactics of war and repression. Beginning in 1965, joint military operations and exercises were initiated throughout Latin America through the UNITAS program.

The triumph of the Sandinista Popular Revolution in July 1979 radically changed the relationship of forces in Central America, and for the United States it meant the loss of its firmest ally, General Somoza, and the loss of its principal military apparatus in the area, the Nicaraguan National Guard; it was then that the Carter administration turned its attention toward Honduras. This country offered extraordinary advantages according to official U.S. analyses: its geographic location, the relatively less intense nature of its internal social conflicts, the weaker economic power of the local bourgeoisie—the weakest of all in Central America—and the fact that there already existed a state apparatus and military/political structures ready to collaborate with U.S. plans.

At that time the Honduran Armed Forces took on a crucial role and a decisive responsibility; it wasn't enough to try to effectively repress popular movements—rather, they had to be the principal instrument of U.S. strategy in Central America.

In order to implement this policy, the U.S. began the task of modernizing, "technologizing," and professionalizing the Armed Forces, placing trusted officers in command while getting rid of the rebellious officers in their ranks. It is important to understand the enormous amount of military aid received by the Honduran Armed Forces in this context.

The strategy, as defined by the White House, was to build a military enclave in Honduras. In order to achieve this, efforts were made to modernize airports and construct new air strips; the construction of the military base at Puerto Castilla, the radar installations at Mosquitia (Mocorón) and Tegucigalpa (Cerro de Hula), and the 300 Marines officially stationed in the country strengthened this effort. The military enclave was not developed peripherally to the Honduran Armed Forces; rather, it was fully incorporated into the aggressive strategy that the United States was developing in that region.

The Honduran Army is an occupation force parallel to the U.S. Marines. Within this framework of U.S. political/military strategy, joint military exercises during the last three years have played a far-reaching role quite different from that prior to 1979. Current military exercises have several simultaneous objectives:

- To prepare the Honduran Army for war in the region, particularly with intent to attack Nicaragua;
- To prepare the Honduran Armed Forces for war against Honduran patriots;
- To prepare U.S. Armed Forces to attack Nicaragua and other people who fight for their freedom;
- To try to subdue the Central American peoples, especially Nicaraguans and Salvadorans;
- To create a practical and natural infrastructure for war;
- To convert Honduras gradually but increasingly into an occupied country and a docile instrument of American policies.

Operations prior to 1979 were generic and did not necessarily have a concrete enemy. Today we see a series of military operations of increasing complexity that are a part of a defined American strategy to prepare military, political and ideological conditions for a massive attack on Nicaragua, on Salvadoran patriots, and on the Honduran people who oppose this strategy. We are not dealing with just any military exercise; these are maneuvers preliminary to war.

The Honduran newspaper *El Tiempo*, which is politically opposed to the current government, has pointed out that these military operations are a "peaceful seizure of Honduran territory." The military Ahuas Tara II (Big Pine II) exercises imply a blockade against Nicaragua in addition to the observations made in *El Tiempo*.

Honduran President Roberto Suazo Córdova and Chief of Armed Forces General Gustavo Alvarez Martínez are the main people implicated in this "peaceful seizure" of Honduran territory, the blockade against Nicaragua, and the preparation for war. Some analyses exclusively blame Reagan and his administration for the Honduran situation and its projection in Central America. This is fallacious; the dominant classes in Honduras and "their" Army are very much responsible for what is happening.

Background

The intensified conversion of Honduran Armed Forces into an apparatus prepared to meet the needs of the dominant classes of the region and U.S. interests in this area began in 1979. To meet this objective, many operations have been carried out involving joint military exercises of the U.S. and Honduran Armies, since 1965, among which are the following:

1965 "Halcon Vista" An operation that took place in October along the Caribbean and Central American coast and in which Guatemala, Honduras, Costa Rica, El Salvador, [Somoza's] Nicaragua, and the U.S. participated.

1976 "Aguila VI" This operation was carried out through the Central American Defense Council, (CONDECA), and had as its objective "the end of Sandinista guerrilla forces" that were operating in Segovia, Madriz, and Estelí.

1981 "Halcon Vista" These operations were carried out October 7-9 on the Atlantic Coast along Nicaraguan beaches. Their purpose was to show U.S. support for Honduras and to warn Cuba and the Soviet Union that "they wouldn't be permitted to continue intervening in Central America." These operations consisted of naval exercises in which several squads of planes from both countries participated, along with three Honduran ships and six American ships, including the frigate *Fort Snelling* with 650 infantry Marines aboard. These operations were supervised by Wallace Nutting, the Chief of the Southern Command based in Panama.

1981 "Despliegue Combinado" ("Combined Deployment") These took place July 26 in Durzuna in Mosquitia, 40 kilometers north of the Nicaraguan border. Participating in this event were 600 U.S. Marines, 1,000 Honduran soldiers from the Fifth Battalion, two C-130 transport planes, and four helicopters; in addition, on this date the ship *Portland* sailed along the Honduran coast with a crew of 400 men and the potential to transport 375 Marines. Officers of the Fifth Infantry Battalion who were stationed at Comayagua founded Fort Mocorón, which provided support to the counterrevolutionaries operating out of this region. The operation had as its objective the preparation of the Honduran Army in rapid deployment techniques, use of weapons, and logistical support.

1983 Ahuas Tara I (Big Pine I) This operation took place February 1-6 in Durzuna Puerto Lempira, the main city of Mosquitia, on the Nicaraguan border. The participants included: 1,600 U.S. soldiers, among whom were 206 members of the Puerto Rican National Guard; 4,000 Honduran soldiers, representing the Second Infantry Battalion (the Special Tactical Force for anti-guerrilla warfare); the Third Battalion; the Fourth, from Puerto de la Ceiba; the Fifth, from Fort Mocorón; and the Ninth, from Tegucigalpa. In addition, CH-47, UH-58, and UH-60 helicopters were used for troop transport, as well as C-2A observation planes from the U.S. Air Force. Furthermore, the warships U.S.S. Spiegel Grove with 350 men aboard and U.S.S. Boulder with 170 men also participated in this operation.

These military maneuvers were defined as defense against an invasion by a communist army belonging to a hypothetical country named "Corinto." This Honduran territory was defended by the Fourth, Ninth, and Second Battalions, and the Mocorón (Fifth). Obviously, the Honduran troops were victorious, after a heroic struggle. The cost of these operations rose to $5.2 million, financed by the U.S., which also installed radar in Mosquitia, maintained and controlled by U.S. personnel. This radar capability is reinforced by that of Cerro de Hula, 20 kilometers from Tegucigalpa, which has a radius of 320 miles and has access to information in Honduras, El Salvador, and Nicaragua, and a small part of Guatemala. This radar also was installed and is currently operated by U.S. personnel (50 U.S.

soldiers). It was installed to control traffic in Honduran airspace and in the Gulf of Fonseca, which belongs to Honduras, El Salvador, and Nicaragua.

Honduran military and political authorities define these maneuvers as "routine" or "normal," a continuation of those operations that have been in effect since 1965. According to Foreign Minister Edgardo Paz Barnica, "The exercises will be designed to prepare the Honduran Armed Forces technically, and they are of a defensive nature." U.S. Ambassador Negroponte has referred to them as "logical or necessary."

The military aide of the Puerto Rican National Guard, Lorenzo Llenza, said that it was a question of taking advantage of the bilingualism of Puerto Rican soldiers, and that the important thing is not military training, but rather the impression that is caused and the *cultural interchange that is provided* (*La Cruz de los Pueblos,* Puerto Rico, 4/17/83, pp. 32ff; emphases added by INSEH).

Current Maneuvers

"La Flotilla" ("The Small Fleet")

On July 16, sources in the U.S. Marine Corps announced in Washington that a "small fleet" of American ships was heading towards Central America and that the United States would simultaneously carry out military exercises in the region.

Information released later revealed that the "small fleet" consisted of 19 ships in three groups. Some would be stationed in the Caribbean, led by the aircraft carrier *Coral Sea* and the battleship *New Jersey.* The first to arrive would locate in the Gulf of Fonseca, led by the aircraft carrier *Ranger.*

The Pacific Group

This fleet left San Diego, California, with its lead ship the *Ranger,* a 60,000 ton ship with 1,940 men aboard; it was accompanied by the *Horme,* a 6,500 ton ship with MK-10 missile launchers and a 127mm cannon, with two triple torpedo tubes and other accessories.

The 3,370 ton destroyer *Lynde McCorwick,* equipped with MK-11 missile launchers, two 127mm cannons, and a rocket launcher with eight tubes with ASROC torpedoes and two triple tubes with MK-32's, also participated.

The twin frigates *Fije* and *Fletcher,* each at 5,830 tons, each with a Sea Knight helicopter, eight Harpoon rocket launchers and one Sea Sparrow missile launcher, two 127mm cannons, two 20mm cannons, and an MK-32 torpedo system were there. The aircraft carrier *Ranger* was equipped with 70 F-14 Tomcat combat aircraft and an A7 and A6 intercepter.

The Caribbean Groups

With respect to these groups, the Pentagon—as usual in these cases—has not released much information concerning their capabilities, the equipment, or numbers of people involved in the crew, and has limited itself to mentioning that the *New Jersey* would be accompanied by a frigate, a cruiser, and four destroyers ("superficial action group"), and that the ship would complete its mission in the Asiatic Southeast before moving to Central America.

Facts about the ships led by the aircraft carrier *Coral Sea* are also scarce; we only know that the ship was escorted by two destroyers and two frigates, that the capacity is 60,000 tons, and that it has 70 aircraft aboard and a crew of 2,610.

The Caribbean Group comprises the most powerful fleet that has ever been in Caribbean waters. According to American Armed Forces calculations, this operation cost $963,558 (*NYT* News Service).

Although the presence of this fleet has been deemed a routine activity and White House spokesman Larry Speakes has said that "it represents no danger to anyone," it is not for this reason that its true motives have been hidden. U.S. Ambassador Jeane Kirkpatrick has said that the presence of U.S. naval units in Central American waters "has the principal objective of reminding the Sandinista government of Nicaragua that Washington can blockade that country."

Admiral Wesley McDonald, Commander in Chief of the Atlantic Fleet, during his visit to Honduras on August 11, 12, and 13, said in reference to the "small fleet": "Basically the presence of U.S. naval power along the Central American coastline is designed to reaffirm the decision to support allied countries in that area" (*El Heraldo,* Honduras, 8/12/83).

For his part, George Shultz, U.S. Secretary of State, declared: "The U.S. and Honduras are demonstrating with our current military exercises what cooperation and *dissuasion through force mean"* (*Ovaciones* 8/5/83).

U.S. officials acknowledge, then, that the presence of the "small fleet" is a show of force on the part of the U.S. and a clear warning to Cuba and Nicaragua, which Reagan has accused of sponsoring "subversion" in Central America.

Big Pine II

On July 23, [1983], news was released in Tegucigalpa concerning the Big Pine II joint military maneuvers, a U.S.-Honduran co-venture expected to continue from August 1983 through March of 1984 in various regions of Honduras.

The announcement made in Washington simultaneously about the presence of the fleet and the joint military exercises made it seem initially that these are different actions; the presence of U.S. ships and the threat of quarantine and boycott against Cuba and Nicaragua hinder our understanding that in Honduran territory thay are establishing conditions (through military exercises) to convert Honduras into a permanently occupied country, with a military infrastructure such that in the future, aggression against Nicaragua and on the Central American revolutionary movement by Honduran Armed Forces would be possible.

The passage of time permits us to see that we are witnessing a maneuver of great dimensions, reaching almost all of Honduras, which will permit the transport of an enormous quantity of weapons and military equipment, the majority of which will remain in the country. It will facilitate the creation of an infrastructure network (airports, roads) that will then permit rapid and easy movement of troops and military materials.

Official Justification

Honduran as well as American authorities have resorted to many types of arguments to legitimize these maneuvers; Ambassador Negroponte declared in Tegucigalpa that "each year we have had this type of military exercise. At times twice a year. This news doesn't surprise me in the least. It is normal, given the agreements we have made" (*La Tribuna* 6/20/83).

For his part, during the visit of the presidents of Panama and Colombia, General Gustavo Alvarez Martínez stated:

> By disposition and tradition, Honduras is a pacifist nation, but must prepare itself because the 110,000 armed Nicaraguans are not there for a parade. . . .We do not know what Nicaragua will do with these people, and if the United States is helping us to get trained and thus be in better condition to confront this threat, we must be pragmatic about the situation. . . .Don't you think it would be foolish to waste time when Soviet ships are arriving every day in Nicaragua? (*La Tribuna* 7/28/83).

Along the same lines, sources from the Honduran Foreign Ministry announced at a press conference that, "The maneuvers are an attempt to help us attain a military equilibrium with Nicaragua in order to give us equal negotiating power."

Colonel César Elvir Sierra, Chief of Public Relations of the Honduran Army, pointed out that the exercises are a "clear warning to Nicaragua's warlike attitude" (*Uno más Uno*, Mexico, 8/7/83).

Finally, Colonel José A. Bueso Rosa, head of the Joint Chiefs of Staff of the Honduran Armed Forces, declared that "the military exercises that have been held in Honduras do not represent any threat whatsoever to a *neighboring nation,* but rather a benefit to those that execute them" (*El Heraldo* 7/12/83).

The common denominator for all of these arguments about the maneuvers is the threat—veiled or open—to Nicaragua. In spite of this, behind every declaration is hidden the true meaning of these exercises: *the preparation of favorable conditions for future aggression against Nicaragua and against Central American revolutionary forces and the deepening of the repression against the popular organizations of Honduras.*

Description

The Office of International Information of the Honduran government described the maneuvers, pointing out that, "It is a question of several different events that together involve 6,000 Honduran forces and approximately 4,000 U.S. forces."

The head of the Joint Chiefs of Staff, Col. Rosa, has described these maneuvers as "Armed Forces drills, the construction of an infrastructure (landing strips and highways, including the one that would link Olancho and Mosquitia). Medical aid and supplies will be given to the people and other types of Military Civic Action will be implemented" (*La Tribuna* 8/12/83).

These maneuvers have, nevertheless, three main purposes:

1. To carry out mock battles to oust a hypothetical enemy through landing on the Atlantic seaboard;
2. To defend against an attack of armored tanks (the T-55's of Nicaragua?) and to construct anti-tank barriers;
3. To practice aerial artillery attack and defense, control of territory and of internal enemies.

For the implementation of Big Pine II, 12 "elite" American units were mobilized, involving 5,673 men, according to the U.S. State Department (*Tiempo* 8/8/83). Among these "elite" units were the following:

An amphibious unit of Marines (2,000 men)
A supporting Army troop (No. 43) (900 men)
A battalion of the Army Corps of Engineers
An aviation battalion
A unit from the General Headquarters of Air Transport
A unit from the General Headquarters of the Tactical Command
A detachment of air surveillance from the Marine Corps
A Marine construction battalion
A Green Beret Battalion
An advance squadron from the Marine Corps

Honduran military sources pointed out, however, that the U.S. presence "would be limited to 200 Marines, one artillery battalion, one battalion of engineers, one battalion of helicopters, and one military hospital."

A planning task force has divided the maneuvers into successive phases, the first of which was executed from August through September and consisted of the construction of training camps, barracks, and special installations.

The coordination of the exercises is under the supervision of a 40-person "Rapid Deployment Command" from the United States, under the direction of Col. Arnie Schlossberg. These exercises were located in three main places:

1. Palmerola (Comayagua). An air base situated in the center of the country, where the general headquarters of the Rapid Deployment Command are located; the American military hospital will be installed nearby, with 60 beds and 250 doctors. One battalion of helicopters with a crew of 400 men will be stationed here for the purpose of transport of personnel and goods.

2. Puerto Castilla (Colón). A U.S military base, headquarters of the Regional Center for Military Training (CREM), where one artillery battalion with 700 men will be installed, equipped with 24 105mm cannons; the landing strip will be widened for the landing of Hercules aircraft. In November there will be a week of amphibious operations, including the participation of 2,000 Marines, who will "train" members of the Honduran Navy.

Zona Sur (Southern Zone). There will be exercises in the cities of Choluteca and San Lorenzo during September and October [1983]; three or four battalions of Honduran soldiers will participate in this training. One battalion of engineers will arrive at the port of San Lorenzo to construct a landing strip for Hercules C-130's.

Coinciding with these exercises in the Gulf of Fonseca, there will be "some naval patrols" with a crew of 20 people. In Choluteca a training camp for infantry and armored operations will be built.

During the climax of the exercises in Olancho in eastern Honduras, maneuvers will take place involving 11,000 soldiers (5,000 Americans).

And finally, in these maneuvers the four most important military airports in the country will be utilized: the Air Force Base Armando Escalón (in San Pedro Sula), the Air Force Base Palmerola (in Comayagua), the General Air Force Base (in Tegucigalpa), and the Air Force Base Héctor Carraccioli (in La Ceiba). The Galaxi C-5, C-141, and Hercules C-130 planes and the Cheenok, Black Hawk, and UH-1H Huey helicopters will be used to transport artillery, campaign tents, communications equipment, detection equipment, supplies, personal gear and specialized operatives.*

The Significance of These Exercises

Just as they had been planned and are being implemented, the maneuvers increase the operative capacity of the Armed Forces, giving them a military infrastructure that is a decisive factor in their capability to mobilize in case of "aggression or internal subversion." The maneuvers also create new space and greater freedom of action for the Nicaraguan counterrevolutionaries. We must emphasize that the land and sea areas where these operations are to take place are exactly those bordering on Nicaragua, with the exception of Palmerola, which because of its installations and its location is the most important Air Force base of the country.

Big Pine II is, without a doubt, one of the last stages in the preparation of the *invasion of Nicaragua and of intervention and repression in Central America,* which has been incubating since 1979. From a military perspective, Big Pine II is a significant turning point in the war preparations (along with the naval maneuvers)** based on the intensification of the exercises and the preparation of landings. Declarations from the Presidential Palace in Honduras illustrate this: "In a given moment both military operations can

---

* The operations began August 4 with an air bridge headquartered in San Pedro Sula where the C-141's arrived; the supplies were transported in Hercules C-130's to other airports.

** Even though those responsible for the maneuvers indicate that the role of the "small fleet" is limited to the task of coordination through radiocommunications groups.

be fused into one unit following instructions issued from the Pentagon" (AP/UPI).

All that's left is to increase the number of military bases (as proposed by General Gorman) [head of the U.S. Southern Command in Panama—Eds.], to convert Honduras into a country totally occupied by the U.S.; along with this the final step would be to intensify and confirm the participation of Guatemala, which would occur "when the moment is right," according to statements by Gen. Oscár Mejía Víctores,* and to increase the number of "irregular" Somocistas to 15,000 (the number that the CIA deems necessary). The stage and actors are ready for the work to be given by the director.

Opposition to These Maneuvers and to the War

The popular movement of Honduras and legal political organizations are firmly opposed to U.S. intervention and to the joint maneuvers of the Honduran and U.S. forces.

The Popular Unity Front June 25 (FUP-25) described the situation as the "waiting room for war" and the "omen of the Vietnamization of Central America." The Honduran Peasants' Unity Front (FUNACAMH) publicly announced: "We condemn the policy of accepting open U.S. government direction of our military and political arenas; they install military bases, radar, provide weapons and warships to carry out maneuvers in Central American waters, to provoke conflict among our countries—and from all of this, we Central Americans—especially peasants—will be the ones who give our lives in order to satisfy the interests of the U.S. government."

The University Revolutionary Front (FUR), a student organization, demanded of the Liberal Party military government that "young lives not be sacrificed in a war that only favors the designs of one who will be recorded in history as a new Hitler, Ronald Reagan."

The Movement of Christians for Justice (MCJ) proclaimed in a public document, "We Hondurans do not want to see ourselves involved in a war with Nicaragua nor with any country of the world"; furthermore, they demand that "we not contribute to finalizing a war that only benefits and interests the war-oriented government of the U.S." The Committee for the Defense of Human Rights in Honduras (CODEH) also called for an end to war.

Ex-Minister of Labor Gautama Fonseca, in an article published in _El Tiempo_, wrote: "There is nothing more ridiculous under the sun at this time than the docile Honduran acceptance of U.S. intervention." And he added, "The problems of U.S. foreign policy are not our problems. To be an ally is not the same as being a slave."

Christian Democratic Representative Efraín Díaz Arrivillaga strongly criticized U.S. foreign policy in Central America, warning that the only goal of Reagan in this region is "to create a state of war without regard for who is to die."

* Gen. Mejía Víctores came to power in Guatemala in a military coup on August 8, 1983.

The Party of Innovation and Unity (PINU) said that "Honduras should not be a beachhead of foreign intervention, nor a sanctuary for regional forces that try to use our land to serve their own interests."

The newspaper *El Tiempo* pointed out, in an editorial on July 20, "The announcement that this coming August there will be in Honduras massive joint military maneuvers with approximately 5,000 U.S. land/air/sea forces *could not be more ominous for peace in the region and for the future of our nation.*"

In Central America the opposition has been unanimous; the President of Costa Rica, Luis Alberto Monge, criticized the maneuvers, saying that "they will not contribute at this time to creating an atmosphere for dialogue in the region."

Panama's President Ricardo de la Spriella considered that "the military maneuvers presently being held in Central America are unnecessary." He also pointed out that "sending soldiers and a war fleet to Honduras will not in the least help to diminish tensions in the region."

The Farabundo Martí National Liberation Front of El Salvador (FMLN) has stated, "The naval maneuvers begun by the U.S. in the Pacific Ocean in front of El Salvador and Nicaragua contradict the work done by Special U.S. Ambassador to Central America Richard Stone." They go on to say that the aggressive vehemence "with which the U.S. threatens Central America is clearly indicated by the breadth of their military maneuvers."

Meanwhile, the Salvadoran Church demonstrated its concern, and a spokesperson stated, "These military actions will not make anyone happy who really desires a peaceful regional solution to our problems." And Monsignor Rivera y Damas [of El Salvador] declared that these maneuvers are a clear symptom of foreign intervention in Central American affairs.

In Nicaragua, the Sandinista Workers' Central (CST) judged these maneuvers as being the prelude to a more aggressive intervention, and Commander Tomás Borge stated, "These operations are desperate reactions to a political defeat that the U.S. government has suffered in the face of our peace proposals."

Foreign ministers and presidents of organizations from all four countries of the Contadora Group have expressed their worry and opposition and are now strongly criticizing these operations as disruptive of efforts for peace and detente in the region.

Conclusions

1. The military maneuvers that have been held since 1979 have different objectives than those held prior to 1979, due in part to changes in the correlation of forces, with the Sandinista Revolution, the Salvadoran and Guatemalan struggles, and the new, repressive, interventionist, and aggressive tasks for Central America assigned to the new Central American Bunker.

2. The maneuvers since 1979, as a whole, form part of a unique strategy (with variants) that is preparing the conditions for war against the

self-determination of the Central American peoples. One could say that it is really one great maneuver with several phases.

3. Having become the pivot of this U.S. military strategy in the region, Honduras has been converted into a territory occupied by its own Army and by U.S. Marines.

4. Given the above, the "preventative" war that the Army is carrying on against the Honduran people becomes more clearly defined; the popular struggle is being converted into a war of national liberation against foreign invaders and their internal allies, who are revealing clearly their anti-popular and anti-national character.

5. The total occupation of Honduran territory means unequivocally that the popular struggle will take on, in this stage, an eminently "American" character, a situation that will make the political, economic, and social struggle in the region more complex, more profound.

The Price of Honduras: Letter From Suazo Córdova to Reagan

This letter appeared (in Spanish) in El Heraldo *(Honduras) on September 19, 1983. We reprint it here as a vivid example of the economic subservience to the U.S. that is a consequence of the U.S. military occupation of Honduras.*

Tegucigalpa, D.C.
July 18, 1983
PRH—No. 100-83

Dear President Reagan:

After sending my letter of June 29 [1983], it seems to me that it would be useful to develop in greater detail the problems that confront [Honduras]. These problems point to the urgent need for the broadest possible aid program, in order to make effective the preferential treatment which Honduras deserves from its friend and ally [the United States]. In our communications, I have emphasized the following points, which concern our mutual relations:

a) The security of Honduras, the strengthening of its democratic institutions, and the maintenance of a growing economy are vital elements for political stability in Central America and for the security of the United States itself;

b) The present upheaval has created barriers to the political, social, and economic progress that existed in Central America. *We know that social injustice and the abuse of power have been the underlying elements which subversive forces use as their banner for struggle. But the conflict which we now confront is an ideological one: democracy vs. Marxist totalitarianism,* which has converted Central America into a new focus of tensions between your country and Russia, placing Honduras at the center of this conflict.

c. We are allies of the United States because we believe in the same democratic values. We have demonstrated a sense of social responsibility, as demonstrated in the decisions we have made, in spite of the implied political risk.

d) The economic and political emergency demands efforts and

resources that we unfortunately do not have. Our economic system depends upon the harmonious coexistence of the factors of production. However, the private sector, because of the political uncertainty that exists in Central America, the international economic recession, and the high rates of interest, is going through an unprecedented crisis. Similar financial difficulties are faced by the Honduran state. *In addition, the economic crisis, with its attendant unemployment, is the greatest threat to political stability and to the entire socioeconomic framework upon which our system is based.*

The analysis presented above is still valid. Furthermore, the political crisis in the area is worsening, as you frankly and courageously stated before a joint session of the U.S. Congress.

For our part, we have made very serious efforts in the following areas:

a) My government has restored a belief in the democratic system among the Honduran people. We have similar recognition from the international community.

b) We have taken drastic measures in an attempt to cure the financial malaise of the country. We have consented to and are complying with a program of financial stabilization with the International Monetary Fund (IMF). New taxes have been established, and public expenditures have been cut and placed under greater control. We have imposed a similar discipline in order to re-establish equilibrium in the balance of payments, limiting imports solely to essential goods. Without a doubt, the Honduran people are being subjected to a most difficult test, which is reflected in growing unemployment and underemployment.

c) With regard to external security, our Armed Forces are being strengthened to confront the communist threat, a necessity that places great strains on our budget. This program is justified given the vital role which my country is playing as the defender of democracy in Central America.

d) We recognize and are thankful for the aid of your government. In your letter of April 26, you informed me of increases in this aid, but nonetheless, these resources will be insufficient to deal with the crisis that we confront.

e) The private sector continues to stagnate. Day by day, businesses that contribute to production deteriorate, while others close, increasing unemployment and creating social and political instability.

In summary, Mr. President, despite our internal efforts, and despite the aid received from your government, as well as from international financial institutions, the crisis is at its most extreme point. Because of this, I am presenting your government with a special aid program which signifies truly preferential treatment for Honduras in fiscal matters, in the balance of payments, and in terms of aid for the private sector.

I am talking about a three-year program that would attack the root of our problems, maintaining, during this period, a minimal level of economic activity, employment, and a reasonable equilibrium in fiscal matters and in the balance of payments. Projections which have been prepared by the World Bank and the International Monetary Fund indicate that international economic recovery could be achieved during this period, enabling our productive sector once again to sustain an acceptable growth in levels of income, so that our economy could once again function with its own resources.

This medium-term project is justified because we anticipate that the Central American crisis will not be totally resolved, since it will not be an easy task to overcome the negative effects of organized subversion on the private sector, which translate into serious disruptions of investments, and the profound dislocation of the social fabric.

Re-establishing stability in Central America will require the rest of this decade, with the constant application of programs for substantial social and economic change, and this depends on decisive support from the international community.

As you are aware, this is particularly true and necessary with respect to the government and people of the United States, and is evidenced in the reactions in the Congress and Senate of your country, such as the recent initiative by Senators Jackson and Mathias to promote a "Marshall-type Plan" for our region.

Groups of businessmen, unionists, peasants, professionals, and members of cooperatives from Honduras have made trips to the United States in order to seek support for strengthening the private sector and the state's finances. They have been speaking with members of the State Department, the Security Council, the Congress, the Senate, and with private business leaders.

As a result of all these considerations, and complementary to what I outlined in my letter of June 19, I am raising for your consideration a proposal for economic assistance going beyond that which Your Excellency informed me of in your attentive letter of April 26. The plan comprises the following areas.

1. A Program of Guarantees for the Honduran Private Sector by the United States Government. The proposal is for the Agency for International Development (AID) to extend guarantees to the Honduran banking sector in order to obtain lines of credit from North American banks up to $200 million, and in order to reactivate lines of credit and suppliers' credits for more than the $300 million which our economy has lost.

This program would have the effect of re-establishing this source of financing, which was completely cut off because Central America is considered to be a high political risk.

Since we need to have this foreign exchange as quickly as possible, and since AID will surely have to get legislative approval, we raise for your consideration that it might be possible to establish, as a financial bridge, the following mechanism:

a) Authorize the Export-Import Bank to extend these guarantees up to $100 million.

b) That the appropriate North American governmental agency guarantee to U.S. banks advance payments to the Honduran Central Bank of up to $100 million for the sale of the next three years' worth of export production (bananas, coffee, sugar, meat, etc.). These funds are in addition to the $40 million which has been obtained from foreign private banks for the renegotiation of the foreign debt.

c) The government of Honduras would guarantee the allocation of the foreign exchange needed to pay off contractual obligations.

The foregoing proposals are the result of informal consultations with representatives of your government about the most expeditious manner of achieving these objectives.

2. Programs of Budget Assistance. This would be an extraordinary program of budget assistance to the government of Honduras. In my letter of June 29, I once again provided justification for a request of $150 million for our fiscal year 1983. However, to complement our internal efforts, and to cover in part the foreseeable fiscal and balance of payments deficits for 1984 and 1985, for which the national economy will not be able to generate necessary resources, in spite of the austerity measures and the discipline we are applying, I request in addition from you at least $100 million annually for the next two years as cited above.

3. Plan for Industrial Recovery. In order to ensure the greatest impact and the best utilization of the resources to be provided, we propose that a complementary plan of industrial recovery be set in motion so that industrial enterprises which are currently established, but which are now in serious financial difficulty, may begin to function again; the current investment of these companies is on the order of $300-400 million. This plan does not require additional financial assistance, but rather seeks mechanisms to make U.S. investment in Honduras more viable.

For the reasons which I have given you above, Mr. President, we hope that our request for a preferential program of foreign assistance for Honduras will be given the special consideration that it deserves.

I am sure, Mr. President, that as you are fully convinced of the strategic importance of Honduras and of our role as the stabilizer of the Central American region, you will give your personal consideration and support to our request.

Sincere greetings,

Roberto Suazo Córdova,
Constitutional President
of the Republic of Honduras

The Panama Canal
and the
Central American Crisis

Marco A. Gandasegui

Marco A. Gandasegui is executive secretary of the Center for Latin American Studies (CELA) in Panama and professor at the University of Panama. This essay was presented at an October 1983 conference in Ottawa, Canada. Minor editing has been done for U.S. publication.

After 80 years of U.S. military occupation, the Panamanian Isthmus has become the strategic stronghold of Washington's interests in Latin America and the Caribbean. Throughout the 20th century, the U.S. has carved out its hemispheric expansion based on its control of the Panama Canal.

Trade between the Pacific basin countries and the large Atlantic industrial nations goes through the manmade waterway; and as Senator Huey Long once stated, the "natural" outlet of the Mississippi River to the Pacific Ocean is the Panama Canal. World trade patterns, and especially Latin America's, are strongly influenced by the Canal, which was U.S.-built and remains under U.S. control.

U.S. Militarization of World Trade

In 1906, President Roosevelt militarized the Canal's construction. Because of civilian contracting failures, Roosevelt was able to make Congress agree on the need to convert the Canal into a government project. Between 1906 and 1979, the Canal was operated under corporation laws with one sole action holder: the Secretary of the Army. The U.S. military presence has always been a constant and important part of the Canal. The president of the Panama Canal Company and Canal Zone governor, between 1906 and 1979, had been a general from the Army Corps of Engineers. The new Canal treaties that took effect in 1979 changed the title to administrator of the Panama Canal Commission but conserved the rank and procedure.

Before World War II the U.S. was able to destabilize practically every country in the Caribbean basin. Military interventions in Nicaragua, Santo Domingo, Haiti, Cuba, Mexico, and Venezuela, and threats to Colombia and support of English repression in the West Indies became a trademark of U.S. policy. However, it was during the war, and more so immediately after the last shots were fired in Europe and the Pacific, that U.S. intervention became a permanent feature of Latin American affairs.

South America—for over 100 years a close trading partner with Britain, France, and Germany—was taken over by U.S. interests. South America's trade with the U.S. rose from below 10% before the war to over 50% at present. Central America, the Caribbean, and Mexico became even more dependent on U.S. industry and finance. The ships traveling through the Canal gave true testimony to this flourishing trade between the U.S. and its southern neighbors.

To ensure the new relations and their stability, the U.S. set up in the Panama Canal Zone—without any specific permission from the Panamanian government—a large military network involved in training Latin American armies, selling U.S. equipment, and preparing special political destabilization teams. After World War II, the U.S. prepared itself for a new kind of war to be staged on new fields and on new political grounds.

U.S. Militarization of Latin America

The U.S. government quickly strengthened Somoza's Nicaragua to undermine Guatemala's traditional leading role in the Central American region (1946-1952). It built up Trujillo's dictatorship in Santo Domingo as a police force in the Caribbean (1946-1956). It toppled the Liberal government in Venezuela and replaced it with Pérez Jiménez (1952-1958). It destabilized prospering Argentina, by conspiring with the Army and one of the most backward oligarchies to crush the welfare-state project under Perón (1955). It was able to create havoc in postrevolutionary Bolivia (1952-1958), where a road to stability is still out of sight. In the midst of these drastic changes taking place across the continent, the West Indian territories became independent states with the U.S. proclaiming itself their custodian.

Overriding this tendency, the Cuban Revolution broke loose from U.S. domination, spreading its message throughout the region, and making the U.S. aware that its "backyard" could and was going to fight back. After destroying serious threats of "insubordination" in Guatemala, Venezuela, and Santo Domingo during the early post-Cuban Revolution period, the U.S. focused attention on the Southern Cone countries.

Economic policies set up by International Monetary Fund (IMF) advisers and accepted in these countries (1955-1960) led to a rapid proletarianization of urban middle class sectors and a mass of rural petty bourgeoisie and peasants. The old labor-based socialist movements were quick to move in and organize these new groups. The threat faced by the

U.S. was not of guerrilla warfare but of general popular mobilization. A new strategy had to be created to cope with the Southern Cone situation. Instead of striking at small and fast moving "targets" that found shelter in the rural areas, the task became how to destroy a massive "target" based mainly in the cities centered around the industrial core.

Never before had so much innocent bloodshed and suffering been seen in Latin America as from this "final solution" put into effect in the Southern Cone countries. The successive coups in Brazil (1964, 1967), Uruguay (1973), Chile (1973), and Argentina (1976) blasted away at these popular movements, partially destroying them, and leaving behind over 100,000 deaths and disappearances.

FSLN Overcomes U.S. Strategy

The latter half of the '70s witnessed the Central American uprising. The Frente Sandinista de Liberación Nacional (FSLN) was able to address itself to the main questions concerning the road to victory. Combining guerrilla warfare (in the tradition of the 1950s and 1960s) with massive mobilizations that included every social sector, even the anti-Somoza bourgeoisie, and with strong involvement from the working class, the FSLN was able to defeat the National Guard and its U.S. advisers in 1979.

Over 6,000 Somoza National Guardsmen had been trained in special schools in the Panama Canal Zone. During the last phase of the Sandinista popular uprising, planes loaded with all sorts of equipment flew daily from military air bases in the "Zone" to the old Mercedes airport in Managua. By early 1979, the U.S. was aware that it could not save the Somoza regime. Its antiguerrilla-warfare tactics were completely outdated, and its massive destruction tactics were also inadequate because of popular urban organization and the full support of the middle strata for the FSLN. (The "Retreat to Masaya"* was spectacular in the sense that it showed the masses' degree of organization and capacity to mobilize under extreme conditions, a situation never even thought of in the earlier '70s in the Southern Cone countries.)

Weeks before the Sandinista triumph, the U.S. cut its military shipments to Somoza. Through the Panamanian government of Gen. Torrijos, the U.S. had been able to initiate negotiations with the FSLN leaders in search of a political alternative that would enable the U.S. to accept a peace settlement. The agreement included provisions for a civilian government with Conservative Party members (viz., Alfonso Robelo, Violeta Chamorro), a fusion of the National Guard and the FSLN Army, a special training program for the latter in the Canal Zone, the FSLN's transformation into a political party, and a new loan package for economic reconstruction. Under

---

* The "Retreat to Masaya" refers to a historical transformation of error into victory when the FSLN, having failed in an offensive on Managua, successfully mobilized thousands of the capital's residents to retreat safely to the town of Masaya to escape bombardment by the National Guard.

pressure from Torrijos and other Latin American leaders, and from the rising death toll provoked by Somoza's indiscriminate bombing, the FSLN accepted the terms. Most fortunately for Nicaragua, despite Somoza's forced acceptance of the agreement, the National Guard and other die-hards balked. The FSLN quickly put aside the agreement and defeated the last quarters of resistance.

U.S. at a Standstill in El Salvador

Alongside Nicaragua, another social volcano had already started to erupt, lighting the region with its powerful bursts of human energy. El Salvador, for so many years under military rule and handpicked by the U.S. to become the region's industrial backbone, had evolved another popular strategy unfamiliar to Washington's outpost in the Canal Zone. While military shipments soared to keep the Salvadoran Army equipped, the different mass fronts and their respective guerrilla-war detachments seemed to multiply.

After several visits from U.S. advisers and military groups based in the Canal Zone, it was decided that changes had to be introduced in the old schema of domination-repression set up in El Salvador. The October 1979 coup invited the involvement of the middle class strata (through the Christian Democratic and Social Democratic-MNR parties), with the Communist Party's acquiescence, in hopes of creating a stronger political center. The coup was unable to take away the hegemony of the political right over vast sectors of the rural petty bourgeoisie. At the same time, the powerful mass fronts, organized beyond CP or Social Democratic control, still held the key to any future settlement.

The U.S. strategy was to give the Army new allies from the centrist parties. The right's reaction short-circuited the plan. As a result of the terrorist methods applied in the ultra-right, the Army was divided, and the Social Democrats abandoned the provisional government, followed by the CP. The Christian Democrats decided to stay on, after receiving a definite pledge of support from the U.S.

Once the social forces were polarized again, the U.S. struggled to save the Army's unity. The right's paramilitary death squads were no match for the powerful popular armies reorganized under the FMLN. The Army was actually the only tool the U.S. had to resist the popular uprising, yet the Army's survival depended on the paramilitary intelligence network's capacity to gather information concerning popular movements. The Christian Democrats were a handy veil of legitimacy with which to cover up the whole operation.

Once this was understood, the FMLN staged its series of offensives aimed at destroying the Army's morale. Washington became aware that its political project had floundered and had no other alternative than to keep on supporting the Army. In a period of almost four years the U.S. has poured around one billion dollars in military assistance into the smallest of all the Latin American countries (only 8,000 square miles).

Most of this build-up has been staged from the Canal Zone. U.S. Southern Command General W. Nutting and his successor, General Paul Gorman, have direct control over military operations in El Salvador.

The present situation has evolved considerably. While the U.S. understood it would lose the war in El Salvador if it did not strengthen the Army, this was not the solution it was seeking. The Reagan administration went on to attack what it felt was El Salvador's lifeline: the Sandinista Revolution.

Reagan's Final Solution for Central America

Another billion dollars is being pumped into covert and overt operations in Honduras and Costa Rica. The biggest effort is focused on 5,000 U.S. soldiers maneuvering on the border between Nicaragua and Honduras. While the Somoza National Guardsmen continue to pour into Nicaragua through the northern border (between 2,000 and 5,000 as of October 1983), the U.S. Marines will shut off the *contras'* rearguard from any possible major counteroffensive by the popular Sandinista forces. By moving in behind the *contras,* just behind the border, the U.S. Marines will try to guarantee Somoza's Guardsmen enough room to set up some sort of government inside Nicaraguan territory. If the U.S. is successful in drilling a hole into the Sandinistas' northern border, it would then start bringing in its own forces to control the conquered territory and push the *contras* on, always staying close behind, so that the Sandinistas would not be able to cut in behind the invading Somocistas. While the U.S. bases set up in Honduras would support the northern border penetration, the southern border would receive help from the Panama Canal bases.* At the same time, the U.S. air-carriers and other heavy battleships off Nicaragua's shores would start shelling selected points such as the capital, Managua.

The White House does not yet believe this plan could topple the Sandinista government. It would, of course, create such chaos that the Nicaraguan people would be set back decades in their pursuit for economic, social, and political development. Moreover, by keeping the Sandinistas busy, the U.S. believes it could then launch a general offensive against the FMLN forces in El Salvador, who would thus be lacking their alleged "Nicaraguan support."

The Canal Zone's Commitment to War in Central America

The Panama Canal bases are playing a leading role in the overall U.S. strategy that includes covert actions against Nicaragua and overt backing of the Salvadoran regime. According to recent publications, there are presently 20 U.S. bases in the Canal area. These bases, according to the

---

* The Panamanian journal *Bayano* reported in May 1983 that 500 Somocistas were airlifted from the Canal area to a location called Raity inside Nicaragua.

Canal treaties, should be dismantled in the year 2000. The same treaties state that the training facilities run by the U.S. in the area should have been shut down by October 1, 1983.

The U.S. Army School of the Americas (USARSA) has trained over 90,000 troops in over three decades. In 1982 it received over 2,500 officers from different Latin American armies. In 1981 over half the "student body" was made up of 445 Salvadoran soldiers. Robert McNamara, former Defense Secretary and World Bank president, stated his case clearly to Congress in 1963 when he recognized the importance of U.S. training programs as a "stepping stone" for Latin America's "future leaders": Pinochet (Chile), Videla (Argentina), Banzer (Bolivia), D'Aubisson (El Salvador), Alvarez (Honduras), Mejía (Guatemala), etc.

USARSA not only trains soldiers in Panama; in 1981 it worked through 24 teams inside El Salvador. According to the Panamanian journal *Diálogo Social,* the number rose to 33 in 1982. Back in 1973, *Diálogo Social* and *Tareas Mensual* (also published in Panama) denounced the presence of U.S. Air Force pilots during direct hits on the Moneda Palace in the military coup that overthrew Chile's Popular Unity government. At that time, the pilots were based in the Panama Canal Zone.

Aware of the Canal area's strategic importance for U.S. hegemony in the hemisphere, the Reagan administration will not give up its firm hold over military action and training policies there. The Panamanian government, under U.S. pressure, recently declared its willingness to grant an extension to USARSA's operations. *Diálogo Social* reported that Colonel Roberto Díaz (Panama's Chief of Staff) is open to hosting a so-called Military Sciences Academy under the control of the U.S. and Panama, for Latin American armies where USARSA operates presently. Along similar lines, one of the Contadora Group's many peace proposals for the region was a training school under multinational control. More than anything, the Contadora governments are looking for stability at a time when Washington is pursuing destabilizing tactics.

"A New Interamerican Policy for the Eighties," the so-called Santa Fe document, on which Reagan based his 1980 presidential campaign platform on hemispheric issues, is very precise about the importance of the Panama Canal for U.S. strategic planning. "The Panama Canal," it states, "has a vital strategic value for the American Republics. . . . If we place this importance in the proper context—the Treaty of Reciprocal Assistance (Rio Treaty) signed at the International Conference of American States in 1947—this body could subordinate the Panama Canal to the Interamerican Defense Junta." The Santa Fe proposal is even more precise when it threatens to "move the Interamerican Defense Junta to the Panama Canal. . . . We would set up a security zone under the Junta's 19 members' flags. . . . We would let the Soviets know of our willingness, desire and capacity to defend our vital interests."

The Panama Canal's strategic military importance cannot be denied.

It has been vital to U.S. capital's interests in the Southern Cone and Central America. U.S. presence in the region has been a major obstacle to over 150 years of struggle by the Panamanian people to assure the peaceful use of the Isthmus by all nations of the world. This goal can only be reached when the U.S. relinquishes its military bases in the area and recognizes Panama's sovereign rights as well as those pertaining to Latin American countries, in general.

U.S. capital, however, will not abandon its Panamanian stronghold. This is the reason U.S. domination must be challenged. Whole nations have already paved the way. We believe strongly that once the peoples of Latin America and North America unite, the Panama Canal will play a very different role. It will become the funnel through which people of the world can freely communicate and trade without fear of military attacks, threats, or blackmail.

PART 3

Nicaragua's Search for Peace

Nicaragua's Proposal for Peace, July 19, 1983

This six-point peace proposal was announced by Comandante Daniel Ortega Saavedra, Coordinator of the Nicaraguan Government Junta of National Reconstruction, at the fourth anniversary celebration of the Nicaraguan Revolution in the city of León, July 19, 1983.

With historic responsibility, taking into account the grave situation which the Central American region is undergoing, which has turned it into an important focus of international tension as a result of the present U.S. administration's policy, the National Directorate of the Frente Sandinista de Liberación Nacional considers it the inevitable moral obligation of all Central American governments and the political leaders of the United States to avoid the tragedy of a generalized war for our peoples.

Therefore, due to this pressing and noble goal, it recognizes the value of the positive proposals resulting from the meeting of the heads of state of Mexico, Colombia, Venezuela, and Panama held last weekend in Cancun, Mexico, which constitute a new step in the search for peace in Central America that has given life to the Contadora Group.

The National Directorate of the Frente Sandinista de Liberación Nacional shares the criteria expressed by the heads of state of the Contadora Group that "the use of force as an alternative solution does not solve but rather aggravates underlying tensions. Peace in Central America can only be a reality to the degree that the fundamental principles of coexistence between nations are respected: nonintervention, self-determination, the sovereign equality of states, cooperation for economic and social development, peaceful solutions to controversies, as well as the free and authentic expression of popular will."

We share such criteria because our ideals and principles—popular power; socio-economic changes benefiting the large majority in our country; our homeland's sovereignty and complete independence; the resolve

Translation of this address was provided by the government of Nicaragua, with minor editing for U.S. publication.

to build a free, democratic, pluralistic, and new society free of exploitation—are facts and convictions rooted deep in the hearts of millions of Nicaraguans. The Sandinista Popular Revolution is an irreversible political reality with national and international repercussions acknowledged by the entire world.

Nicaragua does not have expansionist ambitions nor does it intend to impose its sociopolitical system on other countries. We do not have economic investments abroad nor do we have dreams of imperial domination. For those reasons, our people do not need or want war. For Nicaragua, its commitment never to attack any country is a matter of principle.

The Frente Sandinista de Liberación Nacional—which has struggled and will continue to struggle to assure a peaceful and secure existence for our people, conscious of the deterioration in the regional situation, and consistent with the latest constructive steps of the governments of the Contadora Group—has decided to make a new effort to contribute to peace. In spite of our absolute conviction that the greatest threat to peace in the region demands bilateral solutions, the Government of National Reconstruction will accept the proposal sponsored by the Contadora Group that the beginning of the negotiation process be multilateral. Therefore, all excuses can be done with, and those who claim they are interested in peace can take concrete steps to develop the process of laying the foundations for peace.

Moreover, taking into account that the heads of state have entrusted their foreign ministers "to elaborate specific proposals that should be presented for the consideration of the Central American countries at the next joint meeting of foreign ministers," and that the biggest danger to peace in the region may arise from the exacerbation of already existing military conflicts, the Frente Sandinista de Liberación Nacional proposes that the discussion of the following points be started immediately:

1. A commitment to end any prevailing situation of war through the immediate signing of a nonaggression pact between Nicaragua and Honduras.

2. The absolute end to all supplies of weapons by any country to the forces in conflict in El Salvador so that the people may resolve their problems without foreign interference.

3. The absolute end to all military support, in the form of arms supplies, training, use of territory to launch attacks, or any other form of aggression, to forces adverse to any of the Central American governments.

4. Commitments to ensure absolute respect for the Central American people's self-determination, and noninterference in the internal affairs of each country.

5. The end to aggression and economic discrimination against any country in Central America.

6. No installation of foreign military bases on Central American territory, and the suspension of military exercises in the Central American region which include the participation of foreign armies.

Progress in the resolution of these points would automatically contribute to the discussion of other points which also trouble Central American states, and which are listed on the Contadora Group's agenda with the goal of finding an acceptable and lasting solution for the security and stability of the countries in the region.

When agreements are reached and approved in the assembly of the Contadora Group, the United Nations Security Council, as the highest international body charged with watching over international peace and security, would have to supervise and guarantee compliance with said accords by all countries.

Nicaragua states its willingness to accept all commitments derived from those accords with total responsibility, and demonstrates this by accepting the point of view of the heads of state of the Contadora Group that "The task of settling specific differences between countries must initially be undertaken by the signing of memoranda of understanding and the creation of commissions which would allow all parties to develop joint actions and to guarantee effective control over their territories, especially in the border zones."

While these initiatives materialize, the people of Nicaragua will remain completely mobilized, ready to raise a wall of patriotism and rifles against which all aggressions will shatter.

León, July 19, 1983
"Year of Struggle for Peace and Sovereignty"

Address to the United Nations General Assembly

Comandante Daniel Ortega Saavedra

The following are excerpts from the Address to the 38th General Assembly of the United Nations given by Commander of the Revolution Daniel Ortega Saavedra, Coordinator of the Government Junta of National Reconstruction, on September 27, 1983.

Mr. President, Distinguished Delegates:

The Central American region is not exempt from the upsurge of military, political, and economic tensions. Our peoples, historically deprived of the benefits of development, victims of injustice and a lack of freedom, are today assertively demanding these rights. The current struggle of the Central American peoples has its roots in the expansionist policies of the United States of America.

In the year 1855 this expansionist policy, which grabbed extensive territory from Mexico, had a military presence in Nicaragua through William Walker* and his mercenaries, who were finally defeated and expelled after a bloody struggle. Since that time the different U.S. administrations have endeavored to stabilize brutal regimes in the region, which were to become their principal instrument of domination. Since that time in the history of our peoples, there has been one landing of U.S. soldiers after another, direct interventions aimed at propping up tyrannical governments and drowning the people's struggle in blood. That was how the government of the United States became the best friend of tyrants such as Somoza, Ubico [Guatemala], Carías [Honduras], and Hernández [El Salvador].

Translation of this address was provided by the government of Nicaragua, with minor editing for U.S. publication.

* William Walker (1824-60), a U.S. adventurer, carried out a private operation and militarily seized control of Nicaragua in 1855. The U.S. recognized Walker's government in 1856 — Eds.

And that was how the United States government became the greatest enemy of our peoples.

U.S. democracy has meant hunger and exploitation for the peasants and workers in our region. And it has meant fabulous wealth for the exploiting minorities.

The triumph of the Nicaraguan Revolution was but the final product of this long struggle against U.S. domination, which began in 1855 against Walker, and which culminated in July 19, 1979, with the overthrow of Anastasio Somoza.

Our revolution triumphed over this unjust U.S. policy, and while it is true that in the months following this victory the possibility of new relations with the United States opened up, the taking of office of the new administration in 1981 cut short this effort. Once more it was the policy of the Big Stick, the policy of gunboats, the policy of terror.

We could say that from that moment on, since January 1981, the new U.S. administration declared war on the people of Nicaragua. The strategy was a clear one: military aggression, more economic aggression, more slander campaigns, more attempts to isolate us internationally, all with the goal of destabilizing the Nicaraguan Revolution to bring about its destruction.

Thus, they proposed to undermine the struggle of the peoples of the region and in particular the struggle of the people of El Salvador. Crushing the Nicaraguan Revolution would mean crushing the possibilities for change in Central America and would maintain the situation of injustice and lack of freedom, according to the thinking of the U.S. administration's strategists. They decided, therefore, to implement a strategy of military encirclement against the fighting people of El Salvador and against the liberated people of Nicaragua. From that time on, the U.S. military presence in the region has been on the increase, openly in El Salvador and Honduras and covertly in Costa Rica.

There immediately followed actions by the Guardsmen of the Somoza regime. Armed, financed, and directed by the U.S. government through the CIA and Pentagon, they began their criminal operations against our people from their bases of operations in Honduran territory.

Joining these aggressive actions from Costa Rican territory were foreign mercenaries, counterrevolutionaries of Nicaraguan origin, and more Somoza Guardsmen. From its military base in the Southern Command in Panama, the United States began spy flights over our territory with RC-135, SR-71, and U-2 planes. To date there have been 203 spy flights, 512 violations of our airspace by Honduran Air Force planes and others provided by the CIA to the counterrevolutionaries, who have penetrated our territory on supply, information, and attack missions from their operational bases in Honduras and Costa Rica.

In the same period between 1981 and 1983, on 34 occasions we have detected the presence of U.S. naval vessels in our territorial waters, totaling 56 violations of our territorial waters—24 from Honduran territory and 32 from Costa Rican territory. These activities are designed to infiltrate and supply counterrevolutionary groups. These operations by the U.S. administration, for which $19 million were initially appropriated, were of a covert nature at the time. In the first months of 1982 the Central Intelligence Agency had already designed a plan for military escalation, to be put into operation toward the end of that year. The response of our people was immediate: between December 1982 and January of this year, the aggressions were defeated. In the month of February, the United States carried out joint military maneuvers with the Honduran Army, in order to provide support to the counterrevolutionaries, who had embarked on a new invasion. They were again defeated.

In the months of July and September, the government of the United States made new attempts at invasion through the CIA, relying on the counterrevolutionaries and the Honduran Army. At the same time, they continued conducting joint maneuvers with Honduran Armed Forces in the area bordering on Nicaragua. In September, they began an exercise called "Big Pine II," with the objectives of creating a military situation involving the Honduran Army in the support of the Army of El Salvador, and threatening our revolution with a show of force, without in any way ruling out a blockade and direct aggression.

These Big Pine military maneuvers have been accompanied by naval maneuvers without precedent in the region, involving 19 warships with 16,484 troops on board and 5,000 more troops on Honduran soil.

The systematic military aggressions by the government of the United States have become increasingly overt and from 1981 to 1983 have taken a toll of 717 Nicaraguans killed, including civilians and members of the Armed Forces. Of these, 41 were teachers, and 154 were workers linked to production centers. Also during this time, 529 people—workers, students, and technicians—have been kidnapped; 514 have been wounded. In defense of their sovereignty, our armed people have annihilated 1,636 counterrevolutionaries and wounded 280. To the consequences of the policy of the United States we must add the losses our country has suffered due to the destructions of ports, damages to production facilities, destruction of construction equipment, health centers, schools, and daycare centers, representing a total of $108.5 million in damages, *amounting to one quarter of our annual investments.* [Emphasis added—Eds.]

This month a new form of attack was initiated in an attempt to "normalize" the escalation against Nicaragua. Rocket-equipped planes coming from Costa Rican territory as well as Honduran territory have dropped 500 pound bombs on the Augusto César Sandino International Airport, schools, houses, and fuel tanks in the port of Corinto. These bombings continue to occur. Also part of this new U.S. escalation was the blowing up of an oil receiving station located two miles from our shores in the Pacific Ocean, and other criminal actions aimed at seriously affecting our economy.

As we pointed out before, this aggressive activity was part of the increased U.S. military presence in the region, which included the establishment of military and naval bases with new airports in its military operations against the Salvadoran patriots, and an increase in pressure on the governments in the region to involve them even further in the current actions against Nicaragua.

Mr. President, Distinguished Delegates, the efforts carried out to contain the aggressive policy of the United States in the region, to promote dialogue and negotiation in pursuit of a political solution, have also been significant. This organization, through the Security Council and the Secretary General, has watched the situation closely and been active in these efforts. The Movement of Non-Aligned Countries has also assumed a position clearly condemning the aggressive destabilizing and interventionist policy in the region, and has given its support to the efforts aimed at finding a political solution. In this peace effort, Mexico and France have made a valuable contribution in promoting dialogue. The activity undertaken by Mexico, Venezuela, Panama, and Colombia in the Contadora Group has been solidly supported by all those genuinely interested in the search for peace. The position assumed by members of the U.S. Congress and by important sectors of the U.S. media, intellectuals, the religious community, and the public at large is consistent with the desire for peace on the part of the peoples of Central America who reject these aggressive policies.

We can say that from very different ideological positions throughout the world there is agreement in condemning the aggressive and bellicose escalation in the Central American region and in demanding that dialogue be the means of resolving the problems. But the U.S. administration tramples on all these efforts, rejecting them in practice, and is swiftly carrying forward its aggressive plans.

The U.S. administration is trying to ignore the defeat that its policy has suffered in the region. It has failed in its attempt to destroy the Salvadoran patriots. It has also failed in its attempts to send thousands of Somocista mercenaries against the Nicaraguan people. Our people are inflicting more casualties on them every day and more of them are deserting.

Where are the successes of U.S. policy in Central America? Where are its victories in El Salvador? Where are its "freedom fighters"? The policy of military attacks and aggressions has already failed and the only alternative left to the U.S. administration is greater and ever more direct involvement.

This explains the presence of the U.S. warships, the presence of the U.S. soldiers, the visit by Mr. Caspar Weinberger (Secretary of Defense), the statements by Mr. Fred Iklé (Under Secretary of Defense), the demands made by Mr. George Shultz (Secretary of State), Mr. William Clark (National Security Adviser), and Mr. William Casey (Director, CIA), and the approval of a new appropriation of $19 million to continue to support covert operations against Nicaragua, despite the House of Representatives' vote against these operations.

Mr. President, Distinguished Delegates, Nicaragua struggled against imperialist domination and the Somoza dictatorship in search of peace, in search of justice, in search of freedom. Nicaragua cultivates and defends this vocation for peace, which is nothing more than the sacred right our peoples have to demand peace, win peace, and defend peace.

Yesterday we heard President Reagan state that in Central America as in Southern Africa, the United States is trying to be persuasive about not depending on the use of force. We also heard him say that the United States is trying to construct a framework for peaceful negotiations, thereby pursuing a policy of keeping the major powers out of the conflicts of the Third World.

We must therefore expect an immediate halt to the aggressions, the immediate withdrawal of the U.S. warships from our territorial waters and from the region, the withdrawal of U.S. government support for the armed activities of the Somocista Guardsmen and other counterrevolutionary mercenaries, and an end to the covert operations.

Only concrete steps such as these would prove the existence of an authentic political will on the part of the U.S. to support peace initiatives, and the process of dialogue and negotiation, in order to guarantee the security of all the Central American states and the strict compliance with Security Council Resolution 530 (which supports the Contadora Group efforts to resolve differences through frank dialogue).

It will be necessary to seek security for states which are being attacked. Nicaragua is the most threatened and attacked nation on our continent, threatened and attacked by an extraregional power. For that reason, in the measure that military aggression increases, we have the right and the sovereign responsibility to supply our people with more and better arms.

We reiterate that the United States must withdraw its aggressive forces from the region and desist from its policy of aggression. Accords must be reached offering security to the states of the region first and foremost. Then we will be able to discuss problems of weapons and advisers.

The U.S. government has gone along offering different pretexts to justify its aggressive policy in the region. It has called Nicaragua a threat because of the alleged arms traffic to El Salvador; on other occasions it has come down to the alleged East-West confrontation underway in the region. They have also voiced concerns about the state of democracy in Nicaragua. Most recently, however, they have stated quite clearly that the problem is the very existence of a free Nicaragua.

All of this indicates the lack of consistency and the instability of U.S. policy and the inability today, as in the past, of U.S. strategists to see the root of the problem: the expansionist policy they first employed in the last century and which they continue defending at the present.

Nicaragua has won its right to be free, and this right must be respected.

Nicaragua has defined itself, and therefore acts, as a nonaligned country, and this right must be respected.

Nicaragua is building its democracy, and its sovereign right to choose its own internal system, its own brand of democracy, is a right of our people that cannot be negotiated, cannot be discussed, and must be respected.

Mr. President, Distinguished Delegates, avoiding a conflagration in Central America is an obligation that concerns the entire international community, defenders of the principles contained in the Charter of our United Nations. In the course of this year the Movement of Non-Aligned Countries, meeting first in an Extraordinary Ministerial Meeting of its Coordination Bureau in Managua last January, and then in March in New Delhi during the Seventh Summit of Heads of State and Government, has manifested its resolute support for the efforts that are underway to attain a peaceful solution to the problems of our region.

The Security Council, in its resolution Number 530, also issued an urgent call to all states to support the efforts of the Contadora Group aimed at resolving differences by means of frank and constructive dialogue.

Despite the appeals and the efforts, the situation in Central America becomes more complicated every day. The aggressions against Nicaragua resume and intensify; threats, intimidation, intervention occur there in an attempt to place the so-called "vital interests" of a great power above the delicate efforts being made to achieve peace and coexistence in Central America on the basis of full respect of all the nations of the region.

Nicaragua will never attack any country, but it will defend itself from all aggressions, no matter how big or powerful the aggressor may be. And we know that the United States, that great military power, is threatening Nicaragua.

Whenever Nicaragua has been attacked or invaded, it has defended itself, it has fought, and we Nicaraguans will always be ready and willing to resist and defeat future imperialist interventions.

In the face of this situation, this Assembly must give new impetus and support to the efforts in search of peace, by means of a new and urgent appeal to all states, to refrain from taking actions and to rescind decisions already taken that aggravate the situation in the region.

Toward this end, today Nicaragua is requesting that the Central American question; the threats to peace, sovereignty, and the exercise of the right to free self-determination of the Central American people; and the peace initiatives be considered as urgent items on the agenda of this 38th plenary session of the General Assembly.

Mr. President, Distinguished Delegates, this 38th General Assembly of the United Nations has brought us together in moments of great pain and suffering for our peoples, and of unprecedented threats to the future of humanity. There is still time to avoid a catastrophe. Voices, wills, but above all actions will have to be mobilized to denounce and unmask the irrational positions and strengthen the rational ones. This is not the time to ignore the situation. This is not the time for timid and wavering positions. Even at the risk of facing yet more difficult situations, what is at stake goes beyond individual interests. It is an obligation of all and in this case of those of us who do not possess atomic weapons or economic power to demand peace and to struggle for peace with all the moral strength of our peoples.

Thank you very much.

PART 4

Defending the Revolution

The Ingenuity of the People

These excerpts from three articles that appeared in Barricada *in October 1983—in the wake of the most destructive wave of CIA-planned sabotage directed at vital economic targets—demonstrate the capacity of the Nicaraguan people to rebuild what the con-tras have destroyed. Such reconstruction represents a vital stage in defending the Nicaraguan Revolution. In a country lacking spare parts as well as the foreign ex-change needed to buy them, as a result of the U.S.-imposed economic blockade, it is indeed the creativity of the people that makes reconstruction possible. These articles in* Barricada *serve also as a political education to all Nicaraguans about the less visible heroes of the revolutionary process.*

I. Innovative Workers Reconstruct Southern Electrical Towers

(*Barricada* October 18, 1983)

The workers from the Nicaraguan Energy Institute (INE) gave their most recent demonstration of innovative genius at the site where the towers supporting 69,000 volt cables were destroyed, here at the Costa Rican border. The two towers were blown up by agents of the CIA and the traitor [Edén] Pastora on September 28, 1983. There were difficulties in going into the area and the work of fixing the cables had to be delayed until October 3, 1983.

From the Nicaraguan side, it was difficult to see the towers, because of the mountains, but from Costa Rica it was easy to see them. According to the *compañeros* David Lorío, Augusto Fletes, Daniel Blanco, and Leopoldo Robleto, the workers got to the towers via small roads. They had the rainy season and the threat of criminal aggression by counterrevolutionaries against them. Still, said David Lorío, the lines had to be installed as soon as possible.

Build new towers? Impossible! But Augusto Fletes had the idea that the only way to do this was to set up six pine posts, 50 meters apart (from which the cables would be hung). At the same time, they created some special metallic parts to support the cables with their insulators. . . .

The work of installing the posts and the special pieces to support the 69,000 volt cables took them four days. Now they call it "Fletes's Structure." Augusto Fletes prefers to call it "Nica Style Structure."

According to Lorío it was known that there was no protection on the Costa Rican side. They realized that the counterrevolutionaries were moving around together with Costa Rican guards close to the place where the towers, whose cables bring power from Costa Rica to Honduras and Nicaragua, were destroyed. In contrast [on the Nicaraguan side], the *compañeros* from the Sandinista Popular Army have been guarding the zone constantly to prevent INE workers from being attacked. . . .

Lorío calls the work that they did at the border with Costa Rica temporary. "If it stays there it could last around five years, but we hope soon to be able to rebuild the two towers that were damaged by the counterrevolutionaries."

II. Overcoming the Blockade: The Workshop of the MICONS

(*Barricada*, October 23, 1983)

The workshop of the Ministry of Construction (MICONS) has become a small factory of spare parts that originally came from abroad, making this place a solid front in the struggle against the economic crisis and the blockade, and a bastion of patriotism.

In the immense workshop of the Ministry they have a foundry with ovens to change metals into liquid and mold them into the required shape. They also have ovens to make molds of beach sand and flour. In other words, they already make their own spare parts.

The criminal blockade of Yankee imperialism and the urgent need to have heavy and light machinery functioning have awakened the patriotism and the innovative genius at this central plant of MICONS, with its 1,500 workers.

They manufacture exhaust valves for trucks, nuts for propulsion axles of Caterpillar tractors, bolts and nuts for vulcanization presses, stud bolts for truck tires, pistons for air compressors; they renovate heavy motor parts; and they produce intake and escape valves and supports for scales (that are used to weigh loaded trucks on the roads). . . .

Carlos Cuadra, head of the lathe workshop where the machine parts are made, assures us that what has been done in the Ministry of Construction is of incalculable value. Among the different workshops of the Ministry they call themselves the "artists." Carlos Cuadra explained that the issue begins with the necessity of making machine parts.

If there are no new spare parts for the machines, the broken one is taken and molded on wood. This is done in the carpentry workshop, which is very special and is considered to be an artistic center of production by the inventors in the Ministry of Construction.

The inventors and the foundry workers are like a single arm of the lathe and milling workshop: they join their efforts and their innovative genius. They take the old machine parts, if there are any, draw them on paper sheets, and then make the molds.

In front of the foundry workshop there are hundreds of old parts waiting to be melted down in the oven. When everything is ready, they start to make the molds, mainly out of wood. . . .

The carpenters make the molds. Then the blacksmiths put sand pebbles and flour in specific proportions into the wooden molds. Juan Zamora and Ramón Hernández, two of the workers, told us that they make a good number of molds before they proceed to the melting process. When they consider that everything is ready, they proceed to melt the old parts; liquid iron, for example, is poured into the molds. When the pieces are cold in the molds, they go to the workshop that manufactures parts. . . . [Then] the pieces go to the lathe and milling machines. . . .

Carlos Cuadra showed us with pride the place where they guard the parts as they make them. However, he explained: "As you see, as soon as we make the parts, our *compañeros* the mechanics are waiting to put them onto trucks, tractors, vans, or vulcanization equipment."

He said that they are manufacturing a lot of parts for tractors and trucks—destroyed by criminal counterrevolutionaries hired by the CIA—in Río Blanco and other training schools of the Ministry of Construction in the northern part of the country. The tractors and trucks are in the workshop, being repaired. Some of them, already painted, look almost brand new.

The majority of the creative *compañeros* are high school and university students, according to *Compañero* Cuadra. There are also men like Juan Zamora and Ramón Hernández, who have been working for 30 years in smelting and carpentry. These are the teachers of the young. Juan Zamora says that some young men show a lot of interest in trying to learn what the old ones know, but others don't. He expressed that he will be retiring, and that he wants to pass on all his knowledge about foundry work.

He pointed out that their work is not well known, even though they have been doing it for years. He and Hernández pointed out that only now, with the Sandinista Revolution, their efforts and ingenuity to keep the machinery running are recognized.

In the above-mentioned workshop there are some Swedish internationalists—from the Metallurgical Union of Sweden—who are training workers to run milling machines, radial, parallel, and "revolving" lathes. This last lathe permits us to make hundreds of parts of different sizes. The radial lathe is moved to wherever it is needed.

Our Swedish *compañeros* are leaving in November and they promise to return to give another course on maintenance of the machinery that they donated to the Ministry of Construction. They told us that they were very satisfied with the interest shown by the workers in learning how to run the new machinery and also of the innovative capacity that the workers showed in making new parts.

III. The Heroic Response of the Innovators From MICONS

(*Barricada,* October 24, 1983)

The Ministry of Construction has saved 180 million córdobas in reconstruction of equipment—most of it burned during attacks by the Somocistas. At the Reconstruction Workshop of Heroes and Martyrs of Batahola, for example, the innovators and all the workers send out burned trucks looking as good as new.

Rigoberto Cabrera, the Director of the Workshop, gave as an example the great accomplishment of reconstructing one of the trucks burned by the Somocista assassins, which originally cost 787,000 córdobas. Rebuilding it is costing them an estimated 212,000 córdobas, saving 575,000 córdobas.

In the time of the Somoza dictatorship, reconstructing a vehicle like this would have been impossible. Today it is done because the workers know that the revolution is theirs, and they commit all their ingenuity and political will to keeping the revolutionary state moving ahead.

In the above-mentioned workshop, they are reconstructing trucks and bulldozers (called *patroles* by the people) and fixing and reconstructing diverse types of motors. . . .

Some of the burned vehicles are unusable and are dismantled for spare parts. In most cases, vital parts like the crankshaft of an EBRO or Pegaso truck have been damaged. The innovators look for other crankshafts, make adaptations, and place them in the engines of the trucks. The same occurs with starting motors, gears of transmissions, alternators, transmission axles, electrical equipment, even the upholstery.

There is also continuing reconstruction of machinery that is used to build the roads and highways that the country needs. The innovators have constructed metal cutters, tools not found in the stores that they need for their work.

Guadalupe Gómez, spokesperson of the Ministry of Construction, took us around the plant that today is being expanded and improved. We were shown almost 100 motors that are being checked and waiting to be repaired.

Some of the new parts are ordered from the Central Workshop of the Ministry, where there is a place called "factory of spare parts."

Rigoberto Cabrera introduced us to innovators such as Jacinto López, Miguel Roque, Silvio Morales, Isabel Ortiz, Adolfo Vallecillo, and Arlén Juárez.

The person in charge of the workshop informed us that during 1983 they are planning to reconstruct 177 pieces of equipment, of which 85% have already been done.

He also told us that a Mobile Brigade is in Pantasma making an estimate of the damage done by the criminal Somocistas to the training establishment of the Ministry of Construction there. The damaged equipment will be brought to Managua to be reconstructed in the Central Workshop and in the Workshop of Heroes and Martyrs of Batahola.

Vigilancia Revolucionaria: Guarding the Revolution

In October 1983, during the escalation of CIA-directed attacks against Nicaragua, a delegation organized by U.S. Out of Central America (USOCA) had the opportunity to experience firsthand, from 11 p.m. to 1 a.m., the vigilancia revolucionaria *(revolutionary guard duty) in the El Nicarao section of eastern Managua—a battle zone during the 1970s uprising against Somoza, and still today one of the most combative working class neighborhoods in the city. The document presented here is an edited translation of the taped interviews with officials of the Sandinista Defense Committees (CDS) at the national, zone, and neighborhood levels—who gave the initial briefing and accompanied the delegation through the streets of El Nicarao—and inteviews with a number of the residents of El Nicarao doing* vigilancia revolucionaria.

I. Briefing by Officials of the Sandinista Defense Committees (CDS)

Vigilancia revolucionaria, revolutionary guard duty, is a voluntary task carried out by the Sandinista Defense Committees (CDS) on every block, on every street. The objective is to take care of the community's well-being, to fight delinquency, and to prevent any kind of sabotage against strategic targets of the revolution, as well as any other kind of action attempted by the enemies of our people.

Generally, people do *vigilancia revolucionaria* duty once every eight days. Besides guarding their blocks, the revolutionary guards are also part of other defense work, such as the popular youth militia.

There are two [night] shifts in *vigilancia revolucionaria,* one from 11 p.m. to 2 a.m., the other from 2 a.m. to 5 a.m., but in a massive way our people carry out revolutionary vigilance 24 hours a day, because the enemy strikes not only at night, but at any time during the day. There are housewives working at home and guarding at the same time; 80% of the women in Nicaragua participate in *vigilancia revolucionaria*. Children over 12 years old (the minimum age) also participate.

This *barrio* [neighborhood], El Nicarao, was characterized by its combativeness during the insurrection. As you know, the *barrios* in the eastern part of Managua (where we are now) were the main target of the bombardment [by Somoza's forces—Eds.]. That was because this sector showed a strong determination to fight to the death, to end for good the most disgraceful regime in Latin America, the Somoza regime.

The CDS's were initially [during the insurrection—Eds.] called Civil Defense Committees. We used to keep "safe houses," where we made contact bombs, where we kept arms, and which housed clandestine clinics. Later on, after the triumph, our committees were renamed the Sandinista Defense Committees.

We want you to see here, as you may have seen in other neighborhoods and cities of Nicaragua, the willingness of our people to defend our revolutionary process to the last consequence. Given the level of aggression of which we are victims, it seems our people, even though we are so small and poor, do not allow Mr. Reagan to sleep well. We are not scared of the aggressions or of the blockades. We lack medicines, we are in need of parts to make our machines work, because we have been denied loans; the most basic things needed by the people have been cut off. On July 19, 1979, we decided to make our own destiny and our own history.

Since that date we decided to be a friend of any country in the world that wanted to be our friend; we decided to negotiate with any country of the world, to sell our products to any country of the world, but getting paid for them, and with no conditions imposed. We also decided to buy from any country of the world that wants to sell to us, so that we could begin to move ahead and extricate our country from the economic situation that we are in.

They say we are warlike. We want to live in peace! We don't want the war that they are forcing us to fight to save our sovereignty and our revolution. Reagan's actions through his CIA—for example Corinto, Puerto Sandino, and the Sandino Airport—are not going to intimidate us. [Our enemies] may destroy us but they will never make us kneel down, never. Do you know how many *compañeros* fell in the war to win our freedom? 50,000 brothers, and now there will be another 50,000 with the things the *contras* are doing, sponsored by Reagan. Right here we have buried 15 *compañeros,* young men of this *barrio*. It would make no sense for us to surrender power after shedding so much blood to gain the freedom we enjoy today.

They say that we are the epicenter, that from here we are exporting our revolution to countries such as El Salvador. We aren't exporting our revolution—although it is true that in our hearts we want the triumph of the Salvadoran people. Since you are here tonight with us, we want you to be messengers to tell the North American people that we want to live in peace. . .and to be allowed to make our own history.

Now, to give you more details about how our *barrio* is organized: There are 5,400 of us living in this *barrio*. The CDS's are organized by blocks;

there are 29 CDS's in this *barrio*. We have 1,670 people guarding at the block level; they are the ones who will be watching so that no counterrevolutionary will trespass.

We are also continuing the literacy campaign [initially carried out in 1980—Eds.] through the Sandinista Popular Education Collectives (CEP). We have 7 CEP's with 108 students. There are 50 health *brigadistas* in this *barrio* who work in health campaigns; one *brigadista* for each block is in charge of health matters, such as vaccinating children and dealing with the stagnant puddles on their block. *Brigadistas* are trained to teach people health measures that we didn't know about before, such as how to prevent some illnesses like diarrhea and malaria, how to avoid mosquitos, etc.

In this *barrio* we also have a house where we register people for the military service [instituted in September 1983—Eds.]. We were expecting 4,500 youth between the ages of 17 and 22 to register for our whole zone, and by now we already have registered 80% in only 17 days.

Now we are going to take a little tour so that you can talk with the *compañeros* doing *vigilancia revolucionaria*.

II. Vigilancia Revolucionaria in El Nicarao: Interviews

CDS Official: This is Carmen, who is a guard of this block.

Carmen: How marvelous to see so many *compañeros* and *compañeras!* What can I tell you, there are so many beautiful things to say about our revolution. And that is not because I am Nicaraguan, but because it is the most beautiful revolution. I am a Nicaraguan woman, a proletarian, with 11 children, 6 of them reservists. And although I am their mother and it hurts, they belong to battalions, to the guard, because we belong to the people, because we are good Nicaraguans, we have to struggle to the end even if we have to fight with our fingernails.

What happens is that with Mr. Reagan—if you will excuse me, because you are not responsible; you are our brothers who come here to visit us because of your good will towards the Nicaraguan people; therefore in my name and the name of all the people who live on my block, I thank you a million times for your coming here. As I was saying, what happens is that because Mr. Reagan is everybody's enemy, he does not leave us in peace, not even for a second. The most terrible thing about this man is that he must have no heart, no mother, no songs, no family; he must have none of these, because the pain of all the people that he has attacked in the world matters very little to him—he doesn't suffer for anything.

We can only shout from here and from our border that we will have to fight with him or anyone, but we are going to defend our land. If he weren't causing us so much harm we would not be in the situation that we are. We have to keep being Sandinistas to the very end.

To all of you, please be our *compañeros* and receive the revolutionary embrace of a proletarian mother of 11 children.

CDS: In this house lived the *Compañera* Esperanza Valdes. Last year her brother, who belonged to a reserve battalion, was also killed by one of the Somocista groups, so this is the house of two heroes and martyrs.

These *compañeros* are also revolutionary guards of El Nicarao.

Delegate: Could you tell us what kinds of problems you find in the *vigilancia revolucionaria?*

Guard: Well, at the beginning after the revolution, there remained the legacies of Somocismo—delinquency, robbery, drug addiction, etc. So from the moment of the triumph, *vigilancia revolucionaria* was increased, to try to eradicate all these vices. It is a way of increasing the ability of the people to defend themselves.

Delegate: How old are you?

Guard: 18 years.

Delegate: And how old were you when you started to do revolutionary vigilance?

Guard: Well, I began after the triumph, four years ago.

Delegate: Are you a member of the Sandinista youth?

Guard: Yes, with the revolution there are many different tasks. For example, right now I am only studying at the university, but before, during my vacation, I joined the coffee harvest, that is so important to the country's economy. I also went to the border in a reserve battalion.

CDS: This *compañera* is working with a Popular Education Collective. She belongs to the CDS and has joined the *vigilancia.*

Compañera: We taught our comrades to learn the alphabet and we are in the fifth grade now. We already know how to read, write, add, subtract, and multiply.

CDS: This *compañero* is the most responsible of this block. He is 14 years old.

Delegate: Do you have any message that you would like to send to the North American people?

Guard: Yes, as the *compañero* said before, our policy is the policy of peace. We don't want war, we want to build our revolution. We want to build a new society where we can live in peace. Of course, each time we mobilize, we ask for peace.

CDS: As you can see, we are here in the *barrio* guarding our supply station and our other *compañeros.* In this way, we are guarding our country, because we don't want war. The guard duty that we carry out is the weapon of the people.

If the U.S. government continues to interfere in Nicaragua, the workers will not be able to work in peace. We do not want war. We want your cooperation in speaking with people in your country, because we cannot go there due to our lack of resources. So we need you to carry back the voice of our working class.

We take pride in our Mothers of Heroes and Martyrs. This is the mother of Telma Gutiérrez [who is one of our martyrs].

Telma's mother: I am going to tell you something as a mother, because all Nicaraguan mothers are suffering from the aggressions that we have to endure. They are killing our sons. I have two sons in the military who are at the border, and I believe that although we might become even poorer than we are now, we will keep on fighting. During the time of Somoza, we were like a trench—the youth moved through us and we covered them. We did not have arms, but even so the dictator was overturned. Now that the power belongs to the people, we are going to keep it, no matter what.

CDS: Here we have a young man doing *vigilancia revolucionaria*. He is a reservist of a 50-12 battalion. The role of a reservist is also to defend the revolution, because imperialism, and the *contras,* the mercenary Guardsmen, still want to penetrate into Nicaragua to continue exploiting it. We are here to defend it.

. . .We also have mobile *vigilancia* patrols that go to the houses of the people who are in turn acting as guards of their block.

Guard: Well North American friends, for us it is very important that you have been here to see with your own eyes the readiness of these people, who are being pushed further every day by the enemies of our progress, thinking they can force us to yield. Take with you the message of these humble people to the North American people, that with all our limitations, we want peace. We are not warriors but neither are we going to let them kill us. We are going to defend ourselves.

Because that is the last alternative they are giving us—to defend our revolution, to defend our sovereignty. We will not yield despite all the limitations that we have, despite Reagan's blockade, despite the cuts in loans, despite all the measures; we will fall if we die, but we will not submit in any other way. Reagan is our only enemy in the world right now. He is responsible for this situation. So brothers, thank you, and I hope God will be at your side. We are sorry that you do not have more time so that we could show you our people's constant struggle for peace. We appreciate and hope that you will take this message to your people, as one more trench in our struggle.

Mother: I also want to give you a message as a mother. I am the mother of a martyr, who has been dead for only 9 months. They tortured my son and killed him. We mothers want you to take this message to your country: We do not want more bloodshed in Nicaragua. I, as the mother of a martyr, ask for peace. That is the only thing I wanted to tell you.

Guard: But you can tell Reagan and his gang that in the Sandinista trenches they will not find our people waiting to be their victims. Instead, they will find us with our hands extended, but ready to close into fists—all the *compañeros* from the CDS's, all of the people of our working class. We tell them, "They shall not pass," and we are ready, as you can see right now. I want you to take the spirit our people have expressed with you. Even though there have been some suspicions on the part of some *compañeros* because we are talking to a North American delegation, our people, as you have noticed, know how to identify who are our enemies and who are our friends.

You have already seen the fighting spirit of our people and their willingness to take up arms. Our army will shed a new light on humankind. As the slogan says: Only crystals break, men die standing, and we, the Sandinistas, will be like Ché. On to the victory always. One of our jokes goes: Who gave birth to Reagan? The mule. I complain, said the mule, I did not give birth to that son of a bitch. . . .We will keep striking with force — we will remain implacable, invincible. This rebel people, this untamed people deserve the glory. We hope to have your support.

¡Patria libre o morir!

Women's Participation in the New Nicaragua

Asociación de Mujeres Nicaragüenses "Luisa Amanda Espinoza" (AMNLAE)

This is the translation of the presentation by the Nicaraguan Women's Association at the 15th Latin American Congress of Sociology, held in Managua in October 1983. In the presentation we find the historical roots of the extraordinary participation of women in Nicaragua today in the defense of the country and in the other major tasks of the Revolution.

At this time, when Nicaragua is the victim of the destabilizing policy of U.S. imperialism, which refuses to set aside the use of force against our country;

At this time, when Somocistas are being trained, advised, and coordinated by the CIA, to sow terror at our borders;

At this time, when our airspace is constantly being violated, sophisticated planes spy on our national territory and, in acts of desperate terrorism, are bombing strategic targets built and maintained by our people;

At this time, when the Reagan administration is maintaining U.S. warships in our territorial waters, and 5,000 Yankee Marines are preparing to attack from Honduran territory; when [the U.S.] is also organizing and stimulating the most varied forms of political, economic, and military destabilization internally, and is orchestrating the most sophisticated campaigns of slander at the international level to create a climate of opinion necessary in the international community to justify aggression;

At this time, when Nicaragua is suffering the sudden attacks of the U.S. government on its own or through the Somocistas based in Honduras—attacks designed to destroy the material infrastructure of our country as shown by the sabotage at the port of Corinto;

At this time, when the U.S. government is breaking all international norms and is using $19 million to wipe out lives and sow death in Nicaragua with impunity, ignoring the great efforts of the Contadora Group;

At this time, when Nicaragua is struggling for peace and life while the U.S. government is sowing death in this heroic land;

At this time, when the cowards and traitors are hiding like rats, planning the ways to attack our people, the Nicaraguan Women's Association "Luisa Amanda Espinoza" (AMNLAE) comes before you, participants of the 15th Latin American Congress of Sociology, with two basic objectives: first, to share with you what has been the experience of the participation of Nicaraguan women in the historical development of our society; and second, to affirm before you, sociologists of Latin America and the world, our determination to struggle as part of the people to defend at any cost the Popular Sandinista Revolution, the only guarantee of the gains we have made and will make in the future.

In the world, it is becoming more evident each day that the situation of women and their place in society are indissolubly linked to the economic, political, and social situation of their people as a whole, and that, therefore, the struggle for the equality of women is part of the struggle of the people to fulfill their greatest aspirations, and is part of the struggle for peace as a fundamental step in being able to struggle for development. This is a reality that the women of Nicaragua know from our own experience.

The socioeconomic system of our country condemned women to be the main, and in most cases the only, economic support in our homes. We were supposed to lose all hope of overcoming our being enslaved by a repressive regime and by an economic order that tied us to the chores of the home, that kept us socially marginalized, that conditioned and consolidated the *machista* positions of men and society as a whole, creating stereotypes and assigning roles according to the laws of an economic system of exploitation of man by man, reinforced by the double exploitation of women.

Nevertheless, the glorious history of the struggles of our people against foreign domination has also written in blood the names of thousands of Nicaraguan women, who with the people confronted the oppression and exploitation of the interventionists.

Women patriotically [participated] in the bloody struggles of the Indians against the conqueror [from Spain—Eds.], both on the battlefield and in their refusal to bear children into slavery; in the struggle against being a colony and for independence; against the Yankee filibuster in 1856 [William Walker—Eds.]; in the uprising of General Benjamín Zeledón in 1912; and in the glorious Army of Defense of the National Sovereignty, led by the Father of the Popular Anti-Imperialist Revolution, General of Free Men Augusto César Sandino, in the years 1927-34.

In the development and configuration of our vanguard, the Frente Sandinista de Liberación Nacional (FSLN), the participation of women was growing stronger every day, both in the armed struggle and in mass actions. Women stood out by their participation in the student movement in secondary school as well as the university, coming to hold positions of leadership in the Revolutionary Student Front (FER), a stepping stone for integrating students into the FSLN.

Women stopped viewing civic activity as the only way to fight and went to the front line of fire in the guerrilla war [against Somoza—Eds.], and now maintain their combative spirit to confront the enemy aggressor. On this solid rock, inscribed with the blood and heroic sacrifice of so many revolutionary women, the FSLN brought together this whole accumulated experience and used it in 1977 to found the Association of Women With Respect to the National Problematic (AMPRONAC), an organization to incorporate all women into the struggle to defeat the [Somoza] dictatorship. Since its birth, AMPRONAC had as its primary task to contribute through political action to the overthrow of the dictatorship, understanding that "Only the Popular Sandinista Revolution would abolish the hateful discrimination that women have suffered from men." It was exactly as laid out in the historic program of the FSLN. We can say that AMPRONAC, in the period of the struggle against Somoza, became the example of the most democratic organization, since it was able to unite within its ranks the energy of [many] women, independent of their political affiliation.

The first tasks that they carried out revolved around denunciation of all the crimes committed by the dictatorship and was precisely the consciousness forged in the street mobilizations, in the occupation of churches, in the hunger strikes—the consciousness formed in the face of the teargas bombs, the screams and fire of the machine gun—that transformed our association into a popular organization, which was able to actively integrate women workers, *campesinas,* students, professionals, and the women who sell in the market. All were integrated as part of the single fist that our Sandinista people raised against the Somocista dictatorship heroically and unflinchingly until its final defeat. We learned to conquer fear, we learned to be part of the people, we learned to fight, and we massively joined the march of history for the peace and life of our people.

It is important to point out that at the historical moment of its development, AMPRONAC came to play an important uniting role. As a broad organization, it brought together women of different community groups, religious groups, and political parties around the main task of all progressive sectors of the country: the defeat of the Somoza dictatorship. A concrete expression of this was the organizational contribution that AMPRONAC made to the United People's Movement (MPU), which brought together all the organizations and parties ready to fight for the overthrow of the dictatorship and the installation of Popular Democracy.

We can say in sum that in our history of struggle, AMPRONAC signified the qualitative leap in the participation of Nicaraguan women. We progressed from participating as individual observers, from the time of the first struggles of the colonial era, to the struggle against Yankee intervention led by General Augusto César Sandino, and through the long years of struggle of the FSLN, to having an organized expression such as AMPRONAC, in which women of different social sectors and beliefs found the way to make their contribution to the struggle of all our people against the dictatorship.

Because of this, at the time of the triumph of the Popular Sandinista Revolution, they succeeded in combining two elements that are vital in understanding the degrees of participation of women in Nicaragua today: On one hand, the revolutionary practice of the Nicaraguan women gave the Nicaraguan people an extraordinary learning process. The women learned in practice what we were capable of doing, and our people, without much theoretical discussion, learned what women were capable of doing. That is to say, we women didn't say we were equal—we showed it on the battlefield. On the other hand, with the taking of political power, we gained the real possibility of putting into practice the objectives of the program of the FSLN, which in Point 22 stipulated the struggle for the full emancipation of women.

The combination of the revolutionary practice of women and the political will of the vanguard [FSLN] explain why it was no accident that women assumed with dignity their historic role as the [active] subject of the political, social, and economic transformations. Only in this way have we been able to overcome the obstacles that, as products of underdevelopment inherited from Somocismo, made more difficult the qualitative participation of women and their quantitative integration in the tasks of reconstruction and defense of the Revolution. In contrast to other processes of liberation, AMPRONAC was the organization born in the direct struggle against Somoza and imperialism, and it succeeded in making a practical contribution. It was not born after the triumph, but during the course of that struggle.

AMPRONAC became the Nicaraguan Women's Association "Luisa Amanda Espinoza," an organic instrument of Nicaraguan women. Having contributed to the defeat of the dictatorship, it is now taking on the character of a broad and democratic movement, and is becoming the expression of women to represent their particular rights in society and before the state.

We have two basic routes for accomplishing this: First, the institutional road, through a) our legal representation in the Council of State, where AMNLAE is contributing to a revolutionary transformation, particularly in regard to those Somocista laws that violated the equality of women's rights; b) the Legal Office for Women, created by AMNLAE to guarantee that women receive juridical advice in defending their rights; and c) the Office of Women of the Revolutionary Government, designed to guarantee the integration of women in the plans and programs for national reconstruction.

The second route is promoting the organization of women within their unions, associations, and social sectors, in order to integrate them as a decisive force in the tasks of the revolution and to express in an organized form their concerns and their social, economic, and cultural aspirations. Thus the fundamental objective of AMNLAE is to raise the political and ideological level of women, as well as their cultural and technical level, permitting them to contribute to the construction of the economic bases of the new society in the same way that they were able to contribute to the destruction of the Somocista society.

As we learned to conquer fear in the struggle for liberation, now we have learned to conquer illiteracy, participating in the National Literacy Campaign, continuing the battle against ignorance; 45% of those in the Popular Education Collectives are women.

For many women, the Popular Health Campaigns were the first experience of leaving the closed shelter of their houses and connecting themselves with the rest of the community, learning once again what they are capable of doing and showing the people their capabilities. For other women, members or grassroots leaders of AMNLAE, these same campaigns constituted a significant advance in their technical capacity and in the consolidation of their political capacity as leaders of the base or for central functions. Last year, of the 77,619 health *brigadistas,* 80% were women and of the 8,906 health workers, 75% were women.

Four years after the triumph, the achievements of Nicaraguan women in the Popular Sandinista Revolution are expressed in the constant increase in the participation of women in the different tasks of social construction; in the growth of Centers of Infant Development, the Rural Infant Services, and Infant Dining Rooms.

They are expressed also in the revolutionary laws that institutionalize the full equality of women and recover their rights, converting the popular discussion of the preliminary draft of each law into a great ideological school about the role of women in society and the family, opening up the discussion about family responsibility as a task to be shared by men and women.

Through the discussion and presentation in the Council of State of the Law Regulating the Relations Among Mothers, Fathers and Children (replacing the Law of Paternal Authority), and of the Law of Alimony, which established the broad concept of solidarity and economic, emotional, and moral support among family members, AMNLAE was able to project in all sectors of our society the revolutionary concepts of the family.

The democratic participation of women in 180 assemblies about the Law of Alimony, with the participation of 15,000 people, has meant a qualitative advance in the study, discussion, and collective analysis, making people true participants in [formulating] popular legislation on an increasing basis. Special mention should go, today and always, to the political work carried out by our heroic Mothers of Heroes and Martyrs, who have contributed to strengthening the patriotic and anti-imperialist consciousness of our people.

The organized participation of women in building the new Nicaragua has led to the international recognition of AMNLAE, which is expressed in the moral and concrete solidarity of thousands of women from all parts of the world, from all economic and political systems. These are comrades, marching at our side, peace and life, organized in the Continental Women's Front Against Intervention.

The Continental Women's Front is made up of National Fronts of Women Against Intervention, originating in the plan of struggle of the Continental Meeting of Women for "National Independence and Peace" held in Managua in March 1982, with the participation of more than 300 delegates representing all the countries of the American continent in addition to invited guests from all continents. Since [1982] conscious and peace-loving women have advocated the formation of national fronts in Mexico, the Dominican Republic, Costa Rica, Venezuela, Bolivia, Ecuador, and the U.S., and are in process of formation in Canada, Panama, and Colombia.

AMNLAE also maintains relations with 249 organizations in 114 countries, from whose experiences we have tried to learn, while sharing ours with them. All this has been possible thanks to the Popular Sandinista Revolution, which is fighting for a more just society, free of exploitation and discrimination, and is our only guarantee of future gains.

Nevertheless, we don't want to give the impression that everything is resolved in the Popular Sandinista Revolution. We have difficulties integrating women into production, we need more infant services to resolve the problem of childcare for working women. Nevertheless, the economic limitations of our Revolution, subject to all forms of economic, political, and military aggressions on the part of imperialism, oblige us to use many of our scarce resources in the defense of our country, which is the defense of the life of our people.

We still have problems around understanding the line. Not all our comrades are clear that the problem of women is not, nor can it be, a problem between the men and the women of this country. *Machismo,* as part of the heritage of a society based on exploitation, still persists in many men and women. Unfortunately, it is much easier to destroy oppressive and repressive political and economic structures than the people's mental structures. This is the historical challenge of our Association: to contribute to the formation of new men and women. In any case, the participation of AMNLAE in the process is determined by our contribution to the consolidation of the Revolution; this is the basis for real, not formal, liberation.

Nicaraguan women are fully convinced that women will be free to the extent that both men and women become free: that liberty is not granted but won. For this reason, we shall defend the liberty won by the women and men of our people, just as we won it together, united with our vanguard the FSLN, the only and legitimate force leading the revolutionary process.

That is why today we [women] are 48% of the Sandinista Popular Militia, 60% of those who do *vigilancia revolucionaria* to find the enemy and stop him from advancing and destroying what we have built with such great love and joy.

That is why we formed the Infantry Reserve Battalions and we are integrated into the regular forces of the Sandinista Popular Army and the Sandinista Police.

That is why we are ready to participate voluntarily in the active and reserve ranks of the Patriotic Military Service.

That is why we are organized to participate in production, to substitute for the labor force that is being mobilized to defend our country's borders.

We live in a genuine revolution, which permits us to be subjects of our own history to achieve our freedom, and our struggle is a contribution to the thousands of women in the world today who suffer exploitation and discrimination under repressive and anti-popular regimes.

Above all, for these gains; for the 5,411,000 people who had medical care last year; for the 1,200,000 students in our schools; for the 208,533 children of our humble people who come together daily in the Popular Education Collectives, for the thousands of children who last year didn't suffer even one case of polio, thanks to the Popular Health Campaigns; for all of them; for the thousands of families who have received their land titles through the Agrarian Reform; for this heroic and suffering people which deserves victory, we come before you to ask you to unite with our cry:

Let There Be Peace in Central America!

We Want Peace!

At the Border:
An Interview With Two Soldiers

The following interview was conducted near the Honduran border with Justo Ríos and Cecilio Virgilio, two soldiers in Nicaragua's Reserve Army. It was conducted by staff members of the Institute for the Study of Labor and Economic Crisis (ISLEC) visiting Nicaragua shortly before the July 19, 1983, anniversary of the overthrow of Somoza.

ISLEC: How long have you been on the border here?

Justo: We have gone to the border five times. Now that it's getting close to July 19, we have to be prepared in the areas where the enemy can infiltrate, which are very dangerous. Our comrades in Battalion 4015 have had clashes here, and some of the other companies, such as 4009, have had casualties—18 were killed in an ambush about a month ago.

We have been mobilized to prevent anything happening around July 19. You should see what kind of propaganda our enemies toss out, saying that we are not going to celebrate our anniversary. They do this year after year. And year after year, we mobilize in self-defense. We're not going to let them do what they want, because this revolution has cost us blood, and we have to defend it—for the sake of the martyrs, the heroes we lost.

Cecilio: I have been in this battalion, Battalion 4015, for a year. Our battalion is the vanguard here in the western zone. We have gone out six times and suffered no losses, we have defeated the *contras,* and we will continue defeating them. This is something that has cost us a lot, and we have to defend it.

Just in this year we have had confrontations at San Francisco, San Pedro, and Santo Tomás, and we've been in two battles here in two months. One of them lasted 8 hours, and we succeeded in kicking out the *contras* who were trying to take over the town of Jalapa. There were 90 *contras* killed, and we lost 7 from our battalion. We also got their weapons and other military paraphernalia, including M-16's, and U.S.-made 185mm cannons. In Ocotal, we found the *contras* taking a break, waiting for July 19 to see what was going to happen. Our enemies say we can't celebrate July 19 here in Nicaragua, and we say we can. That's the reason we are here, because we *are* going to celebrate it.

ISLEC: When did you join the revolution, the struggle?

Cecilio: I was working on a banana plantation called La Hacienda de Elisa, and two comrades came around. I couldn't read or write, and they said, "You are in the dark here, you'll never throw off the yoke that way. Haven't you seen the picture in the newspaper of Somoza with his foot on the throat of a peasant farmworker?"

"No," I said. They said, "The FSLN is coming through here, and we need the support of the workers, of everybody." I said, "But they will shoot you and kill you."

"Well, brother," they said, "we are born to die, but isn't it worse to die little by little? Are you going to help us out?"

"Well, what do you want?" I said. "Well, we will write letters to so and so, and you will deliver them, like a messenger," they said. I agreed to do it, and that was when I met Nacho "Mercado" who is now a Comandante.

One thing led to another. I helped them get a truck, and gasoline, then spare tires, then a house that they wanted me to keep secret from the Guard's "ears" (spies). We drove to San José, Costa Rica, to get some weapons. We filled up the truck with arms and drove around to a bunch of places, at night. At Torito, I went right up to the Guards, asking when the bus came through, to keep their attention while the truck got through. They suspected me, and tried to get me to spend the night, but I said I was going to try to hitch a ride on that truck going by. I signalled my comrades in the truck to stop for me. They did, and we got on through. We went to San Francisco where we were trained with arms.

I was sent back to Chinandega with some medicines, but I got caught and was put in jail. They beat me so much, I was afraid they were going to kill me. Three months later, they let us out and had us sweeping the streets, and we escaped to go find our comrades.

This revolution has cost us a lot, and when something costs you a lot, you are proud of it. I really wish the other countries that are oppressed by the imperialist bourgeoisie could also be liberated. Because here, everything has been changing. Everything is different. The older the revolution gets, the more new things you see.

Justo: When I was 22 years old, I joined the revolution. We used to hear about the Cuban Revolution on Radio Free America, but we only heard ugly things that confused us. They said that communism killed every last person, even the old people. We have seen that this is all a lie, but there is no way to be sure of these things until you talk to people from these places.

They used to say those things on the radio so we wouldn't join the struggle. They said the communist terrorists in the mountains want to sow terrorism in Nicaragua. Over time, though, we realized that this wasn't the case. Back then, we weren't very well educated, but when people saw how things were, and how things had been for 20 years, people joined up, not only because they wanted to liberate their own country, but also to save their own lives.

We also had some comrades who fought alongside us, but who were self-interested. They thought that when we won the revolution, they would get a big farm. But we all had to realize that the revolution wasn't just for one person, the revolution was for everybody, for the people. Before, when people fought, they were just defending the interests of the few, but with the revolution we know we defend our interests.

It is true that we don't have everything we want, but we know why. There is a huge crisis on the national level. We have been attacked ever since the revolution triumphed. They haven't let us live in peace — we have always lived in a war. We also have had floods and droughts, and production has fallen back. Our corn has dried up, as well as some of the beans. But thanks to all the friendly countries that support us, and send us food and aid, we are alive, and the revolution is alive.

We don't produce much here in terms of material goods. And what we do produce is for buying useful things that we lack, such as raw materials. We know this, but there are still many comrades who don't understand it. This revolution belongs to the people, and that is why we defend it, because no one else is going to come and defend it. We won't go back to the past. Comrades have fallen and continue to fall, which is why we can't go back. Our slogan "Patria Libre o Morir" (Free Fatherland or Death) is like an oath, because we either live or die, but we aren't going to go backward, no. We are going forward.

ISLEC: Where are your families?

Cecilio: I work here near my father, and my wife and our four children are in Telica, near León. One of my sons is studying in Cuba. I never thought a son of mine would be studying in Cuba, when I grew up not knowing how to read. Now the revolution has changed everything. I'm 37 and my oldest son is 14.

Justo: I was married, but my wife left me because of the revolution. She said, "You are either with me or you can continue with this and go away." I said, "I can't go backwards, I'd rather die. If you want to leave," I told her, "I don't care — I will never betray the revolution. People would say I was a *contra*."

The ones who really will receive the benefits of the revolution won't be us, but our children. Our children are going to be the real owners of the revolution. That is why we are defending it today, and would die for it. I fight because I don't want to die, I want to defend our country's interests. I want to defend our people.

There are those who have land. They live well, and they have been connected to the Guard [Somoza's National Guard — Eds.]. But you can't abuse them. You have to get them to understand, to persuade them. No one can say that we're murderers. This isn't true. We are the people, and we don't go around massacring anybody — we only fight on the border.

ISLEC: Cecilio, is your family involved in the revolution?

Cecilio: Yes, here in Jalapa and in other places. There are eight of us brothers and sisters, and we are all involved in defense. My wife is in AMNLAE—the Women's Association. They do very good work, carrying out *vigilancia revolucionaria* in the towns and districts, helping in the mass organizations, explaining what's going on in the country, and the present political situation. I am very happy that my wife has joined AMNLAE. In addition I have *compañeras* in the Army. Battalion 4015 has a squadron of all women. We say to them, "You aren't going to lay an ambush, we are." And they answer, "Why not, aren't we also part of the revolution? And if you fall, we will jump ahead, because we won't let the revolution be defeated."

ISLEC: Can you tell us what you do on the banana plantation?

Justo: We are banana workers. We support ourselves working in the banana plantations. We do all kinds of work, fertilizing the plants, watering them in summer, shipping the fruit. It's a lot of work, and many tasks have to be done with the machete. We also watch out for the *contras,* who try to destroy our centers of production. They know this is how they can weaken the revolution economically. So, sometimes they harass us, and we can't sleep—we have to be on guard. That's how it has to be. We have to take care of one another. The revolution, the *chavalita* [endearing term for little girl—Eds.] has to be looked out for.

We also have various organizations on the banana plantation: AMNLAE, the CDS, and the July 19 Youth. The CDS's are the eyes and ears of the revolution, they are a high authority and deal with any problem.

ISLEC: How does the Women's Association work on the banana plantation?

Justo: They respond to many issues. Women have to be involved in defending the revolution. Some here are not revolutionary, and they are just working, but AMNLAE lets them know what we are struggling for. For example, some women think it's wrong to take land away from people who paid for it. But if you think about it, they didn't pay for it. I remember my grandfather used to tell me about how the rich always got the fertile land, and got richer all the time, while we just had little houses at the edge of the river. And when the river overflowed, it would carry away the houses and the people with them. We don't want that to happen again. The land belongs to those who work it, not just a few, the minority. That is our struggle.

ISLEC: What is your opinion of what is happening here with the *contras* trained by the U.S.?

Cecilio: In my opinion, the *contras* are dupes. Reagan's policy is to deceive these poor people. It used to be that everything we produced left here, and Somoza was the administrator for the U.S. Now Reagan wants to bring back all the landowners, the García Robelos, all those people. He is going to have a hard time, because our up and coming youth are smarter than he is. Now in Nicaragua, where the rich man goes, so does the poor man. If we have to stand in line to buy a package of beans, they have to stand in line too.

Justo: Here in Jalapa, people were fairly isolated before the revolution. Many believed in Somoza's government. This makes it hard for us. Here, we can't ask just anybody for food, because they might put something in it. They hide the *contras*.

And the worst part is that we can't fire on the *contras* even when they fire into our territory. We see their camps when we get up to the border, but we can't cross, because they would say that we are invading Honduras. We have to be clear about this. We can't give them any excuse to launch a war against us. Our leadership orders us not to violate foreign territory. But if the *contras* cross over into our territory, they won't leave alive.

ISLEC: If you could talk directly with people in the United States, what would you say?

Justo: We know that the working people in the Untied States are suffering the same problems as us, the peasants in poor countries, and it is worse in the capitalist countries. We know they don't agree with what the Reagan administration is doing in Central America. I would tell them that we all have to fight together, because we are one working class—just as the tyrants, the genocidal killers, are one class, and they are united.

We want a new Nicaragua, and we want to build a new socialism, we don't want to go back to the calamities we used to suffer while the people with money lived peaceful lives. We know that this is the case everywhere, and that's why we struggle. In Central America the struggle is for liberation of the people. We want just one Central America, without borders. Compañero Farabundo Martí [leader of the 1932 peasant revolt in El Salvador—Eds.] wanted us to be one. But they came and divided us so that they could dominate us better.

We know that our comrades in the U.S. working class are struggling to stop the aggression against us, and that they help the peasants and working classes in the poor countries. And for our part, we maintain the revolution so that the other countries can also liberate themselves. If we allowed the same people from the past to get back in, we'd be worse off, and the other countries wouldn't be able to free themselves. That's why we defend it. We know that's why Reagan hates us, because we are a counterbalance to him. We are a weight on him.

On the Law of
Patriotic Military Service

*This article is based on a summary of the Law of Patriotic Military Service and
its political context published in the September 1983 issue of* Envío, *publication of
the Instituto Histórico Centroamericano in Managua. Additional research and updating
has been done by the staff of the Institute for the Study of Labor and Economic Crisis.*

Within the context of the increasing escalation of attacks by the CIA-
managed *contras* in the summer of 1983, on August 9, in a regular session
of the Council of State, Nicaraguan Defense Minister Comandante
Humberto Ortega introduced the proposed Patriotic Military Service (SMP)
Law—in essence a law instituting a draft.

Article 24 of the Fundamental Statute of the Republic of Nicaragua,
dated July 20, 1979, one day after the victory which instituted the Sandinista Popular Army, had stated: "Nicaragua's National Guard will be
replaced by a new national Army of a patriotic nature, dedicated to the
defense of the democratic process and to national sovereignty, independence,
and the protection of its territory."

The possibility of obligatory military service had not been mentioned
since 1979 until last July [1983]. On July 19, the Coordinator of the Government Junta, Daniel Ortega, stated that the draft of the military service
law would be presented to the Council of State soon. On August 9, Humberto Ortega introduced it. Subsequently, it went through the regular process
every draft law follows. A special commission of the Council of State was
elected to study the draft and make suggestions, additions, or deletions.
After three weeks of work, the commission presented the working document to the plenary session of the Council of State on August 31. That
same day, 12 of the 51 articles which make up the law were approved. Those
articles included the following points:

- Military service will include both active and reserve duty.
- Active duty means fulfilling military activities in any of the units
  or offices of the Defense Ministry.
- Reserve duty consists of military training and formation.

- Military service is voluntary for women.
- After active duty (which will last two years and can be extended or reduced by six months) the person goes on reserve duty.
- Men between the ages of 18 and 25 will be recruited first.

Within the articles approved on August 31, Patriotic Military Service was defined as "the active participation of the nation in the tasks of defense" and as "the institutionalization of military service which the militia and reservists have been doing voluntarily for the last four years." Military service should be understood as an "effort to achieve better organization in the defense of the country."

Initial Reactions to the SMP Law

Immediately after the draft of the law was published, various organizations, religious communities, and institutions began to make their positions public. The majority expressed their support for the new proposal. The parties in the Revolutionary Patriotic Front, Basic Christian Communities, evangelical institutions like the Evangelical Committee for Assistance to the Poor (CEPAD), and the Eje Ecuménico all announced their support; however, they also presented suggestions for changes in the bill. CEPAD, reflecting the concerns of many of its members, such as the Mennonite Church, has begun a dialogue with the government. The purpose would be to allow some form of alternative service to members of traditionally pacifist denominations.

Throughout Nicaragua the mass organizations quickly held meetings to study the draft as did the unions and the other associations that have representatives on the Council of State. *In just two weeks, over 290 block committees had held meetings.* Seminars were also held by CONAPRO (the association of professionals), ANDEN (the teachers' association), UPN (the journalists' association), etc.

Of these, the most vocal was AMNLAE, the women's association, which proposed that because of the historic role women played in the revolution, obligatory service should be for all and not just for men. Initially the bill stipulated that women from ages 18 to 40 could join the reserves only, according to the needs and specifications of the Defense Ministry; and further, that only technically or professionally trained women would be eligible for participation in the Reserve Army.

After two weeks of consultation with its members, AMNLAE presented a motion in the Council of State to give women from ages 18 to 40 the opportunity to sign up voluntarily for active or reserve duty, and without distinction as to training or academic background. In the words of the Secretary General of AMNLAE, "We women demand our right to take part in [Patriotic Military Service], in accordance with the limitations imposed by history, but also according to our capabilities." After intense debate, on August 31 the AMNLAE amendment was approved by the Council of State.

The first negative public reaction to the draft was from the Social Christian Party. After deciding to withdraw its representative from the Council of State's special commission to study the draft, it published a document which was very critical of the law. An earlier document of the Social Democratic Party also expressed its opposition. But without a doubt, the document of the Nicaraguan Episcopal Conference was the most negative and produced the strongest internal reaction. (For further details, see p. 143, "Two Opposing Views on Defending Nicaragua.")

The Law in Effect

After continued debate throughout the country at all levels, the Patriotic Military Service bill was approved by the Council of State and signed into law on September 13, 1983. The first registration period was set for October 1-31, 1983, for Nicaraguan men between the ages of 18 and 22. Throughout the month of October, amidst political opposition from sectors of the Church and religious sects, as well as from anti-government political parties, actively urging Nicaraguan youth to defy the law, the newspapers carried stories daily about the progress of the registration. By the end of October, over 100,000 Nicaraguans were registered (*Barricada International* 11/7/83).

The spirit with which the majority of Nicaraguans responded to the law is captured in the words of Sra. Antonia Cortés, a revolutionary Christian mother in Managua:

We have a full right to organize ourselves for various types of defense. The Patriotic Military Service is a necessity of the highest priority in order to protect our national sovereignty in the face of so many acts of aggression by the U.S. government. . . . If there is military service in other countries where there is no aggression, then we have all the more reason to impel our Patriotic Military Service, sending our sons to register (*Nuevo Diario* 10/20/83).

PART 5

Christians and the Revolutionary State

The FSLN Position on Religion

National Directorate of the FSLN

This official statement on religion by the National Directorate of the FSLN, issued in 1980, is widely regarded by leading international theologians as the most advanced position taken by a revolutionary party in power in the world today. It is important both because it provides the context for understanding the significance of the current debates among Christians and within the Church in Nicaragua, and because it stands as a counter to the international campaign by anti-Sandinista forces to manipulate the religious issue as a form of ideological warfare against the Nicaraguan government. This document was first published in the October 7, 1980, issue of Barricada; *we reprint here by permission (with minor editing) the translation by Intercontinental Press, published in* Sandinistas Speak *by Borge, Fonseca, Ortega, and Wheelock (New York: Pathfinder Press, 1982).*

For some time the enemies of our people—driven from power once and for all—have been carrying on an obstinate campaign of distortions and lies about various aspects of the revolution, with the aim of confusing the people. This campaign of ideological confusion seeks to promote anti-Sandinista fears and attitudes among the people, while at the same time politically wearing down the FSLN through interminable polemics that never seek honest conclusions, but in fact seek precisely the opposite.

The question of religion has a special place in these campaigns of confusion, since a large percentage of the Nicaraguan people have very deep-rooted religious sentiments. In this regard, the reactionaries' efforts have been aimed at spreading the idea that the FSLN is using religion now in order to later suppress it. Clearly, the purpose of such propaganda is to manipulate our people's honest faith in order to provoke a *political* reaction against the FSLN and the revolution.

This campaign is particularly vicious because it takes up matters that touch very deep feelings of many Nicaraguans. Given the importance of the question, and in order to orient our membership, clarify things for our people, and prevent further manipulation of this subject, the National Directorate of the FSLN has decided to issue this document expressing its official position on religion.

Christian patriots and revolutionaries are an integral part of the Sandinista Popular Revolution, and they have been for many years. The participation of Christians—both lay people and clergy—in the FSLN and the Government of National Reconstruction is a logical outgrowth of their outstanding participation at the people's side throughout the struggle against the dictatorship.

Through their interpretation of their faith, many FSLN members and fighters were motivated to join the revolutionary struggle and therefore the FSLN. Many gave not only their valiant support to our cause, but were also examples of dedication, even to the point of shedding their blood to water the seed of liberation.

How could we forget our beloved martyrs Oscar Pérez Cassar, Oscar Robelo, Sergio Guerrero, Arlen Siu, Guadalupe Moreno, and Leonardo Matute, or the dozens of Messengers of the Word* murdered by the Somocista National Guard in the mountains of our country, or so many other brothers and sisters.

We should give special mention to the revolutionary work and heroic sacrifice of Catholic priest and Sandinista member Gaspar García Laviana. He represented the highest synthesis of Christian vocation and revolutionary consciousness.

All these were humble men and women who knew how to fulfill their duty as patriots and revolutionaries without getting bogged down in long philosophical discussions. They now live eternally in the memory of the people, who will never forget their sacrifice.

But the participation of Christians was not limited to serving as fighters in the Sandinista Front. Many Christians, lay people and clergy, who never participated in the ranks of the FSLN, although some were linked to it, professed and practiced their faith in accord with our people's need for liberation. The Catholic Church and some evangelical churches even participated as institutions in the people's victory over the Somoza regime of horror.

On various occasions the Catholic bishops bravely denounced the crimes and abuses of the dictatorship. Monsignor Obando y Bravo and Monsignor Salazar y Espinoza, among others, were abused by Somocista gangs. It was a group of priests and monks who exposed to the world the disappearance of 3,000 peasants in the mountains in the north of our country.

Many Christians of different denominations carried a liberating message to the people. Some even gave refuge and food to the Sandinistas who were mercilessly persecuted by Somocismo.

People gathered in the religious houses to hear underground news

---

* The "Messengers of the Word" were lay Christians who proselytized among peasants in the early 1970s. They often played a role in organizing opposition to the Somoza dictatorship in the countryside.

bulletins when the Somocista repression prevented independent radio sta
tions from broadcasting.

Because of their brave participation in the struggle, the Catholic Church
and Christians in general suffered persecution and death. Many religious
figures also were mistreated, were expelled from our country, faced a thousand obstacles to the exercise of their Christian faith. Many religious
buildings were broken into, pillaged, bombed, and assaulted in attempts
to murder *compañeros* inside, as was the case with El Calvario Church in
León and the chapels in the mountains.

To a degree unprecedented in any other revolutionary movement in
Latin America and perhaps the world, Christians have been an integral
part of our revolutionary history. This fact opens up new and interesting
possibilities for the participation of Christians in revolutions in other places,
not only during the struggle for power, but also later in the stage of building
the new society.

In the new conditions that are posed by the revolutionary process, we
Christian and non-Christian revolutionaries must come together around
the task of providing continuity to this extremely valuable experience,
extending it into the future. We must perfect the forms of conscious participation among all the revolutionaries in Nicaragua, whatever their
philosophical positions and religious beliefs.

FSLN's Positions on Religion

1) The FSLN sees freedom to profess a religious faith as an inalienable
right which is fully guaranteed by the revolutionary government. This principle was included in our Revolutionary Program long ago, and we will
maintain it in practice in the future. Furthermore, in the new Nicaragua
no one can be discriminated against for publicly professing or spreading
their religious beliefs. Those who profess no religious faith have the very
same right.

2) Some authors have asserted that religion is a mechanism for
spreading false consciousness among people, which serves to justify the
exploitation of one class by another. This assertion undoubtedly has historical
validity to the extent that in different historical epochs religion has served
as a theoretical basis for political domination. Suffice it to recall the role
that the missionaries played in the process of domination and colonization
of the Indians of our country.

However, we Sandinistas state that our experience shows that when
Christians, basing themselves on their faith, are capable of responding to
the needs of people and of history, those very beliefs lead them to revolutionary activism. *Our experience shows us that one can be a believer and a consistent
revolutionary at the same time, and that there is no insoluble contradiction between
the two* [Emphasis added—Eds.].

3) The FSLN is the organization of Nicaraguan revolutionaries, who
have voluntarily come together to transform the social, economic, and
political situation in our country in line with a known program and strategy.

All those who agree with our objectives and proposals, and have the personal qualities demanded by our organization, have every right to participate actively in our ranks, whatever their religious beliefs. Evidence of this is provided by the fact that there are three Catholic priests in the Sandinista Assembly.

Many Christians are members of the FSLN, and there will be Christians within the Frente Sandinista de Liberación Nacional as long as there are revolutionary Christians in Nicaragua.

4) As a vanguard conscious of the immense responsibilities that have fallen upon its shoulders, the FSLN zealously seeks to maintain the strength and unity of its organization around the explicit objectives for which it was formed. Within the framework of the FSLN, there is no place for religious proselytism. This would undermine the specific character of our vanguard and introduce factors of disunity, since the Frente Sandinista de Liberación Nacional includes *compañeros* of various religions and of no religion.

Outside the framework of the FSLN, Christian activists—whether they be priests, pastors, members of religious orders, or lay people—all have the right to express their convictions publicly. This cannot be used to detract from their work in the FSLN or from the confidence that they have gained as a result of their revolutionary activity.

5) The FSLN has a profound respect for all the religious celebrations and traditions of our people. It is striving to restore the true meaning of these occasions by attacking various evils and forms of corruption that were introduced into them in the past.

We feel that this respect must be expressed not only by ensuring conditions for the free expression of these traditions, but also by seeing that they are not used for political or commercial ends. If in the future any Sandinista activist departs from this principle, we state now that this in no way represents the FSLN's position.

Of course, if other political parties or individuals try to turn the people's religious festivals or activities into political acts against the revolution (as has happened in some instances in the past), the FSLN declares it also has a right to defend the people and the revolution in these same conditions.

6) No Sandinista member should, in any official capacity, offer an opinion on the interpretation of religious questions that are solely the concern of the various churches. These questions must be decided by the Christians among themselves. If a Sandinista who is also a Christian intervenes in the polemics of that kind, he does so in a personal capacity, in his capacity as a Christian.

7) Some reactionary ideologists have accused the FSLN of trying to divide the Church. Nothing could be further from the truth or more ill-intentioned than this accusation. If there are divisions within the religions, they exist completely independently of the will and activity of the FSLN.

A study of history shows that around major political events members of the Catholic Church have always taken different and even contradictory positions. Missionaries came with the Spanish colonizers, and they used the cross to consecrate the slave labor that had been initiated by the sword. But against them arose the firmness of Bartolomé de las Casas, the defender of the Indians.*

In the beginning of the last century many priests fought for the independence of Central America, some with weapons in hand. And on the other extreme there were priests who defended the privileges of the crown in Latin America with equal vehemence.

After liberation from the colonial yoke, we find the anti-interventionist positions of Monsignor Pereira y Castellón, who called for defense of the nation's interests against the North American invasion. During the Somoza epoch the figure of Monsignor Calderón y Padilla stands out in his attack upon the Somozas' vice, corruption, and abuse of power against the poor.

And today there is the massive revolutionary commitment among revolutionary Christians.

Earlier we mentioned the participation of many Christians in the people's revolutionary struggle. But we must also point out that some, like León Pallais and others, remained at Somoza's side to the end.

We should not forget that in that period there were priests who proudly paraded their military ranks and official positions—of course no one demanded that they give up their posts. But we should also not forget that in contrast to these sad examples we have the immense figure of Gaspar García L. and so many other Sandinista martyrs of Christian origin.

This situation continues in the present stage. An immense majority of the Christians actively support and participate in the revolution. But there is also a minority who maintain political positions opposed to the revolution.

Naturally we Sandinistas are good friends of the revolutionary Christians but not of the counterrevolutionaries, even though they call themselves Christians.

The FSLN, however, maintains communications on all levels with different churches, with the ranks and the hierarchy, without regard to their political positions.

We do not foster or provoke activities to divide the churches. That question is the exclusive concern of the Christians and does not involve political organizations. If divisions do exist, the churches must look for the causes within themselves and not attribute them to supposed malicious outside influences. Speaking frankly, we would look kindly upon a church that took part, in an unprejudiced, mature, and responsible manner, in the common effort to expand continually the dialogue and participation that our revolutionary process has opened.

8) Another matter that has recently been the subject of discussion is

---

* Bartolomé de las Casas (1474-1566), a Spanish Dominican, was known as the "protector of the Indians" for his defense of the rights of the Indians against the Spanish settlers.

the participation of priests and members of religious orders in the Government of National Reconstruction. In regard to this, we declare that every Nicaraguan citizen has the right to participate in carrying out political affairs in our country, whatever their civil state, and the Government of National Reconstruction guarantees this right, which is backed up by the law.

The priest *compañeros* who have taken posts in the government, in response to the FSLN's call and their obligations as citizens, have thus far carried out extraordinary work. Facing great and difficult problems, our country needs the participation of all patriots to move forward. It especially needs those who had the chance to receive higher education, which was denied to the majority of our people.

Therefore, the FSLN will continue to ask all those lay and clerical citizens whose experience or qualifications might be needed for our process to participate.

If any of the religious *compañeros* decide to give up their governmental responsibilities for their own special reasons, that too is their right. Exercising the right to participate in and fulfill one's patriotic obligation is a matter of personal conscience.

9) The revolution and the state have origins, goals, and spheres of action that are different from those of religion. For the revolutionary state, religion is a personal matter. It is the concern of individuals, churches, and special associations organized around religious aims.

Like every modern state, the revolutionary state is secular and cannot adopt any religion because it is the representative of all the people, believers as well as nonbelievers.

By issuing this official communiqué, the National Directorate of the Frente Sandinista de Liberación Nacional hopes not only to clarify the question under discussion, but also and especially to remind the revolutionary militants of the FSLN and the churches of their duties and responsibilities in the construction of our country, which has been held down by 159 years of pillage, repression, and dependence.

Building Nicaragua's future is a historic challenge that transcends our borders and inspires other peoples in their struggle for liberation and to create the new man, and it is a right and a duty of all Nicaraguans, regardless of their religious beliefs.

Sandino Yesterday, Sandino Today, Sandino Always!

Free Homeland or Death!

Two Opposing Views on Defending Nicaragua: Bishops vs. Christian Base Organizations

I. Introduction
by James and Margaret Goff,
Centro Ecuménico Antonio Valdivieso

A recently enacted law of obligatory military service [see above in this volume—Eds.] is being used here by the Catholic Bishops' Conference as a new point of attack against the Sandinista government. Here are translations of three statements which illustrate the conflict.

The first is the text of the episcopal document. The bishops base the right to "conscientious objection" to military duty on the allegation that the new law provides conscripts for the service of a particular party, not for the service of the nation. Furthermore, they claim that in the Army soldiers will receive "political indoctrination in favor of the Sandinista Party." The bishops state that the new law "follows the general lines of all totalitarian types of legislation."

The charges are being sharply contradicted by numerous Christian groups in the country—Protestant as well as Catholic—all of whom see the episcopacy as seeking to delegitimize the government. We include two of these statements.

These groups point out that the bishops have made an incursion into a purely political field: "The message of the episcopal conference takes on the nature of an open call to desertion, mass disobedience, and rebellion against the revolutionary state, which it considers totalitarian, illegitimate, and unworthy of the respect of the citizens." Defending the revolutionary state, the groups add:

> The legitimacy of the Sandinista government is a historical and social fact, recognized by the people of Nicaragua and by many peoples of the world. The FSLN is not merely a party in power but an authentic national liberation movement which has restored the dignity and identity of the whole nation.

It should be noted that the Episcopal conference issued its criticism while the new law was still a bill under study in the Council of State [legislature—Eds.]. The bill was subsequently passed, with no major modifications, on September 13 [1983] and immediately signed into law by the Government Junta. The Nicaraguan Episcopal Conference consists of nine bishops. Contrary to custom, only the secretary of the Conference signed the message.

II. General Considerations on Military Service
by the Nicaraguan Episcopal Conference

The bill on military service now under debate in the Council of State has provoked some ill-feeling and concern among a large number of Nicaraguans. Vis-à-vis this situation the Episcopal Conference cannot remain silent, since Catholics expect a moral orientation and a standard of conduct to adhere to. Therefore, we bishops, after mature reflection, offer Catholics and all Nicaraguans of good will the following brief ideas.

General Considerations on Military Service

The army is an armed institution of the state, the legitimacy of which stems from the need to defend national sovereignty and the integrity of the state's territory in the event of possible foreign attacks or domestic uprisings.

In this sense, the II Vatican Council refers explicitly to the army whose purpose is "service to the country" and which must function as "an agent of security and freedom of the people" (cf. *Gaudium et Spes*, 79). But the legitimacy of the army's existence as an armed power of the state would be a vain thing if the state itself had no authentic moral power to oblige the citizens, within limits established by law, to be incorporated into the armed forces and render military service to the country. Consequently, it must be admitted that obligatory military recruitment is a legitimate power of the state and in principle is not contrary to any ethical or moral standard.

Nevertheless, the state must respect the just freedom of individuals and take into account the religious or ethical beliefs of the citizens. Thus, the II Vatican Council, picking up the echo of an almost universal feeling, said that, "It seems right that laws make humane provisions for the case of those who for reasons of conscience refuse to bear arms, provided, however, that they accept some other form of service to the human community" (GS, 79).

But along with this "classic concept" of army and military service, there has appeared a "revolutionary concept," based on a new understanding

This document and the two documents that follow were translated by James and Margaret Goff of the Centro Ecuménico Antonio Valdivieso (Antonio Valdivieso Ecumenical Center) in Managua, Nicaragua. Minor editing has been done for U.S. publication.

The first document was translated from "Conferencia Episcopal sugiere 'Objeción de Conciencia': Nadie puede ser obligado a tomar armas por un partido," in La Prensa *(Managua), September 1, 1983, p. 1.*

of law and the state, and its institutions. Totalitarian ideologies have created a new type of law, based on the most radical juridical positivism and on the pre-eminence of society over the individual. In this new ordering of law, personal and individual values are subject to social and collective values, under the discretion of the state.

It has been impossible in practice to legitimate this revolutionary socio-juridical conception by the free acceptance of the people; rather, it has been imposed, de facto, by force of arms and other means of state coercive power. It can be easily verified that in all countries with totalitarian governments, a highly politicized army has been created as a defense of the government's own ideology, and at the same time as a means to force the people to receive political indoctrination.

The fundamental error of this juridico-political system is that it creates an identity of the state with the party and of the party with the people or their interests. This absolute dictatorship of a political party, which is constituted by force as the only arbiter and owner of the state, its institutions, and every type of social activity, poses the problem of its legitimacy as well as the legitimacy of its institutions, including the army (cf. Universal Declaration of the Rights of Man, United Nations, Art. 21.3).

If "armed power," which should be the exclusive right of the state, becomes "armed power" at the service of a political party, even the possibility of a democratic and pluralistic state and diverse social forces is automatically denied. To force citizens to join an "army-political party" without their being in agreement with the ideology of that political party is an assault on freedom of thought, opinion, and association (cf. Universal Declaration of the Rights of Man, United Nations, Arts. 18, 19, 20).

Consequently, no one can be obliged to take up arms to defend an ideology with which he does not agree, nor to perform obligatory military service in favor of a political party.

The Patriotic Military Service Bill

The first Proclamation of the Government of National Reconstruction, on June 18, 1979, states that "it is proposed to organize a national Army which will embody the interests of the Nicaraguan people and defend our integrity and sovereignty." In the Government Program presented in that Proclamation, fundamental bases are defined for the organization of a new national Army. And in this Program it states: "A new national Army will be organized whose fundamental principles will be the defense of the democratic process and the sovereignty and independence of the nation as well as the integrity of its territory" (Art. 1, 12).

In accordance with these principles, the Coordinator of the Government Junta, Commander Daniel Ortega, in a speech on July 19, 1983, said, "It is the decision of the National Directorate, backed by the Government Junta, as soon as possible to submit for approval a bill that will establish Patriotic Military Service" (*Barricada,* July 20, 1983, p. 3, col. 4). The complete text of this bill was published in several national newspapers on August 10, 1983.

This bill is highly politicized in its basic points, has a partisan character, and follows the general lines of all totalitarian-type legislation. Patriotic Military Service is defined as "active participation of all the people in defense activities, and therefore it is an obligation of all Nicaraguans to defend with arms the sovereignty and independence of the nation and the Sandinista Popular Revolution" (Art. 2).

In this article, "the sovereignty and independence of the nation" and the "Sandinista Popular Revolution" are unduly linked.

It is not correct to mix, confuse, or identify the concepts of fatherland, state, revolution, and Sandinismo. Each of these words has a distinct, specific content and very diverse juridico-political values.

Furthermore, the initial popular revolutionary social movement has become a political party.

Military Service does not pretend only "to provide instruction in the most advanced military techniques" ("Whereas," no. VII); it will also "promote in our young people a sense of revolutionary ethics and discipline" ("Whereas," no. VII). That is to say, the Army will become an obligatory center of political indoctrination in favor of the Sandinista Party.

To take advantage of military discipline ideologically, to "manipulate" people and subject them by force to a given ideology, is a serious attack against freedom of thought and opinion.

These principles and the bases listed in Article 4,2.4.5., distort and contradict the true sense of the First Proclamation of the Government and of the Program then presented.

For all of these reasons, the attitude toward this bill, for all those who do not share the Sandinista Party ideology, has to be that of "conscientious objection." And no one should be punished, persecuted, or discriminated against for adopting this position.

On proposing these reflections for the consideration of Catholics, we only wish to illuminate the moral and ethical aspects of this problem and to exhort everyone to search for a peaceful way to solve the serious problems that face our society.

True peace is the fruit of justice, not of violence.

May the Virgin Mary, Queen of Peace, help us to live according to charity so that this Holy Year of Reconciliation may produce in each of us and in our society sincere fruits of justice, love, and peace.

Managua, August 29, 1983

Nicaraguan Episcopal Conference

Certified by Msgr. Leovigildo López Fitoria,
Bishop of Granada
Secretary, Nicaraguan Episcopal Conference

III. Christian Groups Respond to the Nicaraguan Bishops' Communiqué on Military Service

1. We Speak Out of Our Christian Faith

We raise our voices, motivated by the Word of the Lord, which exhorts us to "speak and act as those who are to be judged under the law of liberty" (James 2:12-13), and by the teaching of the II Vatican Council, which indicates that, "Obedience demands that we prudently look for new avenues for the greater good of the Church and confidently propose our plans and urgently expose the needs of the flock committed to us" (Decree on the Ministry and Life of Priests, No. 15).

We do this because the message issued by the Nicaraguan Episcopal Conference as a "moral orientation" and "standard of conduct" on the bill of obligatory military service is causing grave uneasiness and concern for many Christians of the country.

In a matter of such seriousness for the survival of Nicaragua, which is now the victim of aggression, it seems to us necessary to discuss, deliberate, and decide as a community (*in ecclesia*), because the II Vatican Council has taught us that, "It is the mission of the Church to establish dialogue with the human society in which it lives" (Decree on the Bishops' Pastoral Office in the Church, No. 13). The Council said to the bishops: "Always regard the priests as sons and friends and be ready to listen to them" (ibid., No. 16). And it said to the priests that they are "necessary helpers and counselors in the ministry (Decree on the Ministry and Life of Priests, No. 7), who should "listen to the laity willingly and together with them read the signs of the times" (ibid., No. 9), because "they cannot be of service to men if they remain strangers to the life and conditions of men" (ibid., No. 3).

It deeply grieves us that the Episcopal Conference should echo the "ill-feeling and concern" that exists in part of the Nicaraguan people without being able to see "the joys and the hopes, the griefs and the anxieties of the men of this age, *especially those who are poor or in any way afflicted*" (Pastoral Constitution on the Church in the Modern World, No. 1).

We are saddened over the destiny of hundreds of *campesinos* who have been kidnapped and tortured and of those who are exposed to death every day on our borders, "keeping watch night and day, laboring on the work with one hand and holding his weapon with the other" (Nehemiah 4:11, 17).

Many parents rightly expect of the bishops of Nicaragua a word of encouragement and consolation, but it never comes. Have our bishops forgotten by chance the immense sacrifice of the people who took up arms, making use of their legitimate right to defense against the Somoza tyranny? Is it not true that today our people have to defend themselves with arms

Translated from "Al pueblo de Nicaragua y al mundo," in El Nuevo Diario *(Managua), September 13, 1983, p.2.*

in order to protect their lives or face the alternative of letting themselves be overcome by the foreign invader and his mercenaries?

It is surprising that the Nicaraguan Episcopal Conference is not sensitive to the statements and gestures of solidarity from hundreds of groups in all parts of the world, and that it does not echo the Contadora Group's peace-making effort or the forceful words of Archbishop John R. Roach, President of the U.S. Episcopal Conference, who opposes Ronald Reagan's interventionist plans.

It is surprising that the Nicaraguan Bishops' Conference does not listen to the encouraging words of support for the people that the delegates of over 400 million Protestant and Orthodox Christians of the world addressed to us from the VI Assembly of the World Council of Churches held recently in Vancouver, British Columbia.

2. Analysis of the Document

The statement of our bishops denies to the Nicaraguan state a right that no Catholic Episcopal Conference questions in any state today, be it capitalist or socialist. In doing this, it tries to support its thesis in the conciliar doctrine which affirms the validity of conscientious objection.

However, for the Council (and, in general, for pacifist movements) conscientious objection to military service is based on the refusal of some citizens to use arms, even in the case of legitimate defense, and thus does not question in any way the legitimacy of the state. Therefore, the II Vatican Council and the document of the Nicaraguan Episcopal Conference are not talking about the same thing. On the contrary, given the condition which our country is experiencing—of threats and aggression—the message of the Episcopal Conference takes on the nature of an open call to desertion, mass disobedience, and rebellion against the revolutionary state, which it considers totalitarian, illegitimate, and unworthy of the respect of the citizens.

It seems especially serious to us that such a summary condemnation is being pronounced at the very moment when the Reagan administration intends to justify its aggression against the people of Nicaragua with an identical pretext. The Episcopal Conference thus assumes joint responsibility for any attack or invasion against our territory, inasmuch as with its words it contributes, in effect, to undermining international solidarity, which is so necessary for the subsistence of our dignified and suffering people.

It concerns us that the Episcopal Conference, which with such intrepid earnestness requires political pluralism of the state, should deny the same right within the Nicaraguan Church. It concerns us that there are bishops who are trying to make an anti-Sandinista, anti-national party out of the Church in our country. It should be asked if the members of the Episcopal Conference speak in this case as behooves pastors of the Church, according to Catholic tradition, or as private citizens from a partisan political option.

The bishops' pronouncement is not founded on any biblical text, any Church document, or any antecedent in the practice of the Church vis-à-vis the State. It is the first position taken by an episcopacy in the history of the contemporary Church that makes obligatory military service illegitimate. Thus, by expressing our nonconformity we do not question any Church directive; we oppose at the political level the taking of a political stand which aspires—without achieving it—to having the backing of the magisterium of the Church. With this attitude the Church hierarchy is abandoning the country at the time of greatest danger.

3. The Nicaraguan Government Is Legitimate

The legitimacy of the Sandinista government is a historical and social fact, recognized by the people of Nicaragua and by many people of the world. The FSLN is not merely a party in power but an authentic national liberation movement which has restored the dignity and identity of the whole nation. It is the FSLN which has returned to the state, the Army, and the Nicaraguan nationality their purpose—that of being agents at the service of the great majority of the people.

It is the Sandinista Popular Revolution which has made possible agrarian reform, the literacy campaign, the health and adult education campaigns, and the entire immense cultural process which we are experiencing. For the first time in our history our national sovereignty is sound.

All these acts legitimate the revolutionary government. Political, Church, and diplomatic authorities of the highest level throughout the world recognize this. The extraordinary circumstances which surround the triumph of the revolution do not impair the sources of its historic legitimacy: the superb gesture of Augusto César Sandino against U.S. intervention and oligarchic domination; the sacrifice and blood of our heroes and martyrs; the support of all the people in arms that overthrew the tyranny and that now participate with enthusiasm in production and defense, in the mass organizations and in reconstruction tasks; and a political project open to the participation of various political parties.

4. The Christian vis-à-vis the State

Since New Testament days Christians have shown on the one hand an attitude of respect for the state and on the other an attitude of distrust. Obedience to political powers obliges conscience and is founded on the fact that all authority comes from God and is the vehicle of divine justice (Romans 13:1-7). But this is not true when moral standards are trampled on in an arbitrary, violent, and tyrannical way. In this case a conflictive situation arises which is resolved with the well-known principle given by Peter to the first Christian community: "We must obey God rather than men" (Acts 5:29).

Those who have authority in the state may oblige men in conscience only if their authority is in harmony with the moral order and in the final instance intrinsically related to the authority of God (cf. *Pacem in terris,* 49). Only when authority violates the moral order does it lose all obligatory power (ibid., 61). Where public authority oversteps its competence, citizens may defend their rights against the abuse of this authority provided that in so doing they nevertheless "obey to the extent that the objective common good demands" (*Gaudium et Spes,* 74).

The magisterium of the Church, especially in its most recent documents, exhorts Christians and all men of good will to consider duties to the state among the principles and obligations of conscience (GS, 30, 75). Military service forms part of a citizen's duties; it is unjust to resort to subterfuges and frauds to evade the obligation to defend the nation (Romans 12:6-7; GS, 30). When circumstances give the state the right to a defensive war, those who render military service are agents of security, freedom, and true peace (GS, 79, 5).

5. People Have the Right to Organize Their Defense

For centuries the magisterium of the Catholic Church has affirmed the sacred right of peoples to their defense. The II Vatican Council solemnly reiterated this: "As long as the danger of war remains and there is no competent and sufficiently powerful authority at the international level, governments cannot be denied the right to legitimate defense once every means of peaceful settlement has been exhausted" (GS, 79).

The Council also established the right of governments to organize armies that, like the Army of Nicaragua, serve the nation, defending national integrity, security, and sovereignty: "Those who are pledged to the service of their country as members of the armed forces should regard themselves as agents of security and freedom on behalf of their people" (GS, 79). The Nicaraguan bishops themselves therefore admit that "obligatory military recruitment is a legitimate power of the state and is not opposed in principle to any ethical or moral standard." By what supreme design should Nicaragua be the exception to this rule? Our bishops say that the Nicaraguan state is totalitarian, but we ask: What totalitarian state would tolerate, without taking immediate repressive measures, any group—even if it were the hierarchy—publicly proclaiming its illegitimacy and publicly calling on the people to desert it at a time of threat and danger?

When it delegitimizes the government of Nicaragua, the Episcopal Conference excludes itself from the democratic and revolutionary dialogue underway to solve the real problems of our country. In Nicaragua, the constitution of a really new power is at stake, and we Christians have to respond to this challenge. It is our obligation to watch so that in Nicaragua there emerges an authentic popular democracy and the revolutionary power is not diverted from this goal. The example of Bishop Rubén López Ardón (Estelí) is encouraging. His gesture of donating 500,000 *córdobas* for a housing project of the revolutionary government, immediately following the episcopal communiqué, implicitly affirms the legitimacy of our revolutionary state and backs its humanistic efforts.

Also encouraging are the words of Bishop Carlos Santi (Matagalpa), who, indicating that he was uninformed of the communiqué of the other bishops, stated that it was the duty of Christians to be willing to defend their country and that there was no argument in the Bible against military service (*El Nuevo Diario*, September 6, 1983). Bishop Salvador Schlaefer (Bluefields) has spoken along the same line. The People of God, in other words, have a full right to participate in the national effort to shape a more just and human society.

It is disconcerting that there are those who, [addressing] a simple bill still open to amendments and changes, choose condemnation instead of a constructive and productive dialogue. The episcopacy refuses to exert a positive influence in the drafting of a just and humane law of military service adapted to the needs and rights of our citizens.

We think that the principle of the Council continues to shine forth and be valid for our country in these times of aggression by the great power of the North: "It is one thing to undertake military action for the just defense of the people and something else again to seek the subjugation of other Nations" (GS, 79).

We say to Christians and people of good will in the whole world: Support the just cause of the people of Nicaragua! Form a cordon of international solidarity to protect us from the invasion that Ronald Reagan has planned against our country!

Signed by:

> For the Association for the Development of Peoples: Ketxu Amenzua, General Coordinator

> For the Antonio Valdivieso Ecumenical Center: Fr. Uriel Molina, Director; Sr. Luz Beatriz Arrellano, Coordinator of the Secretariat of Solidarity; Dr. José Argüello, Director of Communications

> Friar Rolando Ugalde, Justice and Peace Commission of the Dominican Order; Fr. Donald Mendoza, Director, Colegio Calazans, León

> For the "Gaspar García Laviana" Christian Community of Granada: Frank López Pérez; José Menocal; Mariana de Muñoz; Modesto Ruiz Gómez; Silvio Castillo Jerez; Zacarías Bustos; Eduardo Cortés

> Msgr. Sergio Méndez Arceo, Co-President of Christian Solidarity International

> For the La Salle Pedagogical Institute of Managua: Bro. Edwin Maradiaga; Bro. Narciso Mayorga; Bro. Salvador Chamorro; Bro. Francisco Torres Christian; Bro. José Luis Contreras

> For the Christian Revolutionary Movement "Gaspar García Laviana" of Masaya: Norma Ramírez; Arnoldo García; Javier Alvarado; Bernardo Fuentes Telica; Haydeé Cuarezma; Concepción Zamora; Dominga Méndez; Concepción Mercado; Brigida Martínez; Pastora Pavón; Carmelita Vásquez; Soledad Mercado; Juana Alarcón; Pedro Gutiérrez

> Sr. María Luisa Atienza; Frei Betto; Friar Plácido Erdozaín

Christian Organizations:
Obando Document Is Strictly Political

We are Christian groups committed to the process of the New Nicaragua and we are expressing our feelings about the message of the Episcopal Conference on the Patriotic Military Service (PMS) bill. From the beginning of our criticism of the document we want to affirm that in the judgment made by the bishops of Nicaragua of the situation and the consequences that they bring out, their message becomes an incursion into a strictly political arena.

In our judgment the document of the Episcopal Conference — if we omit the salutation and the final words — is situated exclusively in the political sphere. And we think that in this sphere there can be and in fact are legitimately different Christian positions. Paul VI, in his Apostolic Letter on the 80th anniversary of *Rerum Novarum*, expressly tells us the following:

> It is up to the Christian communities, with the help of the Holy Spirit, in communion with the bishops who hold responsibility, and in dialogue with other Christian brethren and all men of good will, to discern the options and commitments which are called for in order to bring about the social, political and economic changes seen in many cases to be urgently needed (No. 4).

Paul VI makes that statement after saying that from Rome he is unable to speak a universally valid word on the very complex situations that pertain to each country in the world today and should not be expected to do so. Rather, according to the Pope, it is up to "the Christian Communities to analyze with objectivity the situation which is proper to their country, to shed on it the light of the gospel and to draw. . . norms of judgment and directives for action from the social teaching of the Church." Based on this text of the Pope we can say the following:

a) As Christian communities we have the right and duty to determine the position we should take vis-à-vis the PMS and with regard to the situation of military aggression our country is experiencing. We do this from within the communion of the Church.

b) We deplore the fact that in a matter of such importance the Episcopal Conference published this declaration without carrying on ample dialogue with the Christian community (Christian groups, priests, nuns, and laypeople who work in the respective dioceses).

c) We also deplore the fact that there has not been — as both the Pope and the importance of the matter demand — any dialogue with other brothers and sisters of good will. It seems that this dialogue has been held only with the representatives of the opposition political parties.

Translated from "Varias Organizaciones Cristianas se pronuncian: Documento Obando se inscribe en Campo Político," in El Nuevo Diario *(Managua), September 8, 1983.*

The Context That the Document "Omits"

In their document, the bishops of Nicaragua show themselves to be totally uninformed about the global situation of the country and the aggression of which the people are the victims. They show no interest at all in the presence of the U.S. fleet, which is stationed off the coasts of Nicaragua. Nor is it of any importance to them that there are continuous incursions by counterrevolutionaries or increasing attacks by the Honduran Army on our country and an aggressive ongoing intervention by the U.S. administration in the political affairs of Central America.

Neither are the bishops interested in the more than 700 dead over which Nicaraguan homes are in mourning. The bishops make no mention of the achievements of the National Reconstruction Process, achievements which the people will defend even at the cost of their lives, in the name of a legitimate defense in which they seek to preserve and deepen the conquests they have gained since July 19, 1979.

We affirm that this episcopal document, of a totally political character, by delegitimizing the Nicaraguan state, coincides at the present time with the accusations being made by other political sectors of the opposition, as, for example, with the following statement made by the Social Democratic Party:

> We are extremely concerned that a bill like the one on military service should once again confirm the intention of the FSLN National Directorate to destabilize what still lacks equilibrium— the truly free State of Nicaragua and the Nicaraguans—as a result of deviations in the Revolutionary Process. . . .

> This law of military service is an intensification of the dictatorship of power that a few persons have in their hands, while approximately three million Nicaraguans are subjected to them.

In this sense the Episcopal Conference simply took as an excuse the pronouncement on Patriotic Military Service to throw out blanket statements against our country's Revolutionary Process.

From "Omission" to Delegitimization

What the Episcopal Conference is interested in is the disqualification and condemnation of what it calls "Revolutionary Law," which is simply the right that the people have to defend their Revolutionary Process from the attacks of the counterrevolutionaries.

Furthermore, the bishops forget that the "classic law" to which they refer and of course they become zealous and strong defenders, is the law of capitalists and oppressor nations. Besides, this position attacks the revolutionary movements of the region (El Salvador, Guatemala, etc.), which struggle for the liberation of their peoples. In the present context, according to the episcopal document, the only "political" army is Nicaragua's. Does that mean that the armies of the United States or Honduras, or of the counterrevolution are apolitical? And was the old Somoza Guard apolitical?

We have reflected much on the Bible, and there we find the inspiration for, and significant examples of, the legitimate defense of the people. It is enough just to remember a passage from the book of Nehemiah:

> I arose and said to the nobles and to the officials and to the rest of the people. . ."Remember the Lord, who is great and terrible, and fight for your brethren, your sons, your daughters, your wives, and your homes."
>
> When our enemies heard that it was known to us and that God had frustrated their plan, we all returned to the wall, each to his work. From that day on, half of my servants worked on construction, and half held the spears, shields, bows and coats of mail; and the leaders stood behind all the house of Judah, who were building on the wall. Those who carried burdens were laden in such a way that each with one hand labored on the work and with the other held his weapon (Nehemiah 4:14-17).

"Apparent" Conscientious Objection

As we have said, at the heart of the episcopal document is the delegitimization of our Process and of the Nicaraguan state. In dealing with the law of Patriotic Military Service, the document presents "conscientious objection" as one of its arguments. The conscientious objection of which the episcopal document speaks, however, is not a true conscientious objection, nor is it the objection of conscience which the II Vatican Council recognizes. Let us look at this step by step.

a) *According to the Council.* The II Vatican Council accepts the validity of authentic conscientious objection for people who refuse to physically take up arms for real reasons of conscience. Such people ask for an exception to a just law which, for reasons of conscience, they feel they cannot obey. At the same time, they promise to serve the community in other tasks during a situation of war. The bishops of Nicaragua cite Vatican II in support of their position. But the bishops do not say that the Council speaks of this objection in the context of the inhumanity of wars of extermination or conquest. It is necessary to emphasize that conscientious objection grew out of the context of imperialist aggression, such as that in Vietnam. Honest citizens "in conscience" objected to participating in genocidal attacks on oppressed peoples. Absurdly, the Episcopal Conference compares the defense of our people to this type of genocidal aggression.

Furthermore, on speaking of the objection of conscience as something that can take place in a situation of war, Vatican II presents us with some affirmations that the Nicaraguan bishops do not speak about. The Council clearly distinguishes between defense and aggression. And the Council's document recognizes that incumbent upon the heads of state and ministers is the duty to protect the security of the people. Lastly, Vatican II, on speaking of defensive armies, recognizes that those who serve the country in the army "should regard themselves as agents of security and freedom on behalf of their people. As long as they fulfill this role properly, they are making a genuine contribution to the establishment of peace" (*Gaudium et Spes,* No. 79).

b) *The Bishops at Medellín.* Finally, on this point of conscientious objection vis-à-vis the pacifist position, it is also necessary to remember what the Latin American bishops said at Medellín: "The Christian is peaceful and not ashamed of it. He is not simply a pacifist, for he can fight, but he prefers peace to war" (Peace, No. 15).

c) *Discrepancy on the Ideological Level.* What the bishops present is discrepancy on an ideological level rather than conscientious objection to taking up arms. According to their reasoning, in any country of the world where there is a law of obligatory military service, all those with different ideas from those of their government are excused from obeying that law.

d) *Civil Disobedience.* What the bishops of Nicaragua are proposing is not just disobedience to a law (PMS) that they consider unjust—since they admit that other states (those that are not revolutionary) can legitimately adopt this same kind of law. What they oppose is the legitimacy of the present Nicaraguan state and the legitimacy of our Revolutionary Process. The Episcopal Conference, in making this radical judgment, contradicts the real, active, and organized participation of the people in health, the promotion of literacy, the harvesting of coffee and cotton, in cooperatives, revolutionary vigilance, etc. The document says not one word about the Process in which we live, in line with the recently approved Law of Political Parties, nor does it mention the date already set for elections.

In summary, the episcopal document does not really speak of conscientious objection (exception to a law), nor about civil disobedience to a concrete law. What the bishops really talk about is general and generalized disobedience. They oppose our legitimate Revolutionary Process, recognized in the United Nations and recently supported by Nicaragua's election to the Security Council, and this against the express vote of the United States.

Conclusion

Without doubt, the bishops of Nicaragua can make a judgment on the Law of Patriotic Military Service. But we think that judgment should be based on objective data about our situation and on some evangelical principles which enlighten from the point of view of faith the difficult and tragic situation that a people who are mainly Christian face because of a prolonged and growing aggression. The Episcopal Conference presents some very serious statements about the situation of our Process without giving proof. It is here, in the analysis of the situation and in the general affirmation that disqualifies all our Revolutionary Process, that our principal differences lie.

Our fundamental interest is that our Church in truth be faithful to the poor and thereby to the gospel, and that our Process may continue to grow and mature. We are committed to defending the Process of the New Nicaragua, a Process of justice for the poor who before were exploited.

But with pain and sadness we see that the episcopal document does not defend the cause of the poor. Instead, it defends the interests of the bourgeoisie, because it only recognizes the bourgeois state as legitimate. And it defends the interests of imperialism, because it does not condemn the aggression it makes against us. It is this aggression that has made urgent the Law of Patriotic Military Service.

Vis-à-vis the position of the bishops of Nicaragua, the parties of the Right, and imperialism, we reiterate our support for the Revolutionary Process. And by being a part of the tasks of consolidation and defense, we confirm that between Christianity and Revolution there is no contradiction. And if we now participate actively in health campaigns, adult education, revolutionary vigilance, mass organizations, militia and infantry reserve battalions, tomorrow we will be participating as soldiers or reservists in defense of our Process for the New Nicaragua. We are ready to give our lives, inspired and strengthened by the words of the gospel: "No one shows greater love than he who lays down his life for his friends."

Signed by:

Basic Christian Communities

Central American Historical Institute (IHCA)

Center of Education and Agrarian Promotion (CEPA)

Commission for Youth Promotion:
    Christian Students for the Revolution (ECR)
    Christian Youth Basic Communities (CJCB)
    Revolutionary Christian University Students (UCR)

Conference of Religious (CONFER)

Eje Ecuménico

El Tayacán

Community of Christians in the Revolution

PART 6

Democracy in the New Nicaragua

"Cara al Pueblo":
Popular Democracy in Practice

"Cara al Pueblo" ("Face the People") is an encounter and dialogue between top officials of the Nicaraguan government and the Nicaraguan people—a unique example of mass democracy in the new Nicaragua. It is held weekly in a neighborhood or community, and segments are subsequently shown over national television. Residents of the community have an opportunity to raise the concrete daily problems they are experiencing, and the government officials are held accountable to give explanations if not solutions to the problems. Their honesty (which Nicaraguans have come to expect) is striking to foreign observers, as is the determination to solve concrete problems through a joint effort between the government and the people through their mass organizations—all this in the midst of external attack. Certainly it stands in stark contrast to the lies and deliberate obfuscation shown by U.S. government officials on such television programs as "Face the Nation." In addition, "Cara al Pueblo" is a public forum at which government leaders provide political education in the broadest sense—both in giving people an explanation of the current situation, and in answering popular concerns about such crucial and difficult issues as: Why are counterrevolutionaries not given the death sentence? In a June 1983 "Cara al Pueblo," for example, Comandante Daniel Ortega spoke at length on the question: What is the difference between a nonrevolutionary person (i.e., someone with low understanding or consciousness and low participation in the revolution) and a conscious counterrevolutionary?

Members of a delegation organized by U.S. Out of Central America (USOCA) in October 1983 had the opportunity to attend the session of "Cara al Pueblo" in the Managua neighborhood of Acahualinca. The following is excerpted from a transcript (translated and edited at the Institute for the Study of Labor and Economic Crisis) of the October 7, 1983, session attended by the USOCA delegation. The questions came from community members and responsables of the community Sandinista Defense Committee (CDS). Except where indicated that the answers were given by Comandante Daniel Ortega, they were provided by top-level government officials: among those present at the Acahualinca "Cara al Pueblo" were the Vice-Minister of Health, the Chief of the Sandinista Police, the Vice-Minister of the Nicaraguan Energy Institute, the Vice-Minister of the Managua Reconstruction Junta, officials from the Patriotic Military Service, and the Ministry of Internal Commerce.

Ortega: Good evening, *compañeros*. How are you? Fine? Wonderful!

We were here some time ago for the inauguration of a people's store. It has been a while—about two years, I think.

We are pleased about the participation of this *barrio* [neighborhood] in the *vigilancia revolucionaria*. Your participation has been wonderful, and so is the low crime rate in this neighborhood. I think that the *vigilancia revolucionaria* is important as support for the police and for our effort against delinquency and counterrevolutionary activities. Clearly, there is a high level of participation here. This has been a combative *barrio*, not just recently but since the time of the struggle against Somoza's dictatorship.

I would like to recall an occasion where here in this *barrio*, Acahualinca, over there in that area, in that low section at the edge of the lake, we had strong Frente Sandinista activity. We are talking about 1965, 1966. The Frente Sandinista had a support house there. The first classrooms where we taught reading and writing to adults and to children who couldn't attend school were housed there. *Compañeros* such as Enrique Lorén, Francisco Moreno, Carlos Reina, and Joseito Escobar were involved in those activities.

During that time, the Neighborhood Committees were formed, the Sandinista Defense Committees that were organized in areas of Managua and here in Acahualinca, and there was a great deal of participation. And as we were saying, good work was done, a lot of teaching as well as active participation in the struggle against Somoza.

So, now we are in better shape than in those times because we have been able to get rid of Somoza, the National Guard, and the power they represented. But we are always fighting against Somocismo—which means fighting against those who wanted Somoza in power in Nicaragua. And those who wanted Somoza in power were the U.S. policymakers. No one will be able to forget how the United States used Somoza to liquidate Sandino [in 1934] and subsequently supported the Somoza dictatorship for many years. We all know that tale.

So now we are still facing Somocismo here, since they want to see it revived in Nicaragua. And who wants to see this? The United States would like to see us return to a Somocista regime.

Do you agree that we should return to Somocismo?

People: No!

Ortega: Do you support those Somocista Guards—who, by the way, *have* been captured?

People: No!

Ortega: They have now formed a command structure and have named Adolfo Calero Portocarrero president. And now information is being released that these people from the FDN ["Nicaraguan Democratic Force"—Somocista *contras* based mainly in Honduras—Eds.] who have U.S. support will ask for help from CONDECA when the time is right. They are announcing this, and we shall see what CONDECA has to say about this. They calmly declare from Tegucigalpa that they will solicit aid from CONDECA when they need it. Just as they have announced from Tegucigalpa that they will attack ships that bring petroleum from Mexico to Nicaragua.

It's funny. . .every time we make public accusations to the world, the Honduran Office of Foreign Affairs appears. . . . For example, when we denounced the situation of the airplane that was shot down, in which Hondurans were directly implicated, they stated that it was a Nicaraguan lie. But on the other hand, in Tegucigalpa, spokesmen for the FDN—for the Guards—are calmly making statements about attacking ships that bring petroleum from Mexico to Nicaragua.

We can see clearly that [the Hondurans] are totally supporting them. This support is becoming more apparent on the part of the Honduran Army, above all the Honduran military command, especially [Gen. Gustavo] Alvarez—and it's all tolerated by that poor Honduran President. I say *poor Honduran President,* because he really isn't to blame, he doesn't give any orders, he only maintains Alvarez's policies.

There is a similar situation in Costa Rica. Statements have also been released from San José, Costa Rica. Robelo* lives there, and Robelo is always reaffirming that bombardments against Managua will continue; that they will repeat the bombings of the airport, and things like that. What this shows is that the United States is actively promoting the efforts to create conflicts between Costa Rica and Nicaragua. The CIA is working in Costa Rica in spite of the fact that the Costa Rican government does not give support to this counterrevolutionary activity; the CIA has become involved in Costa Rica and has imposed counterrevolutionary activity.

The night before last, our Foreign Ministry spoke with Costa Rican authorities and informed them that there was a concentration of counter-revolutionaries from ARDE ["Democratic Revolutionary Alliance"—a leading *contra* organization—Eds.] and the FDN. In Costa Rica the FDN and ARDE are already working together, and they are concentrated near a point called La Vuelta, quite near the Nicaraguan border. This was denounced in Costa Rica so that authorities would take necessary measures, and a new confrontation could be avoided. The Guards and that traitor [Edén] Pastora are particularly interested in fomenting a conflict between Nicaragua and Costa Rica, and the best place for doing so is Peñas Blancas. So what did they do? They dispersed their forces, in the face of the denunciation that was made, because that day they were going to fight in the early morning hours; today at daybreak they were going to attack us. Then, afterwards, they distributed themselves facing the towns of Cárdenas, Papaturro, Orosí, and Peñas Blancas. There they have all their counter-revolutionary forces distributed [on the Costa Rican side of the border].

---

* Alfonso Robelo, a businessman who left the Government Junta in 1980, and subsequently became a *contra* leader.

Today, at 2:30 p.m., there was a mortar attack on our outpost at El Naranjo from Costa Rican territory facing El Naranjo. Then this afternoon we noted a mobilization in the Peñas Blancas zone, which made us believe that an attack was being prepared from around Peñas Blancas. And this is being brought to the attention of Costa Rican authorities, just as the presence—with the location—of two artillery aircraft, based in Costa Rica for launching a new attack on Nicaragua, is also being brought to the attention of Costa Rican authorities.

As we said, the Costa Rican government has a position: but what is happening? The CIA, basing itself on Somocista Guards and that traitor Pastora, has developed activities designed to provoke a confrontation between Costa Rica and Nicaragua and in this way to isolate Nicaragua. But we are finding out about these provocations and informing Costa Rican authorities, so they will take measures, and all this is being made public in Costa Rica.

Another thing—yesterday at 6:00, from Honduras, on the border with Nicaragua, there were air operations, and some places were attacked. Near Las Manos, an airplane penetrated 20 kilometers to the northeast of Ocotál, flying over a zone called "El Guayusín"; two bombs were aimed at the village of San Fernando. But [the *contras*] are aware that we have anti-aircraft artillery, so they are cautious, and because of the altitude at which the bombs were launched, they did not fall on the village target. Also, yesterday morning, at "Guapinol" near Wiwilí, another plane penetrated Nicaraguan territory and flew over that area, strafing "El Portillo," "Las Nubes," and "Cerro el Horno." These are concrete examples of the kinds of attack that we suffer every day, and that are accompanied by U.S. Air Force exploratory actions. For example, yesterday while these attacks were going on, an RC-135 aircraft, one of those spy planes that the U.S. uses, was flying over our territory. That is, we are confronted with blatant, shameless, open actions against our people, actions in which the U.S. is openly implicated. The U.S. is above all the principal cause of tension. Of course we are confident that these actions will continue to be defeated, they cannot be successful [in their goal]; although these attacks can do us a great deal of harm, they cannot stop the Nicaraguan Revolution.

We must remember, on the other hand, that Nicaragua is insisting upon the importance of real dialogue, because we Sandinistas are not interested in permanent warfare, we do not want you to march permanently to the beat of constant alert and defense. Above all, we are interested in having our youth study and produce. . .that is to say, we need a climate of peace.

But these people will not let us live in a peaceful environment. We have said that we will maintain our will in this respect, and they have in some cases misinterpreted our desire for peace. They have said that our desire for peace is a product of their covert operations, that it is a product of warships—as if they were scaring us with this, when really it is a responsible position on the part of our revolutionary government, on the part of the National Directorate of the Frente Sandinista.

But let's put these topics aside for now; I wanted to give you a little background before we begin our dialogue. Let's turn to hearing the many questions that you must have for us. Those who would like to ask a question, please raise your hand.

Question: Hello. My name is Juan García; I am the Responsible for Organization of the Acahualinca Neighborhood Committee Jacinto Baca Jeréz. Comandante Daniel Ortega, Coordinator of the Government Junta, and distinguished *compañeros* who have come to visit us: The *barrio* of Acahualinca would like to warmly thank you for visiting us now when we so sorely need someone to respond to our neighborhood's problems. *Compañero* Coordinator, I would like to read to you how this *barrio* has worked together during the last four years.

"*Compañero* member of the Government Junta of National Reconstruction: the Neighborhood Committee Jacinto Baca Jeréz, on behalf of the heroic and militant *barrio* of Acahualinca, sends you warmest revolutionary and anti-imperialist greetings. *Compañero* Coordinator of the Government Junta of National Reconstruction, Revolutionary Comandante Daniel Ortega Saavedra, and other distinguished guests, *Compañeros:* Since July 19, 1979, this *barrio*, one of the areas most highly marginalized by the Somocista tyranny, through its heroism and revolutionary combative spirit, and through the blood shed by the heroes and martyrs of Acahualinca, has won the right to be free and independent from imperialism and from the oppressors of our brothers and sisters in Latin America, who are still struggling for their liberation. We would like to report to you our achievements during the four years of the revolution: in collaboration with [the government], we have relocated 2,000 families who were living in unsanitary and unhealthy conditions. They have been moved to places where any human being can live in dignity. Together with the Managua Reconstruction Junta, we have paved 1,300 meters of streets with gutters, running water, and sewage lines. Together with our *compañeros* from the Nicaraguan Energy Institute (INE), we have installed 2,000 meters of electric power lines and have put 43 units into public service. In order to defend the achievements and progress we have made, our CDS organization in the Acahualinca *barrio* has done the following: we have organized 32 CDS's, with 860 *vigilantes revolucionarios* and 25 of our *compañeros* are in the 5015, 8221, and 2883 Battalions. In each battalion we have 14 *compañeros* integrated in territorial militias. We are working on the Patriotic Military Service Project, and we will be enlisting 800 youth between the ages of 17 and 22 on October 17, 18, and 19.

At this time we have the following problems:

1) The supply of basic goods like corn and [cooking] oil does not totally meet our needs and does not arrive regularly.

2) We need more houses, to solve our problem of having our children

grow up in unhealthy conditions.

3) We have a very bad public transportation system; we have only a few units, which do not give decent services;

4) The relocation of our neighbors of the northern sector is one of the problems that the Housing Institute should solve immediately. This would be the area including 84th Street east to the lake. . . .

In brotherhood, Neighborhood Committee Jacinto Baca Jeréz.

Answer: Good Evening, representatives of our revolutionary state. We represent the Ministry of Internal Commerce. We will address the problems brought to our attention regarding corn [and cooking oil].

We all know, since it is public knowledge, that we have had a problem with the harvest of "first-class" corn this year. First of all, remember that there was a drought this year, and those who cultivate corn—primarily small producers—did not gather a good harvest. That is to say, we have a serious problem in the production that is not anyone's fault. . .we can blame nature. . .and we had to import corn. So we are presently consuming imported corn, which we must purchase with foreign exchange. We can't buy it with córdobas as we do inside our country, and the money we have to spend on the international market is scarce.

We are all aware of our monetary problems, the problem of aggression, of how every day they raise the price of the products we purchase. Corn bought outside our country is incredibly expensive, so what we've tried to do is buy corn from several countries and distribute it equitably on a national level. The problem is that we can't purchase quantities sufficient to satisfy all the demand, so we must buy what we can with the few dollars we have. We are not importing corn to create an abundance now; we are bringing in corn mainly for the poultry industry and for rations among those who make tortillas or *chicha* [a corn beverage called "finol"].

At this moment we aren't capable of distributing corn in a consistent fashion. We must face the production problem, and we will overcome it because our people have never been defeated by anything—not even those aircraft and imperialist attacks.

In terms of cooking oil, we have reached rather high production levels, but when it came time for distribution, we said that we would distribute it to our entire population. So we have set up a per capita system, a certain amount rationed to everyone in our country, regardless of age, sex, etc. In some cases this quota could not be reached. We have been told that in this area they are distributing one half-liter per person a month. I believe this is the ration that is being distributed in Managua. In some places there are mistakes, and some people get too much at the beginning. I think the store is distributing a little more than that, but what has been established for Managua is the amount rationed.

We are seeing a real effort being made in this area; for instance, oil comes from cotton, and we are trying to sow 170,000 *manzanas* (square blocks). This will give us more oil, but not until 1984. The oil that we are presently consuming is [derived from] crude oil that we buy abroad and refine in Managua. We are importing oil at a cost of more than $25 million per year in order to supply our country.

At the moment we can't raise the ration. What we can do in the Ministry is to see that this oil is equitably and consistently supplied to all sectors—in our case, in Managua. These are some of the problems that we have. As far as the problem of the oil not reaching you regularly, this is our mistake; we will examine the situation and see how we can improve things. But right now, we can't raise the ration.

Question: *Compañeros.* One of our main concerns is: What do we have to do to solve supply problems, in particular that of rice, as we receive only three pounds per person each month?

Answer: About the rice. In almost all of Managua we have rationed rice to three pounds per person. We know that there are other sectors where more rice is being supplied through other channels; let's say that we are now taking measures to correct this. But what we have presently assigned is three pounds per person. . . .The problem with the rice is that we can't give you more right now.

To mention a specific case that is affecting the rice problem, as we all know, we have one rice-producing zone near Jalapa. We get a high yield from this area that supplies us on a national level. With the [*contra*] gang operations there, one sector [had to] arm itself in that region, which is cultivated by some private growers. In order to distribute the rice, we also need trucks, which we don't have at the moment, so we have had to hold this rice out in the fields. Then we have to send machinery in there, too. All these things have been targets for attack—including our own *compañeros*—as you have seen in the newspapers—who found themselves riding combines with guns trying to harvest the rice there. But the truth is that—even with all our efforts—production decreased by more than 1,500 to 2,000 *manzanas*. Let's do a little calculating: we were going to harvest X amount, less what we lost because of the *contra* gangs, less what we could not produce because we needed parts for our machinery and we couldn't get loans, less what we lost because of the areas we couldn't cultivate. . . .Now we have a much smaller quantity, which we must distribute among everyone in our country over the period of a year. This leaves us with the ration of three pounds per person.

As Comandante [Ortega] has said, we are fighting for peace. If we had been in a state of peace we would have harvested not only those 1,000-plus *manzanas,* but much more, and we wouldn't have had this problem with the rice now. We can't resort to magic and make a silo appear. . . .Right now we can't tell you that it will get better; we are making great efforts and our National Directorate has ordered that other regions be planted, but even with that we still face the ever-present threat of imperialism;

they will be there ready to attack us, wherever we try to plant. We saw this when they attacked the port at Zelaya. So wherever we may be, they'll be there to attack.

Another problem—we need to have more control over distribution. . .to find a better way to supply the rice. It's a problem of transport: how can we distribute those rations of rice better? But beyond this, it must be clear that there are situations beyond our control: we are being attacked, they are trying to keep us from eating, to put it in simple words. This is the reality of the situation. . . .

Question: Good evening. *Compañeros,* my name is Alfonso. I would like to direct this question to Comandante Ortega, to tell him this concern of ours. We all know that counterrevolutionary groups supported by imperialism have been overtly and covertly attacking us. We have captured three pilots whose job it was to supply these counterrevolutionary gangs. The Acahualinca *barrio* is asking for punishment to make an example of these counterrevolutionaries who came into our country to supply the Somocistas. We would like the maximum sentence, and not only this, but a punishment that would be a lesson to other counterrevolutionaries and to everyone who causes bloodshed in our country. Thank you very much.

People: THE FIRING SQUAD! THE FIRING SQUAD! TO THE WALL!

Answer: I believe that there is more than enough reason to demand the maximum sentence for these pilots who have been captured, whose airplanes were shot down, who have participated in the Guards' "clean-up operations," as they refer to their bombardment and killing of the Nicaraguan people. Once they were able to leave Nicaragua they went to work, brutally shedding the blood of the Nicaraguan people. The maximum sentence established by the revolution is 30 years imprisonment—a sentence that was given to many who had committed genocide and were captured after the triumph of the revolution, and was also applied immediately during the moment of triumph to the National Guardsmen. This sentence is still in effect. This is what has been established, and the Popular Anti-Somocista Tribunals surely will hear and punish the *contras*. We are certain they will give them the maximum sentence, given that there is now no death penalty in Nicaragua. Logically, we can't change this sentence from one day to the next. But we have the obligation in this case to apply the maximum sentence, and we also have the obligation to listen to the people who are asking for stiffer sentences, which is something we must discuss.

Question: Good evening, *compañeros,* members of our Government Junta, *Compañero* Daniel Ortega Saavedra, and visitors. My name is Ramón López. As a Block Coordinator, I have the following concern: in February my sector was relocated; at a "Cara al Pueblo" meeting with the Minister of the Managua Reconstruction Junta, we told him our concern about getting a garbage truck. He promised us that there would be two trucks a week passing by. But to date they haven't come, not even one.

Answer: *Compañero,* we are really very sorry that we have not kept our promise to you. The day before yesterday, at 4:30 a.m., we met with the people who clean, and we were very satisfied to see the efforts that these people are making. These *compañeros* begin work at 4:30 a.m., and there are 35 zones in Managua and 35 teams made up of squads of 5. Among this group there is a great deal of concern about improving their work, and they even told us that while they begin at 4:30 a.m., they do not have a fixed quitting time. Workers who start on the 4:30 a.m. shift also work the second shift, which starts at 11:00 a.m. And of course we have that same old problem of trucks that break down on us, leaving us with zones that we can't service.

This doesn't really have anything to do with your situation, but I wanted you to understand some of the limitations within which we work. We will look into why we haven't kept our promise right away. . . .We believe that we should first respond to the agreements we have made with you — even though there are some jobs we didn't plan for. This is our position — and has always been our position — but sometimes things slip through the cracks and we are really sorry; we hope that this won't happen again, and if it does, please come and see us. We have an office where we take care of the CDS's. We are here [to serve you]. So if a few more weeks go by without trucks, remind us, because you let a lot of time go by before you brought this to our attention. . . .

Question: Good evening. My name is Ruth Velez Cantadero, responsible for the [CDS] Social Front [for several blocks] and I am in charge of 40 families in *vigilancia revolucionaria.* On behalf of our entire neighborhood, we ask that you be less generous with those individuals captured by our militia, who even give their lives for our glorious country. We come before you to ask that there be no more pardons, that you not be swept along by the generosity of our revolution, with these individuals who criminally attack our country, morally and materially damaging our country. Consequently we ask [you to pass] the law that we have been demanding in our glorious mass mobilizations, that law of execution: the firing squad! That is all, *compañero,* and thank you.

People: WITHOUT WOMEN'S PARTICIPATION. . .THERE IS NO REVOLUTION! FIRING SQUAD, FIRING SQUAD FOR ASSASSINS!

Question: Good evening, *Compañero* Daniel Ortega Saavedra. My name is Carlos Alberto Rodríguez, responsible for Social Defense at the *barrio* level. . . .Almost our entire community has problems with inadequate transportation, because, as you realize, the majority of us are workers. The buses leave at 6:00 a.m., and a construction worker who must be at work at 6:00 can't take the bus at 6:00; he should take the bus at 5:00 a.m. in order to get to work on time. We ask you on behalf of this community if you couldn't give us 10 more buses in order to improve transportation in Acahualinca. [Applause]

Answer: Good evening, *compañeros.* Perhaps you already know something about the transportation situation; at the national level it is critical. But we will review the situation with the two routes that service this area and we'll see how we can find an answer to this critical problem that is affecting you. *Compañeros,* we ask that you be patient; as soon as these buses are reactivated, we will be solving your problems. Thank you.

Ortega: Well, *compañeros,* we have heard here a lot of questions concerning different problems in the community, and the problems that you have raised also come up in other *barrios* all across the country. Certainly, there are problems that can be resolved in a better way in spite of our limitations; this is why it is so important that these problems be raised directly by you and that these *compañeros* who work in the Ministries hear all of your concerns in order to find more practical solution[s]. For example, with the problem of transportation and of no access to transportation here: Surely, as our *compañeros* from Transportation are informed of your concerns, they will be able to take steps to see that buses are working in your area; they will become more responsible in their work, and they could also consider the possibility of [adding other buses].

But clearly, with all the problems that have been expressed here, energy problems, problems with water, housing problems, problems with transportation and supply, these are all problems that we would be confronting more adequately if we did not have to defend our country. I already explained how rice production is affected. But it has also meant something else to us, in all types of production, independent of the effects nature has. To take the example of corn: the reality is that when a farm worker, someone who produces, has to be mobilized in a reserve battalion, or in his Popular Sandinista Militia, this *compañero* at that time stops producing. This indirectly affects the production of corn.

U.S. aggression against Nicaragua has imposed a high degree of sacrifice on us. The aggression has raised the difficult issues of supply—for example, of energy and drinking water—and issues of transportation. Why? On the one hand, the U.S. has not limited itself to subjecting us to the Somocista Guards who bomb our strategic economic targets; they are also assuring that Nicaragua receives no [international economic] aid, no assistance, no loans. Well, what does this mean? We must purchase means of transportation outside our country, for example, since we do not produce them here; but it is difficult for us to get lines of credit in order to purchase means of transportation on the international market. Everything we have that is related to energy is imported. The same for maintenance of the buses—we need parts, and what do we buy parts with? Foreign exchange. [But this too is a problem] as production is also affected by the attacks: our exports, such as cotton, coffee, sugar, sometimes have to be reduced in volume, although we have made great efforts to increase production in the midst of this crisis situation, and we succeeded last year.

But we are also confronting another problem which is beyond our control: the fact that other countries fix the prices of the products that we sell internationally. What other countries? Rich countries, those rich countries that pay us whatever price they like (of course a low price). Meanwhile, the products they sell us—the medicines, the parts, the tractors, the buses, everything that has to do with electricity—all of this they sell to us at high prices. Then each year they charge us higher prices and pay us less for what we produce. So we are exploited by rich countries—beginning with the United States itself, which doesn't pay a fair price for products from small, impoverished countries. It isn't that we are *poor* countries, rather that they have made us poor, they have exploited us, they have ransacked us, and they continue to exploit us economically.

We have obtained our political liberation, we are struggling for social liberation. Health service in this country is still not as good as it should be; not everyone in this country has a place to live, not everyone in this country is educated, because there are countless barefoot children and children who can't go to school in this country. So, we are fighting in this sense. . .while being constantly exploited by those powerful countries.

And on top of the economic injustice, we face the direct aggression—for example, at Puerto Benjamín Zeledón, on the Atlantic Coast near the mining area. . .where the U.S. blew up some gas storage tanks. This practically paralyzed our production of gold. It paralyzed our fishing industry in the area, because the fishing boats use this fuel, and we have no fuel for these fishing boats. How long will it take to solve this problem?. . .

And who headed the mission [to blow up oil pipelines at Puerto Sandino]. . .who guided it. . .who directed it? The United States government. It isn't that we want to blame the United States for everything bad. We have even made efforts to see that relations of mutual respect are established between the United States and Nicaragua. What is happening is that this U.S. administration, in office since 1981, has declared war on us. At first they did it in secret—"covert" operations, because they weren't done openly. But these began to become public knowledge in the United States among the American people, concerned congressmen, and journalists. While speaking out so loudly about terrorism against democracy and human rights, the U.S. government practices terrorist activities and the violation of human rights, because it is a totally anti-democratic government. Reagan began openly defending covert operations. And when they were discovered, [his people] devoted themselves to defending the U.S. government's right to declare war on Nicaragua. . . .Without the aggressive policies of Reagan, [exploitation by the rich countries] and the [international economic] crisis would still affect us, but we would be in better shape.

So the questions that you have raised are related to general problems that are affecting our country; some can be solved, others can't be solved immediately, and we must wait until we have the resources to solve them. But the effort is being made, as we say here. You people have the spirit to make the effort, to overcome difficult situations. . . .

Well, *compañeros,* let us end this "Cara al Pueblo" program by singing the hymn of our vanguard, the Frente Sandinista, after our slogan: PATRIOTIC MILITARY SERVICE!

Pluralism and Popular Power: An Interview With Sergio Ramírez Mercado

This interview with Sergio Ramírez Mercado, member of the Government Junta of National Reconstruction, was conducted in May 1983 by Marifeli Pérez-Stable, and appeared in Spanish in Vol. 9, No. 34 of Areito, *published in New York by the Círculo de Cultura Cubana. It was translated at the Institute for the Study of Labor and Economic Crisis.*

Pérez-Stable: After four years of revolution, what is the balance of the political pluralism in Nicaragua?

Ramírez: We have to see the topic of pluralism as an essential part of the project of the revolution. One of the most common weapons utilized by propagandists against the revolution has been to portray pluralism as an imposition used by the right wing against the revolution, even though it is part of the original program of the Frente Sandinista and of the program adopted by the Government of National Reconstruction. The imperialists hope that pluralism will collapse under the pressures that they themselves lay against it, so that they can find easy excuses to isolate the revolution. So for us, pluralism is a concept essential to the revolution, maintained not merely by the recognition of certain right-wing parties so that they can function within the country, but also to make possible the political and democratic participation of different sectors of the population that never before in our history had access to that participation.

The institutional concept of pluralism is expressed in the Council of State [legislature—Eds.]. Almost all the political forces in the country have a guaranteed representation in the Council of State. The right-wing parties do not have a seat in our Council of State because they respond to the interests of imperialism; they want to discredit this institution and our political pluralism generally. But none of the parties stop functioning here through our imposition. There is no restriction. The right-wing parties have their offices open and function normally. They are even organized in what is called the Democratic Coordinating Committee.

Of course, the way to test the practice of this pluralism, the culmination of this practice, will be in the elections of 1985, in which all the parties, including the right-wing parties, will have a guaranteed participation.

Pérez-Stable: What have been the achievements and difficulties in structuring popular power in Nicaragua?

Ramírez: The main difficulty is the absence of a tradition of participation in the country, throughout the 50 years during which the dictatorship discredited the system of representative democracy. The forms of popular participation were born with the revolution and have emerged not only in the political but also in the daily life of the citizenry: the right to speak out, which very few Nicaraguans had; to express themselves on the radio, television, the newspapers; to participate at the grassroots level, in organizations formed on their blocks in their neighborhoods; to participate in social campaigns of the revolution, such as the literacy campaign, adult education, defense campaigns, environmental health, popular cultural centers; and, above all, participation in the national defense, a popular right being fully exercised with massive participation. In reality we could not have carried out a single revolutionary task without popular participaton. Any type of democracy that is established in Nicaragua has to take into account this new form of popular participation, this democratic participation that has emerged in our country.

Pérez-Stable: How do you anticipate satisfying both the demands of political pluralism and popular power, when at times they seem to conflict, to contradict each other?

Ramírez: That is the formula that Nicaragua has to find and offer to the world. When we talk about elections, we don't talk of a one-party election; we mean that through the elections, all parties have a right to express themselves. But here the right-wing parties find themselves in effect limited by the fact that during the course of this interim, before the election takes place, a new form of popular participation has been developed in the country by the Frente Sandinista, as the vanguard of the revolution.

This means that in order for a party to challenge the Frente Sandinista in a popular assembly, it will have to compete with the Frente through popular organization, and with the mystique that the Frente Sandinista inspires in the popular organizations. Here the right-wing parties remain tied to old-fashioned proselytizing, and when election time comes, there is going to be a clash, and a cultural clash at that, between the form of popular participation that has been practiced with the revolution and the mere presentation of an electoral program.

Pérez-Stable: But isn't the electoral process, and the very way in which it is carried out, alien to the popular participation that is part of the revolution?

Ramírez: Well, we will have to see. No, because we haven't yet defined the electoral rules. But we couldn't consider any electoral form that would contradict the revolutionary practice during these years. For example, it would be impossible here to go out and sell candidates in 1985...

Pérez-Stable: That is what I'm referring to.

Ramírez: [It would be impossible] to sell candidates with a smile or a slogan. First, because the level of popular consciousness that the people have developed would not permit it; here the people wouldn't elect public relations fetishes, but candidates of flesh and bone, who would present themselves with political programs having a trajectory. Here the people will tend to elect those who participated in the revolutionary fight to overthrow the dictatorship, people who have stood firm in the struggle against imperialism, who have participated in the defense of the country, that is, people with a record. So a candidate of this nature would have to confront other candidates who don't have that same record, and it would be impossible to think they could fill that void with a slogan, with propaganda, even while having more money to buy air time on TV, or a page in the newspaper, or by giving away little hats, pencils, or sewing machines. That wouldn't be possible.

Pérez-Stable: But how would this process be regulated?

Ramírez: It would have to be regulated in a new electoral form, which we want to create. For example, surely the candidate will be able to present his photograph along with his record. That would have to be the basis.

Pérez-Stable: If the Democratic Party happens to win the Presidential elections in the United States in November 1984, what changes can we expect regarding the U.S. policy towards Nicaragua?

Ramírez: Really that is something very unpredictable for us. First, we would have to see which wing of the Democratic Party won the elections, and, above all, we would have to see if the Democratic Party is in any position to win against Reagan....This change would have to take place before the elections, because otherwise, the accumulation of tensions created by the absurd policy of the U.S. toward Central America will create situations that are increasingly intolerable. The U.S. is lighting a great fire in Central America, and it keeps adding more fuel to that fire. We are very much afraid that these attitudes and actions could lead to events that ultimately not even the U.S. itself will be able to control.

Pérez-Stable: What events are you referring to?

Ramírez: Well, that the aggression against Nicaragua keeps growing. The fact, for example, that the U.S. Congress is discussing whether it is moral or immoral to support the Somocista Guards so that they assassinate, torture, and kidnap in Nicaragua; whether or not this support serves the interests of the U.S., whether or not the President can say that it is necessary to block the sale of arms to El Salvador. All of this is an academic discussion. The fact of the matter is that the U.S. is attacking us, it is financing an aggression that has cost us 500 lives (from January to May of 1983).

This is what should balance the discussion of U.S. policy as to whether it is moral or immoral, just or unjust, legal or illegal, and not a discussion of what effects the covert or overt operations might have, in a place like the U.S. Congress.

That worries us a lot. And we are worried that if the U.S. keeps using Honduras as a base of aggression against Nicaragua, it will rapidly lead to an internal destabilization as well as to serious social conflicts within Honduras. At the same time, if prompt solutions to the situation in El Salvador are not found, the deterioration of the situation will become more and more profound. Central America is becoming as bloody a theater as was Vietnam.

Pérez-Stable: What is involved in the task of creating a new culture in Nicaragua?

Ramírez: As with any country in Latin America, before the triumph Nicaragua had an elite culture, a culture in the hands of a minority, educated, well-read; a minority that had enjoyed the opportunity to see paintings hanging in museums, and to read books to which not many people had access: that is, it was very restricted. But, besides being restricted, the culture in Nicaragua was deficient because the bourgeoisie was never able to create a rich cultural tradition.

What we inherited besides a culture for the minority of the people was an impoverished culture. The only way to make a revolution in the culture of Nicaragua is not by improving on a culture that was elitist, nor by elevating the education of people who were already educated, nor by giving this minority a sense of "modernity" or the tools to improve their "creative" or "perceptive" cultural abilities; rather we do it by broadening the base of participation.

This is a dialectical relationship that has already brought about important results: while guaranteeing the intellectuals, the creators of culture, access to any form of creation, i.e., cultural freedom, at the same time it allows the masses to participate in culture not only as spectators but also as creators. Since 1979 we have been consolidating workshop movements in poetry and theater, and popular participation in dancing and singing, all of which, I would say, have proven to be enriching experiences.

Pérez-Stable: In your own personal terms, how have you reconciled your vocation as a writer with your current responsibilities in the Nicaraguan Revolution?

Ramírez: Well, that reconciliation has been very easy because I have simply stopped writing. So I have not even had that problem. It was very hard trying to combine these two things. In the past I was a professional writer first, dedicating myself to writing. I think that literary production is a profession like any other. I would end up being a bad politician and a bad writer if I tried to do both.

The service to the revolution, besides being creative, is very time-consuming. It demands many hours, day and night. It is a task in which it is not possible to make plans. We do not have plans because the situation we are undergoing is highly affected by conjunctural events. Any schedule in which I would have two hours to write would be canceled in an instant. Anyhow, these years of revolutionary participation have greatly enriched my quality and expanded my material as a writer. What I can say is that I feel ready to return to the task whenever it becomes possible. I have not lost my vocation: I have reaffirmed it.

Law of
Political Parties

The Law of Political Parties was passed by the Council of State on August 17, 1983, after months of debate in the Council of State and throughout the country. The debate permitted an extensive airing of views by parties of extremely varied ideological perspectives, and holding widely diverse views on the functioning of political parties and the nature of the state in a revolutionary society. The law itself is an essential aspect of Nicaraguan pluralism and democracy. The translation of this document was provided by the Nicaraguan government, with minor editing for U.S. publication.

The Council of State of the Republic of Nicaragua, Meeting in Ordinary Session Number 10, on the Seventeenth Day of the Month of August of the Year Nineteen Hundred and Eighty-Three, Year of Struggle for Peace and Sovereignty,

Considering:

1) That it is the duty of the Government of National Reconstruction to strengthen the revolutionary process, guaranteeing the validity and development of democracy, legitimately based on popular participation and political pluralism;

2) That the Nicaraguan legal order is developed and strengthened through the promulgation of new laws which express the will of the Nicaraguan people to advance toward the institutionalization of the Popular Sandinista Revolution;

3) That in order to promote national unity and preserve peace in our homeland, practical actions are required which will lead all democratic and patriotic political forces to assume together the responsibility for reconstruction and defense;

4) That the Fundamental Law and the Law of Rights and Guarantees of Nicaraguans establish the rights of citizens to organize and participate in political parties or groups;

5) That it is consequently necessary to establish the legal framework for the Political Parties which exist in the country so that, inspired by the spirit of national unity and political pluralism, they may contribute to

national reconstruction, strengthen the defense of our homeland, and join in the search for peace in Nicaragua and the world.

Therefore: In the use of its powers,

Decrees the following "Law of Political Parties":

Chapter I: Object of the Law

Art. 1 The present Law regulates the exercise of the right of all citizens to organize Political Parties or to form part of them and establishes the regulations that will govern their establishment, authorization, functioning, suspension, and cancellation. This Law is of public order.

Chapter II: On Political Parties

Art. 2 Political Parties are groups of Nicaraguan citizens in ideological agreement, formed with the goal of achieving, among other things, political power in order to carry out a program that would respond to the needs of national development. Political Parties are institutions of Public Law.

Art. 3 Only groups legally recognized as Political Parties will enjoy the rights and guarantees and be bound to fulfill the obligations established by this and other Laws of the Republic.

Art. 4 Political Parties can be organized freely in the country with no ideological restrictions whatsoever. The existence of political groups or parties which seek the return of Somocismo or which advocate the establishment of a similar political system is prohibited.

Chapter III: On the Principles and Goals of Political Parties

Art. 5 Political Parties will be governed by their own principles and goals, but they must respect the Fundamental Law and the Law of Rights and Guarantees of Nicaraguans and the basic principles of the Popular Sandinista Revolution, such as its anti-imperialism and its profoundly popular and democratic character.

Chapter IV: Rights and Obligations of Political Parties

Art. 6 Political Parties have the right to:

a) Disseminate their ideological principles, their political programs, their statutes, and declarations of principles.

b) Carry out, at all times, political propaganda and proselytizing throughout the nation, with all the means at their disposal and, during the electoral period, contract with communications media according to their economic possibilities and respecting the right of free enterprise in accordance with legislation in force and the By-laws of this Law.

c) Hold private meetings and public rallies.

d) Criticize public administration and propose constructive solutions.

    e) Form alliances with other Political Parties for general goals and participate with them in specific activities.

    f) Name representatives to the National Assembly of Political Parties.

    g) Apply for membership in the Council of State.

    h) Take part in elections and present their own candidates for the posts open for election.

    i) Possess their own patrimony.

    j) Maintain centers and offices throughout the country.

    k) Raise the funds necessary for their functioning in accordance with the By-laws of the present Law.

Art. 7 Political Parties have the obligation to:

    a) Comply with the legal structure of the country.

    b) Comply with the resolutions of the National Council of Political Parties.

    c) Promote and support the patriotic unity of the nation in order to carry out the tasks of reconstruction and development of the country.

    d) Contribute to the consolidation of the political, economic, and social conquests achieved by our people.

    e) Defend the Revolution against any internal or external attempts to install a regime of oppression and exploitation of the Nicaraguan people.

    f) Fight to preserve the freedom and independence of the country and to defend the national sovereignty and self-determination of the Nicaraguan people.

    g) Foster and promote human rights in the political, economic, and social spheres.

    h) Take responsibility for their acts within the framework of the alliances made with other political parties and of the specific activities that they carry out with them.

Art. 8 The Political Parties that, in accordance with the Fundamental Law and its Reforms, make up the Council of State, will have the duty of naming permanent representatives to that Council.

Chapter V: On the National Assembly and National Council of Political Parties

Art 9 The National Assembly of Political Parties and the National Council of Political Parties, which will be known by their acronyms ANPP and CNPP, will be the decentralized bodies of the State entrusted with the application of the present Law.

Art. 10 The National Assembly of Political Parties will have a consultative character and will be formed by:

a) One delegate named by each of the Political Parties.

b) One delegate named by the Government Junta of National Reconstruction.

The members of the Assembly will have their respective alternates.

The National Assembly of Political Parties will meet in ordinary session twice a year and in extraordinary session when convoked by the National Council of Political Parties or at the request of two thirds of its members.

Art. 11 The functions of the National Assembly of Political Parties will be to:

a) Analyze the annual report or any other report presented by the National Council of Political Parties and make recommendations to the latter.

b) Put forth opinions on matters submitted for its consultation by the National Council of Political Parties.

c) Elect from among its own members the delegates, and their respective alternates, of the Political Parties to the National Council of Political Parties, ensuring as far as possible the representation of different ideological tendencies in the aforementioned Council.

d) Draw up its internal By-laws.

Art. 12 Thirty days after the members of the National Assembly of Political Parties have been selected, the President of the Supreme Court will proceed to administer to them the oath of office.

Art. 13 The period of office of the members of the National Assembly of Political Parties will be from the moment of their nomination to the first election of officials to take place in the country. The Government Junta of National Reconstruction and each Political Party will have the right to remove its delegate from his/her post when it considers it advisable.

Art. 14 Quorum for the ordinary and extraordinary meetings of the National Assembly of Political Parties will exist with the presence of more than half of its members, and its resolutions will be adopted with the agreement of more than half of the members present.

Art. 15 The National Council of Political Parties will be formed by:

a) Four delegates elected by the National Assembly of Political Parties from among its members.

b) The member named by the Government Junta of National Reconstruction to the National Assembly of Political Parties, who will be the Presiding Officer.

c) Three members named by the Council of State.

All delegates to the National Council of Political Parties will have their respective alternates.

The National Council of Political Parties will meet every two weeks or when the President so decides. Quorum will exist with the presence of more than half of its members and its resolutions will be adopted with the agreement of a majority of those present. In the case of a tie, the President will have two votes.

Art. 16 The functions of the National Council of Political Parties will be to:

a) Guarantee the fulfillment of the present Law and its By-laws and to ensure their effective application.

b) Resolve all questions related to the present Law and its By-laws, especially in respect to authorizations, cancellations, or suspensions, assuring that favorable or unfavorable resolutions be taken on the basis of the practical activities of the Political Parties.

c) Take the measures necessary for the execution of its resolutions.

d) Draw up its By-laws and determine its own administrative structure.

e) Call meetings of the ANPP.

f) Present its annual report to the ANPP.

g) Carry out any other functions established by the present Law and its By-laws.

Art. 17 The President of the National Council of Political Parties will have the following functions:

a) Preside over the National Assembly of Political Parties and the National Council of Political Parties.

b) Convoke the National Council of Political Parties.

c) Represent legally the National Council of Political Parties and the National Assembly of Political Parties.

d) Carry out resolutions taken by the CNPP.

e) Name the Executive Secretary of the CNPP, who will serve as such for the ANPP also.

f) Name administrative personnel.

In the case of temporary or permanent absence of the President, his/her functions will be carried out by the appointed substitute, and in the case of permanent absence, the substitute will fill the position until the Government Junta of National Reconstruction names a new President.

Art. 18 The definitive resolutions of the National Council of Political Parties can be appealed for review or relief before the Supreme Court of Justice; for the effects of this Law, Political Parties will have all rights, guarantees, and protection enjoyed by natural persons in the intervention and resolutions of the appeal for relief.

Chapter VI: Constitution of Political Parties

Art. 19 Those persons who wish to establish a Political Party must obtain the authorization of the National Council of Political Parties in order to carry out the activities leading to its formation and fulfill the requirements established by this Law to apply for legal status.

The authorization obtained from the CNPP must specify the activities it authorizes as well as the time period of its validity, which can be no more than ninety days.

Art. 20 Political Parties must be established by means of a Public Document in the presence of a representative of the National Council of Political Parties. The Public Document must contain the following:

a) Name and capacity of the issuer.

b) Name and emblem adopted by the Party.

c) Pledge to carry out its activities in accordance with the Laws of the Nation.

d) Proof of having presented the political principles of the Party.

e) Functioning bodies of the Party and their attributions, names of the members of its National Directorate and those of at least nine provisional Departmental Directorates, and the Legal Representative of the Party.

f) Method of internal election for appointing Party authorities and determining their terms of office.

Chapter VII: Authorization of Political Parties

Art. 21 Political Parties will be authorized and will obtain their legal status by means of resolutions of the National Council of Political Parties, before which the interested parties must introduce applications drawn up in accordance with the requirements established in the present Law.

Art. 22 For their authorization, Political Parties must fulfill the following requirements:

a) Application based on the reasons that they consider proper.

b) Authenticated copy of the Public Documents of Constitution.

c) Political Program of the Party.

d) Principles and Statutes of the Party.

e) Patrimony of the Party.

f) Other requirements established in this Law and its By-laws.

Art. 23 Upon presentation of the application before the National Council of Political Parties, the latter will verify whether it fulfills the requirements of the Law; the National Council of Political Parties within a period of three days will pronounce its decision, ordering the fulfilling of the requirements lacking in the application or declaring admissible or inadmissible such application. In the case in which the application fulfills the requirements of the Law, the National Council of Political Parties will publish a notice in the *Gazette,* the Official Newspaper, so that the Political Parties legally constituted in the country and the Attorney General's Office, which are parties to this procedure, will appear within a period of three days of the publication of the notice.

Art. 24 If opposition exists to the application, the National Council of Political Parties will open hearings for a period of fifteen (15) days for the presentation of all charges, within a period of three days from the end of which, the National Council of Political Parties will pronounce its decision, declaring the application accepted or not accepted.

If no opposition exists, the National Council of Political Parties will pronounce its decision within the following five (5) days.

Art. 25 The appeal for review established in Art. 18 of the present Law will be filed before the Supreme Court of Justice within a period of five (5) days after notification and the appeal for relief in accordance with the procedure established in the Law of Appeal for Relief in force. When thirty (30) days have elapsed from the time of the notification of a favorable resolution, and if there has been no appeal, the resolution will be published in the *Gazette,* the Official Newspaper. As of that date, the applying Party will possess legal status and the rights that Law grants to established Political Parties.

Chapter VIII: Suspension and Cancellation Of Political Parties

Art. 26 The suspension of a Political Party prohibits its functioning for a specified period of time. The cancellation dissolves the Party.

Art. 27 The nonfulfillment of the obligations set out in Art. 7 of the present Law will be grounds for suspension. Also, the Political Parties which form part of the Council of State can be suspended for the following reasons:

a) Official withdrawal from the Council of State.

b) Causes foreseen in the first paragraph of Art. 5 of the General Statutes of the Council of State.

Art. 28 The following are causes for cancellation:

a) Recidivism in the nonfulfillment of the obligations established in Art. 7 of the present Law or its violation during a State of National Emergency.

b) Participation of the Political Party in activities contrary to public order and to the stability of the Institutions of the Government of National Reconstruction without detriment to the resulting penal responsibilities.

c) Self-dissolution of the Political Party or its fusion with another.

Art. 29 The suspension or cancellation of a Political Party will be decided by the National Council of Political Parties. The procedure can be initiated at the request of the Attorney General's Office or of any of the Political Parties that are members of the National Assembly of Political Parties.

Art. 30 Upon receipt of the request for suspension or cancellation of a Political Party, the National Council of Political Parties will pronounce on its admissibility within a period of seven (7) days after the request is presented; the parties which present themselves as such will be notified so that within three days they may express whatever they consider wise.

At the end of this period, hearings will be opened for fifteen days, within five days of the end of which the decision will be pronounced.

Art. 31 Upon the resolution of the National Council of Political Parties as to suspension or cancellation of a Political Party, appeal for review or relief can be made to the Supreme Court of Justice in conformity with Art. 18 of the Law and the appeal will be filed in the same terms and form as those established in Art. 25 of the present Law.

The resolution as to suspension or cancellation of a Political Party by the CNPP will cause the immediate suspension of its functioning.

Art. 32 The resolution of cancellation of a Political Party will order the transfer of its property to the State in the branch of Social Welfare.

Art. 33 When a Political Party has been canceled, it cannot be re-established with the same name, emblem, or the same directorate members.

Chapter IX: General Dispositions

Art. 34 The dispositions of Common Law will be applied in all matters related to Political Parties which have not been foreseen in this Law.

Art. 35 The Council of State will establish the By-laws for the present Law.

Chapter X: Temporary Dispositions

Art. 36 When the present Law goes into effect, legal status will automatically be granted to those Political Parties that, at the present time, form part of the Council of State in conformity with the Fundamental Law and its reforms.

For purposes of record, these Political Parties will present to the National Council of Political Parties the following documents:

a) Principles of the Party

b) Statutes of the Party

c) Political Program of the Party

d) National and Departmental Directorates

e) Patrimony of the Party

Art. 37 The political groups that have applied to the Government Junta of National Reconstruction for membership in the Council of State at least one year before this Law goes into effect, may continue to function as they have been up until the present time, and must, within a period of one month from the publication of this Law, present application to the National Council of Political Parties in accordance with the requirements established in Article 36 of this Law.

This disposition will be valid with regard to each Political Party until the National Council of Political Parties rules as to its authorization.

Art. 38 Within a period of ninety (90) days after the passage of the present Law, the Council of State must discuss and pass its By-laws. This time period can be extended by the Council of State.

Art. 39 The Government Junta of National Reconstruction and the Political Parties legally recognized by the present Law will designate their representatives and alternates who will form part of the National Assembly of Political Parties immediately upon publication of the present Law in the *Gazette,* the Official Newspaper, so that, on the day, hour, and place that they decide, they will constitute themselves as the ANPP and take office in accordance with that established in Art. 12 of the present Law.

The Council of State and the National Assembly of Political Parties will elect their representatives to the CNPP within a period of one month after the establishment of the National Assembly of Political Parties.

Art. 40 From the moment of the entry into effect of the present Law, while its corresponding By-laws are being drawn up, the National Council of Political Parties is authorized to implement the present Law, resolving those matters which present themselves in accordance with the Law, with General Legal Principles, and with the rules of good judgment.

Chapter XI: Entry Into Effect of the Law

Art. 41 The present Law will go into effect upon its publication in the *Gazette,* the Official Newspaper.

GIVEN IN THE CHAMBER OF SESSIONS OF THE COUNCIL OF STATE ON THE SEVENTEENTH DAY OF THE MONTH OF AUGUST OF THE YEAR NINETEEN HUNDRED AND EIGHTY-THREE, YEAR OF STRUGGLE FOR PEACE AND SOVEREIGNTY.

Commander of the Revolution
Carlos Núñez Tellez
President of the Council of State

Sub-Commander
Rafael Solís Cerda
Secretary of the Council of State

Preparing for Elections: An Interview With Comandante Carlos Núñez Tellez

This interview with Comandante Carlos Núñez Tellez, President of the Nicaraguan Council of State (Congress), by Washington Post *journalist Robert McCartney, was conducted in September 1983. It was published in the English edition of* Barricada Internacional, *October 17, 1983; minor editing has been added.*

McCartney: What do you think of the U.S. government's decision to deny you a visa [to the U.S., to study U.S. electoral laws—Eds.]?

Núñez: Evidently this decision is part of the current administration's global foreign policy. In a verbal communication sent to the Council of State by U.S. Ambassador Anthony Quainton, the decision was said to be a response to the political treatment which we had given Under Secretary of State Motley. As I see it, the truth lies elsewhere. I believe that as a part of its global strategy to re-establish U.S. hegemony in the world, the current administration is doing its utmost to prevent those nations which have been affected by that policy from having access to the U.S. public. Hence, they are prevented from providing information on the situation in those nations and on the reasons why these nations are rising up in arms, not against the United States as a nation, but rather against the Reagan administration's current policy.

This decision, as I see it, denies the very principles which gave rise to U.S. democracy. The current government has neither the political nor the moral authority to demand, suggest, or recommend that Nicaragua should follow a new, democratic path when it is not even capable of leaving a small country in peace.

With its decision to prevent the visit of a Council of State delegation, the U.S. government has violated international norms. The parliamentary visit had been arranged at the request of various Democratic and Republican members of Congress who had come to Nicaragua. Its purpose, among other things, was to discuss the issue of elections, which has been used very often as a weapon to attack the Sandinista Revolution within the United States.

We were not simply going to examine the political and electoral system of the United States; we were going to speak to the U.S. public and members of Congress about a great number and variety of topics. We were going to follow up on the discussion begun here in Nicaragua with a number of congressional representatives who had visited us. They had summarized that discussion, saying: "We are aware of this; now we would like you to go and explain it to the U.S. people."

I believe the U.S. government is afraid of what we have to say. I believe that we could have spoken with members of Congress, with the U.S. public, via the mass media, and with the editorial boards of the country's major newspapers. This would have created obstacles for the Reagan administration's policy of confrontation with Congress when the debate over covert operations resumed on September 30. I believe this was one of the arguments which the U.S. administration used to justify the denial of the visa. No consideration seems to have been given to the fact that in doing so, the U.S. government was moving away from the ideals of its own Constitution, from its own democracy, and damaging a legislative body such as Congress.

Moreover, they weren't even concerned with looking at the makeup of the Council of State delegation. It was not only a member of the Frente Sandinista's National Directorate, but rather, included representative and respected Nicaraguans, such as the president of the Supreme Court of Justice, Doctor Roberto Arguello—who is not a Sandinista and who presides over the government's judicial branch; the dean of the Autonomous University at León, Doctor Mariano Fiallos; and other colleagues.

McCartney: You wanted to examine the United States' electoral system. What were you looking for?

Núñez: In the task that was entrusted to us we have attempted to study various Latin American and European models, and we considered that the U.S. experience is one which mustn't be ignored. The Council of State commission—and I myself in particular, on behalf of the Frente Sandinista, the National Directorate, and by mandate of the Government Junta—has been placed in charge of presenting the legislature, the Nicaraguan people, and the various political parties with an electoral bill.

We examined the history of the struggles undertaken in the United States from the first battles against British domination through the Declaration of Independence in 1776. It was in 1789, 13 years after the first declaration, if I'm not mistaken, that the Constitution was passed. With this Constitution, the United States made an important contribution, particularly to the Latin American nations.

For this reason, one finds the executive, legislative, and judicial branches—and in some cases the electoral branch—throughout Latin America. It is an experience which interests us for a very simple reason: we did not emerge or develop as a state in the Middle East, Africa, or Europe. We emerged in Latin America, and we are aware that U.S. hegemony and influence have taken very concrete forms in Latin America.

However, in our particular case, it is clear that the United States, under its various administrations, never left us a democratic heritage. Rather, I would say it has given us a negative past: a history of interventions, war, filibusters, and the black past of the Somoza dictatorship. Yet, when we implemented our program of government, we created an executive branch, a legislative branch, and a judicial branch. What does this mean? That the U.S. political system has something positive to offer, regardless of the fact that we disagree with and categorically reject President Reagan's policies.

I believe that the current administration and the State Department are precisely afraid that we do view matters in this way and hence, block our entry into the country.

McCartney: But the electoral system which is functioning now in Nicaragua is different from those of the past.

Núñez: The electoral system we are referring to has not yet been formulated. We are just beginning to enter that stage. The first question always raised is: "So, are the Sandinistas really going to hold elections, or are they just talking about them to fool people?" This has consistently been raised at the governmental level and even in some of the major U.S. media networks. What we have done during this period—after evaluating the aggressions, the attacks, the presence of Somocista forces in Honduras, the steps the United States has taken to install its military bases in Honduras, the reinforcement they have given to the Salvadoran government, and even the possibility of a direct U.S. intervention in Managua—is to insist that despite any escalation, elections will be held in Nicaragua in 1985.

Now, what kind of elections? This is precisely the task that the Council of State is undertaking at this time: to approve an electoral law. The electoral model chosen will be the result of those international models we have studied—which I have already spoken about—plus the result of consultations held with the country's different political parties.

However, a basic premise of that model will be the participation of all the country's recognized political parties, whether in coalitions or individually. Secondly, in whatever model we choose, the Frente Sandinista will be an organization with equal standing as any other, and based on the support it currently enjoys among the different social sectors and its various organizations, it will participate in those elections with its own platform independent of whether any other parties present theirs.

And thirdly, we will have to consider whether we're going to choose a traditional model such as that of other Latin American nations or if we're going to depart from this Latin American experience in order to give our electoral model the originality characteristic of a revolutionary country.

By this I mean—and this is my personal opinion insofar as I am in charge of this task—that the intention to hold elections in 1985, ensuring the participation of all political parties, must basically be aimed at achieving an electoral model and elections that will break completely with the concepts or understanding of democracy that prevail in the various Latin American, European, or North American countries. Some have felt that we should exactly reproduce one of those models in our country.

In our particular case, it must be an electoral process which not only ensures the active, widespread participation of all the people and their organizations, but also legitimizes a power that we have attained as a result of a long struggle. However, we must also ensure that the electoral process will contribute to consolidating the socioeconomic system we are promoting as well as the political structure which is being built.

That is, this socioeconomic system must represent the interests of the most important sectors of our people and ensure their social benefits. This alone would represent a historical break with the tradition in Latin America.

What has traditionally taken place here? The existing electoral processes have served to either keep military dictatorships in power or reshuffle them. Thus has been the case in Paraguay, Uruguay, Chile, Guatemala, Haiti, and for some time in Bolivia. Electoral processes have served to establish a political and socioeconomic system based on the economic power of a minority while the rest of the population starves. We opt for the opposite. It's fine for that minority to enjoy their privileges and accept the rules of the game; but our option is for the people.

The proposals that each party will make will be dealt with in due time. Our mission right now is to work on the electoral bill and later present our proposals to the different parties, along with the deadline for the bill's completion, the dates for consultation with each political party and for its discussion and approval within the Council of State. Once the electoral law has been passed, we will proceed to organize the system or the apparatus which will be responsible for its implementation. Finally, based on all of this, the exact date for the 1985 elections will be announced in 1984.

McCartney: In the United States, the prevailing concept of elections is that two political parties with differing views and ideas on policies present their platforms and the people choose. But I understand that the elections you are proposing are different, because the electoral system must reinforce and guarantee the process already begun by the revolution. Can you comment on this?

Núñez: As a member of the Frente Sandinista and on behalf of the FSLN, I can confirm that this is undoubtedly the goal, program, and project. That is, to further the revolution, to continue moving it forward, and to safeguard the people's achievements.

The Social Christian Party could advocate a different kind of project should they attain power; they could propose a system of reforms according to their doctrine. The same holds true for the Social Democrats; or perhaps with a reactionary party such as the Conservative Party, which could propose that we return to 1927.

However, I believe that the main question does not lie there. We would not even be able to propose that there be only two major parties here in Nicaragua, without being accused of being totalitarian. In the United States there are two political parties which alternate power. There are also other minority parties which represent no major political force. Since it is an already established system, a power which has existed for years and years, it has become a tradition.

However, Nicaragua is only four years old in that sense. In fact, if you ask if we have a constitution, we would have to say no. We are being pressed for one because of the argument that it is the only way the revolution can maintain its legitimacy. In the U.S., if I am not mistaken, the Constitution was written after independence was attained; it was passed 13 years later, and even then five states refused to sign it.

Furthermore, it would seem to be a historical contradiction that the party which represented the anti-slavery sectors at that time, that is, the Republicans—who had a great leader in Lincoln, a great figure in history—should today be the ones who are seeking to subjugate other nations, denying them the right to develop freely.

In Nicaragua we cannot reproduce another model to the last detail because we would be going against the tide of history and against the interests of our revolution. In theory we are proposing an electoral model which will promote the participation of all parties, each one of them proposing its own program, as will the Frente Sandinista. Our duty at the present time is to fulfill the political commitment of the Frente Sandinista's National Directorate, to carry out elections, to draw up and present an electoral model which will provide for the participation of all our parties.

At this time, we do not contemplate formulating a draft constitution, as objectively it is impossible.

McCartney: With the electoral law, who will the population be voting for? A legislature, an assembly, a president? What will it be like?

Núñez: That has yet to be determined. It is a question that the Council of State must still deal with, taking into account the different opinions that have been voiced. I believe that the crux of the matter lies not in who the people are going to vote for, but rather, in what model: What is going to be presented to the people for them to elect? The questions that need to be addressed here are whether they should vote for a Government Junta of National Reconstruction, not for the currently existing one, but rather for one in which each party proposes its own candidate, and whether they should do so individually or in coalitions. This has not yet been defined, because each party has its own alliances, and we do not yet know whether parties will form coalitions or remain separate.

But in any case, should this be the model we propose—that in Nicaragua the government offers a governing junta and each party has the right to propose its own candidates for it—that would be a contribution for Latin America.

McCartney: So they will be electing a new junta?

Núñez: That's one possibility, that each party would be able to propose a government junta. Another is that each would be able to present its candidates for membership on a government junta. For example, the Conservative Party proposes its party president or vice president as a candidate, and the Social Christian Party or the Frente Sandinista does the same. But what matters is that this can be one option: that in Nicaragua, the executive branch be comprised of a governing junta. That is one of the things we have to decide upon.

Another point that needs to be decided on is whether, instead of a governing junta, candidates should be nominated for the presidency of the republic. And yet another factor that must be included is whether a party must prove that they have a minimum base of support; if they do participate in elections and prove not to have such a base of support, should they be considered a political party in the future? And, in the future constitution and elections, will they participate in a determined fashion?

Some of these questions will have to be decided upon in the formulation of this law or in the bill, which the various parties will be consulted on. Here we do not intend to reproduce the classic parliamentarian regime, nor will we allow ourselves to reproduce the traditional or classic direct elections of Latin America.

Although it's true that the current political system in Nicaragua is a de facto regime, as it was the result of a struggle, internationally there is a political matter which is a formality for us: that this revolution must be legally institutionalized and legitimized, and that this should take place through elections. That's fine, and we are going to hold elections, but we must point out that whoever wins those elections will in the future make all the decisions necessary to continue the transformations in the country. Then the international community, accepting this judicial legitimacy, will have to bravely and whole-heartedly take on Nicaragua's defense. Because at that point, if the United States continues its aggressive policy, it would no longer be attacking a revolution because it does not have liberties, or because it does not hold elections, but rather because the U.S. wants to destroy it, despite the fact that it is an internationally recognized and judicially structured nation.

McCartney: For many people, particularly the U.S. administration and conservatives in Europe, the problem is that you want elections to legitimize the government. It is also understood that you insist that the new government continue the process of transformation which has been initiated . . . that the electoral process and the Law of Political Parties will guarantee economic transformation, political transformation, and so forth.

Núñez: In the first place, one must ask what does it mean to President Reagan and his advisers for elections to be held in Nicaragua? As I see it, it doesn't mean a thing for President Reagan because the essence of his policy is not aimed at maintaining good relations with Nicaragua or recognizing the existence of a government of an independent country seeking its own democratization. To the U.S. President, in his global strategy and ruling philosophy, the hegemony of the United States, especially in a continent like Latin America, must not be damaged by any country seeking independence.

For the current administration, the elections are nothing more than a rhetorical argument used to try to generate favorable U.S. public opinion toward its policy. The fact that we hold elections does not mean that the U.S. administration will halt its aggressive policy.

On the other hand, as the U.S. electoral campaign nears, the current administration's aggressive policy will increase and world tensions will rise, because a call has been made for a crusade to re-establish U.S. power, generate a favorable opinion toward it, and seek the current President's re-election.

I would be more concerned if he were re-elected, and the moral boost that would imply. What would happen in Central America, or in other areas of conflict in the world? What would happen to the human race?

Although history is history, when one runs across events that have already occurred before, they usually acquire much greater dimensions. The language which currently prevails in the world and which is being used by the U.S. administration, cannot be called simply an arrogant and aggressive language; rather I'd say it is a dangerous language. Dangerous on the one hand because it attempts to generate within the U.S. public a sentiment of wanting to defend itself against a great number of countries. But, on the other hand, it feeds into an extreme nationalism that, in turn, can lead to an extremist domestic opinion very dangerous for world peace.

This has been demonstrated in the statements made by the U.S. Defense Secretary, who has simply said, "We must save Central America," by which he means, guarantee U.S. hegemony. He has not said, "We must seek means to negotiate with Nicaragua," but rather, "Nicaragua must be destroyed," and for us this is simply a threat. We ask ourselves: Has the Reagan administration already taken the decision to destroy us? That's why I've said that, faced with this most serious of dangers, we must be prepared.

I don't think the U.S. administration considers elections to be of fundamental importance to improving its relations with Nicaragua. That's simply not the case. What is true is that for the U.S. Congress and public, elections are a very interesting subject where questions are raised; it's true that the major mass media in the United States are interested in elections, as are European political parties and governments, and the countries of the Contadora Group.

So, in part, when we speak of holding elections, we are saying that we are going to fulfill our international commitments, because we do respect them.

But we don't believe, nor do we try to convince ourselves, that if we hold elections Reagan will suspend his aggressive rhetoric and policy, pull out the Somocista Guards or remove the military base from Puerto Castillo, in Honduras. I don't believe elections will achieve that.

McCartney: If the Law of Political Parties and the electoral bill guarantee the domestic changes in the country which have been initiated by the Government Junta and the Council of State, is it possible to say or maintain that the people have elected this transformation process through free elections?

Núñez: I was referring to the U.S. administration. Now let's speak of another phenomenon: what elections mean from the viewpoint of progressive Europeans and Latin Americans or some international organizations.

I believe, and I've said so on other occasions, that in an electoral process the first ones we would invite would be international organizations such as the United Nations, UNESCO, the Non-Aligned Nations Movement, representatives of the Christian Democrat International, the Socialist International, and the Liberal International. These organizations have been very close to our process here in Nicaragua and would serve as a means to ratify the content and projection of the entire electoral process. We have absolutely no fear, as the Frente Sandinista, of losing the electoral process. And as a show of this, we are willing to invite all these personalities or representatives of these bodies to our country.

Now, from the classic point of view, from the point of view of what is understood as an electoral process in any country of the world — even in the famous democracies — it all depends on governmental policies.

For example, everyone knows that the elections in El Salvador were fraudulent and that those they were planning to stage now were going to be just as fraudulent. However, the U.S. administration had approved US$12 million for these fraudulent elections, to be staged over 40,000 dead bodies — over 40,000 Salvadorans who have been assassinated.

In our case, if you ask me whether this means the recognition of a freely elected government by other countries, I would answer that it depends on the structure of those countries, those governments, and those parties. Because if they refuse to recognize that a legitimate process is taking place here, they will not acknowledge that in the midst of a war and with all the aggressions, we make that effort, carry out elections, and we answer respect with respect. Obviously, those governments would be opposed to Nicaragua with or without elections.

Some questions could be asked, such as: Were they free elections? Did the people participate directly? Were the elections fraudulent? The questions asked will depend on them, and would show a clear political behavior.

If the Frente Sandinista wins this type of elections, they will legitimize a policy, a process, and a leadership in order to deepen the revolution, continue with the transformations, establish better rules of the game with private enterprise, religious, and political sectors, etc. That, we believe, should be acknowledged by other countries.

Resolution on the Denial of U.S. Visas to Representatives of Nicaragua

The following resolution was adopted by the Business Meeting of the 1983 Conference of the Latin American Studies Association, Mexico City, September 29, 1983. It was submitted by Marlene Dixon, Ed McCaughan, and Susanne Jonas of the Institute for the Study of Labor and Economic Crisis, San Francisco; Joel Edelstein, University of Colorado at Denver; and Max Azicri, Edinboro University of Pennsylvania.

Whereas the U.S. Department of State [has] denied visas to representatives of the people of Nicaragua on several occasions; and

Whereas these actions deny the rights of the academic community and of the people of the United States to a free exchange of information;

Be it resolved that the Latin American Studies Association condemn these actions to the U.S. Department of State; and

Be it further resolved that the Latin American Studies Association convey this resolution to the Secretary of State and urge the Department of State to permit entry into the United States for representatives of the Nicaraguan government and people.

An Exchange of Views
at the Council of State

On October 21, 1983, a delegation from U.S. Out of Central America (USOCA) held an in-depth meeting and discussion at the Nicaraguan Council of State (Congress) with members of the Foreign Affairs Commission and Subcomandante Rafael Solís, Secretary of the Council of State. The following document is a transcription, translated and edited at the Institute for the Study of Labor and Economic Crisis, of the meeting between the Council of State representatives and the USOCA delegation.

USOCA Spokesperson: First, I would like to take this opportunity to thank all of you for taking the time now to speak with us, during this time of crisis for the country. We are a delegation of people from California organized by USOCA—U.S. Out of Central America. The task of our organization is to mobilize the American people against Reagan's war policies. We recognize the critical role that the people of America must play in opposing what Reagan is doing in Central America. We are a national organization with over 100 chapters across the United States.

We see that one of the most important things that we can do is to educate the American people from all sectors—workers, students, people in the church—about the truth of what is happening in Central America. While there is a very strong feeling against entering into a war with Central America among the American people, it is not organized, and that is what we see as the urgent task before us. . . .

Subcomandante Solís: In the name of the Council of State I want to give you a very cordial welcome to our country and to our legislature, and to express our satisfaction at your being able to be here at this very difficult time for our country. We're here in this meeting as members of the Foreign Affairs Commission of the Council of State, representing different sectors of the Council of State: *Compañera* Angela Rosa Acevedo represents AMNLAE, the women's association; *Compañero* José Luis Villavencencio represents the Association of Nicaraguan Educators; *Compañero* Reinaldo Payán is from the Juventud Sandinista, the Sandinista Youth Association; *Compañera* Yadira Centeno is from the National Confederation of Professionals (CONAPRO); also present, from our legal advisory staff, are

Compañeras Maria Lourdes Vargas and Josefina Ramos. I am here representing the Armed Forces, and I am head of the Defense Commission, but I have also been working in matters related to the work of this Foreign Affairs Commission. I wanted to express great satisfaction at the presentation that the *compañera* gave about USOCA, since it shows the enthusiasm being generated in the United States for the existence of organizations opposing U.S. interventionist policies against Central America and Nicaragua.

I would say that you have come here at one of the most difficult moments of the revolution since the triumph. We're undergoing a new stage of U.S. aggression, because the operations are being directly run by the CIA, and furthermore, very special forces, or commandos, are directing these operations; they are directing their actions against strategic economic targets in the country: for example, our oil pipelines, and the port facilities through which all the foreign trade enters and leaves our country. These actions will probably continue, directed at other strategic targets.

In addition, and in conjunction with these kinds of commando activities, there has also been an intensification of what are called the "task forces" of the counterrevolutionary Somocistas operating in the north of the country. Two days ago, one of these groups came to the town of Pantasma, where they assassinated 47 peasants and *milicianos* (members of the militia). They burned what was there, and practically destroyed the few cooperatives in that area.

These kinds of activities would clearly not be possible without the open support given by the Reagan administration to the counterrevolution—with, of course, the collaboration of the government and army of Honduras, which is no more than an instrument of a bigger power that has occupied Honduras—the same United States Army. Honduras has really been converted into a giant strategic armed base for the United States in the region. Right now there are more than 3,000 U.S. forces, Marines and others, participating in exercises on Honduran soil. And they are going to be increased by November to 5,000.

In the face of this situation of the last two weeks—of an increase in the military activities of the counterrevolutionary forces, the commandos, and the task forces—both the Nicaraguan government and the leadership of the Frente Sandinista have decided that additional emergency measures needed to be taken. These regulations will affect all organizations and all institutions throughout the country, including the state institutions. In short, we are in the stage of preparing the country for a war. And this is different from what we had been preparing for previously. Of course, the Council of State has been involved and included in this entire situation. In the session of two days ago, we discussed extensively the emergency situation facing the country.

We have been working on the process of institutionalization of the revolution, including formulating some of the principal political laws. For example, two months ago we approved the Law of Political Parties. And for the last three weeks we have been discussing a draft of the electoral law, which would basically regulate the elections being prepared for 1985. We certainly have considered all of these activities to be tremendously important, particularly in terms of enabling us to discredit all the accusations made against the revolution from other countries, to the effect that Nicaragua was becoming or was a totalitarian country and that there were not going to be elections here. Since our political decision was to have elections in 1985, of course we needed to be formulating the electoral law. The Law of Political Parties [see above] would guarantee to all of the 10 political parties in Nicaragua their rights, which was necessary if we were getting ready for an election. . . . So these [laws] were already passed and specified, and a commission had started to work on the electoral structure that we would implement here in Nicaragua. Two groups had been traveling to Western Europe and to Latin America to study how elections are held [there]. And we had begun the whole process of discussing with various political parties the best way to run elections in the country.

But the national state of emergency, in existence since last week, will of course affect the work we're doing to prepare for the elections. The new regulations of the state of emergency are going to affect what is happening. We're discussing with the various political parties whether or not to continue the process of preparing for the election, because some of them have already openly proposed that this process should be suspended, for example, the Communist Party of Nicaragua (PCN) and the Movement of Popular Action (MAP). These two parties, which we could call extreme left, have opposed measures of the revolution on various occasions in the past. More recently we have had better relations with them. But obviously we have to take into account their positions. Three political parties that are allies of ours in the Patriotic Front of the Revolution—the Socialist Party, the Liberal Independent Party, and the Popular Social Christian Party—are also discussing internally the situation facing the country and whether or not the electoral process will continue.

The Frente Sandinista as such has not yet taken a position on this question, because we wanted to hear the opinions of the different parties, and until now we have maintained the process of preparing for elections and meetings of the electoral commission. This week the electoral commission met with people from the Communist Party and the Socialist Party, and next week we have meetings planned with other political parties.

Clearly, in a situation of war, one has to focus all the energy of the country on defense. And it is necessary to put aside some of the political activities. Because the most basic thing is to defend the sovereignty of our country. We believe that in the coming months, November and December, there could in fact be such a war, a very serious war. And for this reason the Council of State decided in Wednesday's session to take special measures. One of these was the creation of a special commission within the Council of State, headed by Leticia Herrera, one of the *comandantes*, and vice president of the Council of State, with the purpose of meeting directly with all the social, political, and union organizations of Nicaragua. They will be discussing what measures need to be taken and what are their opinions about the present situation. Within this we are also including the right-wing parties, which are actually opposed to the revolution, and one part of the private sector, also opposed to the revolution, which is headed by COSEP (Higher Council of Private Enterprise). [We are even meeting] with the Catholic Church, because the hierarchy of the church has also opposed the revolution.

In addition, this special commission is going to be in contact with other countries, with other Congresses, with committees of the Parliaments of other countries, informing them about our situation, and explaining to them the measures we have had to take. We've also decided to send a delegation from the Council of State to the United States, if the American Embassy allows us to enter and gives us visas (because they denied them to us a couple of months ago), on the basis of invitations we received from several universities and members of Congress. This will be happening in early November.

In addition, within the Council of State, we have been discussing laws specifically related to defense. We're going to present a draft for a law of civil defense, which would lay out all the measures needing to be taken in the case of war, in order to guarantee that production continues and to protect the civilian population: what will be necessary in the case of bombings, fires, sabotage, what kind of first aid, etc. As you know, about a month and a half ago, we passed the new Law of Patriotic Military Service, and during this month of October, the registration of all of the youth has been at a very high level.

There is a tremendous willingness on the part of the youth of our country to enroll in and become part of the defense. In this law of civil defense we would broaden all of the tasks necessary for the defense of the country— in view of the fact that we now do not see war as a remote possibility, but as something that could happen in a very short period of time. We continue to hope that certain factors could intervene, to prevent these policies of the Reagan administration from being realized; we have always had great faith, and great hopes, in American public opinion and in the U.S. Congress. We feel that the decisions of the Reagan administration are going to be very difficult to change [if we only] deal directly with the administration, since they have clearly taken a position that they cannot coexist with the Nicaraguan Revolution. They're determined to destroy it, and the only solution they see is the military solution.

In addition to our hopes regarding the people and the Congress of the United States, we are also in contact with countries of Western Europe, which have disagreed with the Reagan administration's policy, and with some of the Latin American countries, particularly those within the Contadora Group. Yesterday Foreign Minister D'Escoto presented some proposals to the U.S. Under Secretary of State [Motley], which show Nicaragua's disposition to maintain peace in Central America, and we're waiting to see the response of the Reagan administration to these proposals. We're prepared to guarantee the security of the rest of the countries in the region, and of course the security of the United States, because we have never considered ourselves to be a threat to security.

We believe that there still exists some space within the United States to restrict the Reagan administration's policies. As an example, we have the vote that was taken in the House of Representatives yesterday, which reiterated the opposition to continuing covert aid funds to the *contras* in Nicaragua. It will all continue, however, because there is opposition [to the House vote] in the Senate and, of course, in the administration itself. Nevertheless, it's important to see that the House vote does represent a victory for the anti-interventionist forces in the United States.

I'd like to know if other *compañeros* of the Commission want to add something to this or if the delegates want to ask some questions.

Delegate A: I'm from the Institute for the Study of Labor and Economic Crisis in San Francisco. Members of ISLEC and others sponsored a resolution at the Conference of the Latin American Studies Association in Mexico City two weeks ago denouncing the refusal of the United States to grant visas to members of the Council of State who wanted to travel to the United States to study the electoral process there, among other things. The resolution was adopted at the LASA business meeting.

Since the ideological justification given by the Reagan administration for aggression against Nicaragua is that it wants more democracy, what can we make of its refusal to allow members of the Council of State to enter the United States to study the process there?

Solís: In the first place, from their point of view, the State Department did not give any justification or reason at all for why they denied the visas. The only thing they said was that this wasn't the best time for the commission to come. This was just at the time when the U.S. Congress was discussing covert operations, so obviously they did not think this was a very good time to allow a commission from Nicaragua to come and talk to all the congressmen! Clearly, there is an open contradiction, because on the one hand the Reagan administration justifies itself in terms of defending democracy, and on the other hand it would not allow a commission to come there for the precise purpose of studying the electoral law. *Compañera* Maria Lourdes Vargas, one of the people who did go to the United States, might want to add something; she was there during this whole episode.

Vargas: As adviser to the Council of State, I actually went earlier than the delegation in order to look over the program of interviews and plans for the commission while it was in the United States. It is important to see the level of people that we were going to talk with—we planned to talk with members of Congress, and all this was going to have an effect on the votes, just at the time of the decisions on covert operations. I don't remember all the different names, but they were going to talk to [Congressional leaders like] Byrd, Wright, Tsongas, and others. Also, the delegation of the Council of State was going to have a very big meeting with Presidential candidates

Mondale, Glenn, and McGovern, as well as meetings at important intellectual centers. After Washington, they had other programs in Boston, at Harvard Law School, with the dean of the Law School, with the president of Boston University, and meetings with representatives of different sectors of the people—for example, black, Hispanic, and women's organizations.

Delegate B: I work as a printer in San Francisco. I don't have a question at this point, but I just wanted to say that what has really impressed me is the love for democracy in Nicaragua; and there is much more democracy than we have in the United States. You know Reagan never asked us if we wanted to have the CIA direct activities against Nicaragua. It takes an incredible amount of effort for the people to get through to stop what's going on. The people of the United States want to learn about democracy from the Nicaraguans.

Delegate C: I am a teacher and an educator in the field of early childhood curriculum. In the United States, as the other delegates said, there is nothing structurally set up for the Congress to really seek out the opinions of their constituencies; in fact, if we want to make known what we think we have to actively lobby them. That's clearly not the case here in Nicaragua, and I wanted to ask how the discussions of the state of emergency in the mass organizations and workplaces are linked with discussions going on within the Council of State.

Angela Rosa Acevedo: Those of us who are representatives here directly from the mass organizations can talk about this, because we have our own mechanisms for carrying on these kinds of discussions. In this way the Council of State is establishing links with the Nicaraguan people. First of all, I am here as a representative from a mass organization—when we are here in the Council of State we do not represent ourselves, we do not bring our position. Rather, our position reflects what women at the base are doing. For example, I am from the women's association, so when I am here, I will take the position that has been discussed in the women's association.

Laws come here to the Council of State through a process of discussions that are held through the mass assemblies of popular consultation. For example, the law we presented last year, the Ley de Alimentos (Alimony), generated discussion in 180 assemblies among different sectors of women. Not only did we have these meetings, but there was also great coverage given to them in all of the media—radio, television, and in the newspapers—and this opened up the discussion beyond just the assemblies themselves.

We were planning in October to introduce our fourth Family Law (which refers to the problems of paternity) to the Congress, but we had to lay this aside due to the fact that all our energy has to go to defense.

The emergency measures that the Government Junta and the National Directorate of the FSLN have taken were discussed immediately after they were presented—they were discussed by our leadership throughout the country. And with the same degree of urgency with which the government has presented them, we transmitted them to the base to be discussed in popular assemblies with women of all sectors throughout the country. Obviously, the very conditions of preparation for war have also enabled us to be much more competent in calling these kinds of meetings.

For example, when the bombing in Corinto took place, that very same night—or early morning—our entire leadership was called together to discuss and to implement the mobilization of all the women to protest the action of sabotage. And on that day we were able to mobilize 50,000 women throughout the country, demanding the rejection and denunciation of this act. By the time that the Frente Sandinista held the discussion here in the Council of State about the viewpoint of each organization in relation to the emergency situation, we had already discussed these and came to this discussion with a consensus from the base to the National Directorate.

So, we came with a position prepared. The first point was to participate actively and patriotically in the measures that had been passed by the Government Junta and the National Directorate. Second, we also put forth our plans to implement these regulations and in particular the mechanisms for saving resources in our homes, taking into account that women have to assume new challenges in this process. We already saw the consensus of all the mothers of the martyrs who had fallen in the last four years, during which we had all these attacks from the Reagan administration. This can be summarized in the following points:

The first is a call for unity of everybody in the country, regardless of what party they are from, to support these measures; many of them are Sandinistas, of course, because their children are Sandinistas. Perhaps the best example was expressed by the women from Pantasma, yesterday, when they said that they will shed not one tear; they just want arms to defend their lives. We are demanding our right to live, the right to defend our country.

Given that our desires are just to be able to live in peace and to make the revolution, we made a demand in the Council of State that everything necessary be done to defend the country. We called for the defense of the revolution and defense of the economy. What we have seen as women is that we have made many advances since the time of the revolution and we now have the right to speak and to vote and to participate in this society that we are not willing to give up. We are going to have to pay the price in defending these rights.

Delegate D: There is one statement that I would like to make. When the Reagan administration denied visas to the Nicaraguan representatives, we thought there was something to hide. Since I have been in Nicaragua and gone around with this delegation, I see that the Nicaraguans have nothing to hide! I am a union activist in the U.S., I've been a civil rights activist, and I also fought against the Vietnam War with my sons—to keep my sons from going to Vietnam. When we see how things are projected in the U.S. on television and in the newspapers, we watch it and know that it's not the truth. But you don't know what the real truth is, so you look for a way to find it out.

This is the first opportunity I have had in my life to go to another country and find out what the real truth is. It has really been a process of growth for me, and I will be able to go back to the United States with this delegation from USOCA and really work and fight. I have seen the fight in the people in Nicaragua. You can see it in their faces—traveling around, it has just amazed me. We should take it back to the United States with us and really work to help the people of Nicaragua.

Villavencencio: I would like to make a little comment because the words of the *compañera* unionist have moved me very much. You can really see here the great difference between the sentiment of the American people and the sentiment of the Reagan administration. But more than that, I had assumed that the North American people were apathetic, and now I see differently.

We in Nicaragua want peace and we know that the people of the United States want peace, but it is important to understand that when we are talking about peace from the viewpoint of Nicaragua, we are talking about our lives and about respect for our right to live.

And we will continue, very much strengthened by these words, because it makes us realize that if there is aggression against our country, there will be many delegations coming from the people of the United States to form part of a great human front to fight against any war situation that could be generated in Central America. We are completely sure about that.

We don't want another Vietnam in Central America, and we know that the people of the United States don't want another Vietnam in Central America.

Solís: I want to thank you and give you this copy of the letter that was sent from the head of our Council of State to the U.S. Congress [see above]. We are very, very satisfied with your visit, and we think that this conversation has been productive. We very much hope that delegations will continue to come, because it is the best way to really see what is happening.

PART 7

Perspectives on Revolution, Intervention, and Negotiations

"You Cannot Overthrow a People": An Interview With Comandante Jaime Wheelock Román

Institute for the Study of Labor and Economic Crisis

As the Minister of Agricultural Development and Agrarian Reform in the Nicaraguan government, and as a member of the nine-member National Directorate of the Frente Sandinista, Comandante Jaime Wheelock Román is one of the leading figures of the Nicaraguan Revolution. This interview with Comandante Wheelock was conducted by staff members of the Institute for the Study of Labor and Economic Crisis in Managua in October 1983, and was translated at ISLEC.

ISLEC: Perhaps we could begin by your telling us how you view Reagan's policy toward Nicaragua and the effects of that policy.

Wheelock: Reagan is the main enemy of the principles of nonalignment, mixed economy, and pluralism in Nicaragua [which are the bases of the Program of the Nicaraguan government—Eds.]. First, in terms of nonalignment, we have been forced [because of U.S. aggression] to seek arms from everyone, to look for all ways to defend ourselves, and to gain help in our defense efforts. We know that the United States is attacking us and will not help us militarily. This in some way may affect our alignment, because we are developing a profound mistrust of the United States, and we see increasingly that our friends are the Western European countries, the socialist countries, the Arab countries, and Latin America. We are certainly losing confidence in the United States because of its aggressive policies.

Second, Reagan is the enemy of a mixed economy in Nicaragua. First of all, he is destroying it, undermining it with military actions. In the second place, he is putting psychological pressure on those in the Nicaraguan private sector, who, because of their technological and academic ties to the U.S., understand the enormous military potential of the U.S. and don't want a bomb dropped on their children's room one day. Then, because they are businessmen, they prefer to go and produce somewhere else.

In spite of that, the private sector here has responded to us: Nicaragua, with all its difficulties, today is producing more coffee, more basic grains, more meat, more sugar than what was produced during Somoza's time. It would be impossible to reconstruct an economy and produce more if the 75% of the property owners who are private entrepreneurs didn't produce. Why has our economy been reactivated? Because the private-sector 75% have supported this reactivation, and because the government has subsidized them, has given them incentives, and given them good prices. Moreover, we have made the changes involved in the agrarian reform not with a vindictive spirit but with a humanistic spirit, because those private proprietors are not responsible for being landowners; the responsibility lies with the historical situation that we now wish to change.

Third, Reagan is the enemy of democratization. We have discussions with the political parties in Nicaragua about the elections, but there are parties that Reagan has stirred up, and has made insubordinate and anti-Nicaragua. He has stirred up the [Somocista] Guardsmen, and has undermined the integrity of certain politicians here so that they have joined the Guards. He is giving arms to Robelo and to Pastora to enable them to take the road of armed struggle, not of elections, which are what we want.

So, who is the enemy, Reagan or us? It is he. And in the same way he is really becoming an enemy of his own country. Because we are not in any way a threat to the United States. How can Nicaragua threaten the U.S. if we do not have an air force or navy to threaten the U.S. with? From the military point of view we are completely insignificant. What threatens the U.S. is this kind of policy, because it loses allies and friends for the U.S., while gaining enemies and hostilities; moreover, the attack that [Reagan] is waging against Nicaragua is an attack that can lead to a war. Not only a war in Nicaragua, but a war in Central America, unleashing [an explosive] situation in a sensitive place close to the U.S.

We offer treaties of peace and friendship with the United States, treaties with Honduras, nonaggression pacts with all of Central America, proposals for mutual agreements not to give support to armed insurgent forces [in other countries]. Although we may sympathize with these forces, we don't think that we have to arm them artificially. Revolutions are not exported, but are made by the people. Nobody can export a revolution. We are the most concrete example, aren't we?

So despite our offers of peace and of conditions for a process of hope here in the region, Reagan, because of his lack of historical perspective, and because he acts with a very short-range mentality, looking for a quick victory, is harming the strategic interests of the U.S. itself. So Reagan has become an enemy of Nicaragua, but at the same time also an enemy of the United States—an enemy, I would say, in the historic sense. He says he is defending the U.S., but he is leading his country into a tense situation, into a war, and he is also challenging a world power, the Soviet Union. So this is a road that can only lead to disaster, as they'll see.

What happened in Vietnam? Did they have a victory? Did that policy—the same as Reagan's—win out? There was no triumph, only defeat. Besides the revolution in Vietnam, look at the situation in Laos, in Kampuchea, and what is still to come in that region.

The same thing is happening here. Reagan doesn't see that there are profound internal causes for making [structural] changes. The changes can be revolutionary—overthrow of dictators and subsequently a gradual process of transformation, as in our case—or they can mean a process of transformation without the necessity of overthrowing governments. If there were a political solution in El Salvador, it would not be necessary to overthrow the government there; they could come to an agreement on how to make changes, and how those changes would be expressed politically in Parliament, in a co-government, in elections, or whatever. But if Reagan only sees guerrillas, Sandinistas, terrorists everywhere, there is no possibility [of peaceful solutions]. . . .

ISLEC: Could you tell us how you view the relation of the religious sector in Nicaragua to the revolution?

Wheelock: Our government practices full respect for religious belief and religious life here. Of course, we have problems with some religious people—not because they are religious, but because they are politicians, because they take political positions against the revolution, and these are not religious ideas. For example, Monsignor Obando y Bravo [Archbishop of Nicaragua—Eds.] is religious, as is Ernesto Cardenal [Minister of Culture in the government—Eds.]; nevertheless, Ernesto Cardenal is part of the revolution and Monsignor Obando y Bravo is against the revolution—not because he is a priest but because he is a bourgeois politician, a reactionary politician who never was part of the revolution and never will be. It is a question of one's political formation.

We support and are, I would say, part of the Christian sector. Many people in the Frente Sandinista are Christians. A good part of what is now the National Directorate of the FSLN comes from Christian families and from the Christian movement. Moreover, we can see the humanistic, Christian-based character of the conceptions of social transformation and overall in how these transformations are being carried out in Nicaragua.

ISLEC: How would you assess the balance of forces between the revolution and those who are trying to overthrow it?

Wheelock: We are certain we will triumph. First, because there is no military solution in Nicaragua, and I'll tell you why I say this. We have defeated the Somocista conterrevolution. They are defeated and in a state of decomposition. As much as the U.S. has wanted to unite the Nicaraguan Democratic Force (FDN) the FDN has been falling apart. They wanted to unite the counterrevolutionaries of Steadman Fagoth (who was trying to incite the Miskito [Indian] peasants to rebel) with the FDN, and they did not succeed. There is a division, moreover, between the two forces that are attempting to get the Miskito minorities to revolt. On the one hand there is an organization called the Armed Forces of Resistance (or of the Nicaraguan Revolution), led by Negro Chamorro, which used to be allied with Edén Pastora and now is allied with the FDN, but is also having problems with the FDN. On the other hand, Pastora doesn't want to be connected with the FDN either. That is, everything is a mosaic—it's all mixed up among them. The truth of the matter is that the Nicaraguan people are united and becoming ever stronger, and we are winning in spite of the fact that the *contras* are killing some of our people with arms provided by the CIA.

If there is an invasion, for example, by the Honduran Army, we will defeat them here because we are a formidable force in the defense of our country. Our forces would not serve to attack another country, because in that sense we have a weak army and we have no air force or navy. In fact, the Nicaraguan Army is the weakest army in Central America for the purposes of invading another country. But it is the strongest in terms of defending our country against any aggression—so strong, we believe, that it could defeat all the other armies put together. Because who is going to fight? All of the people, defending the country inch by inch.

You tell me: who in Central America can call upon 400,000 men? We can call up 400,000 or more here in Nicaragua to defend the revolution. We have recently been able to fill the plazas with 400, 500, 600 thousand people, and we are capable of mobilizing them. At this moment our people have mobilized more than 100,000 men from an [economically] active population of 900,000, without any decrease in industrial or agricultural production or in services. You can see for yourselves. What does this mean? That the people are mobilized for all the tasks of the revolution, and at any particular moment we can call up additional military contingents. So we are strong in defense.

But let us suppose that the U.S. intervenes. How would the situation change? There would be a tactical change in the situation, not a strategic change. There would be no military defeat here. What we would have is a change in military tactics. If they occupy one of our cities we would leave the cities. Do you suppose that any government installed through intervention would be capable of confronting 200,000 guerrillas all over the country? Because it *is* a guerrilla war that is being mounted here, with Nicaragua and Central America as its theater of operations. Who will govern Nicaragua with 200,000 guerrilla fighters everywhere? If [*contra* leader Alfonso] Robelo were to be brought here through an intervention, what governmental functions would this Mr. Robelo be able to carry out? There would be no official government functions. So how can there be a military solution [imposed by an intervention]? Here there is no military solution.

Now, we aren't people used to a comfortable situation. We're doing very well [in this situation], since only five years ago we lived a clandestine life in the mountains. How has the situation changed? Now we live in cities, and we have the power to do what we have wanted to do. If someone wants to stop us in a monstrous way, well, we won't be able to do what we wanted to do, but then neither will they.

All of this poses the possibility of a prolonged war here, a very long war that certainly could occur, that probably will occur! If it is so prolonged in Central America, I am sure that it will touch the U.S. border and will somehow be expressed in armed struggle in the United States. I am absolutely sure of this. Now you tell me, what do you think the minorities will do, what will the North American people do, in the face of a U.S. aggression? I'm also sure that North Americans will come to Nicaragua to fight for the Nicaraguan Revolution, because there are many North Americans who support us. And brigades will come from Argentina, from Chile, from Bolivia, from Venezuela; ex-presidents who have promised to come to fight here, not for Nicaragua but against intervention in a small country, which is ready to defend itself and to die for dignity and honor. This will generate protests in the U.S. — and also violent actions.

So, what about Reagan's solution? This is what Reagan wants? we are waiting, we are waiting for him, ready to defend our revolution.

ISLEC: Going back to what we discussed earlier: can you expand upon your view of the situation developing between the U.S. and Nicaragua?

Wheelock: Yesterday, our Foreign Minister delivered new treaty proposals [to the U.S. government]. We are not the ones who want war. They are the ones who want a military solution that doesn't exist. We delivered the treaties, we want peace, we want understanding with the United States. But on their part, they should say once and for all what it is that they want. They say that we export arms to El Salvador. Fine, we can reach agreements for a political solution in all areas. They say that we are a threat to our neighbors. Fine, we can sign treaties of peace, friendship, and nonaggression. We can make a commitment to all of this on the strength of our word and on our honor as revolutionaries.

But I am sure that for Reagan these peace offerings from Nicaragua are an obstacle to his policies, because what he basically wants is to destroy the revolution. Reagan has read a book that is his principal doctrine, *The Real War* by Richard Nixon, which maintains that the Third World War began before the Second. Reagan would like to be the hero, to roll back [the entire socialist bloc]. Hence, he goes around seeing Soviets everywhere, with a completely Manichean and very dangerous view of things, a vision of war. He [says he] wants to avoid World War III, but he is the one unleashing it, creating problems every day.

I don't know what is going to happen in the U.S., but if I were a North American I would not elect him. If I were a Republican I would get rid of him quickly and look for someone else. That is to say, if I am a Republican and I love my home and my family and I want to live peacefully, to fish, to ride in a good car, comfortably, without problems, I'm not going to elect Reagan, because this man is endangering my safety and that of my children. The North American public doesn't realize this—which is one of the most difficult things, because he is deceiving them; the average North American citizen doesn't know how serious the danger is.

There's a fact that I want to tell you, a fact that you can verify: North American citizens have already died down here. You should check over the past month, the soldiers who have died in accidents or from unknown causes in Honduras. Moreover, in a combat two weeks ago in northern Zelaya [in Nicaragua], we found two persons killed; clearly they were foreigners and they looked North American. We're sure they were North American; they could not have been anything else. When we captured counterrevolutionaries, they told us that they got into the country as commandos, and leading them was a North American who came to carry out very specialized sabotage operations. Then suddenly a North American appeared in Honduras, killed by a falling bridge or found dead on the streets from unknown causes. They are dying here in a covert war that will eventually burst into the open.

The best way to guarantee the security of the United States is through an understanding with Nicaragua and acceptance of the need for change in these countries. To attack Nicaragua, to impose military solutions, will lead to guerrilla warfare within the United States. That's the way it is, and that is where things are heading, also involving many other countries in this matter. The pilots that we captured [in October 1983—Eds.] from the plane provided to them by the CIA stated that they had been shown their military and economic targets by CIA officials.

What happens if a Mexican ship is attacked by one of those T-28's that the CIA has given to Pastora or to the FDN? Was it the FDN who sabotaged the Mexican ship? No, it was the CIA who gave the orders. And who does the CIA belong to? Isn't it part of the U.S. government? So isn't it in certain respects a hostile act by the U.S. government against the Mexican ships? I would like to know: when are these things going to happen and what will be the responses? Because Mexico has the right to choose whom to trade with; you cannot take away from Mexico the right to have trade relations with Panama, Costa Rica, Nicaragua, the U.S., or the Soviet Union, because it is a sovereign act. And if tomorrow one of these ships is sunk and 100 Mexican citizens die, isn't the U.S. to blame? Of course the U.S. is to blame, the Reagan administration directly.

This is the path we're all headed on, because they are not going to sink Nicaragua. They can sink a ship but they can't sink Nicaragua. And if the ESSO ships don't come [to deliver oil from Mexico—Eds.], and Nicaragua is left with no oil, there will be another country in the world that will send oil to Nicaragua; I believe in the existence of that country, and I believe that they will deliver the oil in a guaranteed way, so it will not be sunk. That's another kind of situation. You can see how we are headed toward more serious problems.

ISLEC: You've laid it out very clearly. Finally, can you give us your perspective on the long-range prospects for the revolution?

Wheelock: One thing is clear—the people here are determined to go through any type of difficulties presented by the circumstances, because a people that has already experienced freedom and revolution and social transformation is not about to give them up. We made the revolution not just for us, but for the poor, and in this country of 3 million people, 98% are poor. The revolution has been for that 98%, as opposed to 2%. Of the 2%, some are still in the country accepting the norms of the revolution; some are in Miami, and others are dead, like Somoza. If the revolution has favored the whole country, the entire population, and the people count on total support, are [our enemies] really going to be able to overthrow a government that is of the people? Will they really be able to overthrow a people? You cannot overthrow a people; you can kill a people, you can exterminate a people, but you cannot overthrow or defeat a people.

And, if things go badly here, they would have to exterminate all of us. But this is not possible, because in order to exterminate us, they have only two alternatives: one, to drop a lot of atomic bombs that would destroy everyone here; or second, to send an enormous army against us. Well, the alternative of sending a large army against us isn't viable. That army would be destroyed here. Certainly we could be destroyed if they used the bombs. But who would win? Would anyone win with this? Would the United States win? Would the United States have conquered us? No. They would be defeated, they would lose the war with those bombs.

Moreover, there are forces in the United States, democratic forces, the people, the students, the humanists, who oppose these barbarities, these atrocities. What is happening is that the [North American] people are misinformed, they hear a lot about tyranny, about communism, about exportation of arms, and they hear nothing about the atrocities of their government and the CIA. We need the support of the democratic forces within the United States. And, for our part, we shall struggle, we shall advance.

The Unfinished American Revolution and Nicaragua Today

Sergio Ramírez Mercado

This is a speech given by Sergio Ramírez, a member of the Government Junta of National Reconstruction, on July 14, 1983, to the "Conference on Central America" sponsored by the Sandinista Association of Cultural Workers. The conference was attended by a number of delegates from the Institute for the Study of Labor and Economic Crisis. Translation of this speech was provided by the government of Nicaragua, with minor editing for U.S. publication.

Like the rest of Central America, Nicaragua has had an unfavorable relationship with the United States, starting practically from when the United States became a nation and replaced its original project of liberty and democracy with Manifest Destiny.

Due to our unfortunate geographical proximity to the United States and Nicaragua's geographic possibilities for an interoceanic canal route, we have been in the geopolitical sights of one North American administration after another. This proximity and the insatiable thirst for domination fired by the idea of empire which some in the United States used to encourage the perpetual expansion of its borders—and they still want to continue expanding them—created a fundamental historical contradiction. For centuries, Nicaragua has struggled to survive as a nation in the face of the United States' imperial ambitions. From 1855 when we were invaded by the first filibusters until 1979 when the revolution definitively proclaimed national independence—a period which included General Sandino's heroic fight against the 1927 intervention when he laid the ideological foundation for this age-old struggle—now we are again fighting the struggle of all Latin America in these small but solid trenches.

Since this is also a political and ideological struggle, and the arguments of imperialist propaganda only try to mask and justify the military aggression armed, organized, directed, and financed by the Reagan administration, it is useful to look at some of the more blatant falsehoods entoned, like songs of death and perfidy, against our right to independence and to look at them under the light of reason, which is the right of a poor people to struggle for their national identity against the growing attacks of Manifest Destiny, in order to see this web of lies and deceptions so often repeated:

"The Serious Error of the Sandinistas Is That They Try to Export Their Revolution."

Throughout history, revolutions have been exportable, if we care to use that rather commercial term when talking about the dynamic by which ideas circulate across borders. Without the revolution of the 13 North American colonies, there would never have been a French Revolution, nor would Jefferson's ideas have existed without the inspiration of the French Encyclopedists, nor would General Lafayette have left France to fight in the fields of Virginia had he not believed that revolutions have no borders, nor would Benjamin Franklin have spent so many years plotting in European courts had he not thought that his American revolution was exportable.

So the revolution which gave rise to the United States' nationhood has been the most exported revolution in modern history, and the one which employed the greatest number of imported ideological elements as the basis for its thinking, its liberation war, and its innovative laws.

Confronting the despotism of the Spanish monarchs in Hispanic America, a colonial absolutism just like that practiced by England over the then future United States, our creole liberators found that the most brilliant and convincing formulas for ending the colonial yoke came from the north (just like later all our calamities would come from the same place): the example of an implacable and bloody war fought by men intent on substituting the colonial regime with a new political and social order; the crystallization of European Enlightenment's utopian ideas about democracy first put into practice in the New World, a promised land for those philosophical dreams which until then were considered extravagant—a constitutional government and the balance of powers. All these concepts were considered extremist and subversive by the monarchical order, and when they clandestinely spread through Hispanic America they met with persecution, jail, and exile. Reading James Madison then was a *les majesté* crime, just as reading Marx can cost you your life in Guatemala or El Salvador now.

The new United States Constitution and the explosive ideas which inspired it traveled by muleback through Central America as clandestine literature. That nascent republic, governed by radical madmen, extremists, and exporters of revolution, believing only in their own model and rejecting any other, represented a threat to Spain's internal security and strategic interests in the New World when her great colonial empire was ready to crack open. In 1823, when independence had been won in Central America, the first federal constitution was adopted as an attempt to concretize the ephemeral dream of a united Morazán-like Central America, beginning with the same introduction, copied word for word, as the Constitution written by Madison in 1787. Thus the United States was exporting a model and exporting the bloody lesson that such a profound change— the defeat of the British Empire in America—could not be moved forward without rifles, without militarily crushing the enemy, and without emulating the Minutemen, guerrilla combatants as brave as those of El Salvador's FMLN. Facing the emergence of a new order based on new, necessarily subversive ideas, the old order was destroyed in the war, and the old ideas and hundreds of thousands of counterrevolutionary theories underwent a mass exodus to Canada, because revolutions always produce an exodus.

The continent's first armed revolution occurred in the United States. The United States exported its revolution to Spanish America, and in spite of everything that the crown did to repress these clandestine ideas quickly and secretly circulating throughout the Viceroyship of Guatemala and through New Granada, it was impossible to prevent them from taking hold in the minds of thousands of other bearded, barefoot, hungry, and ragged extremists who trafficked in books and pamphlets containing those incendiary speeches and subversive laws. They also trafficked in rifles and ammunition, since those ideas, which already had the power of truth, had to be imposed by force. And they did not hesitate to seek and accept the weapons they needed to assure their liberation army's victories. As Bolívar admitted in his Angostura Speech: "Our army lacked military elements, it had always been unarmed...now the soldiers fighting for independence are not only armed with justice but also with force...such great advantages are due to the unlimited generosity of some foreigners who have seen humanity groan and have seen the cause of reason perish, and they have not observed this calmly but rather have rushed to extend their protectful aid...these friends of humanity are the genuine custodians of the Americas...."

It would not have been possible for Jefferson, Washington, Bolívar, or Morazán during those days of forging a new world on a continent in revolution to prevent their revolutions from being exported, because it was not a matter of ruses to impose models by force, but rather of leading a historical crusade for radical changes which buried the old colonial world.

Morazán, as the ideologue of the great dreams of the Central American federal republic, never thought in provincial terms; nor did he believe that his liberalism would stop at Honduras's borders. On the contrary, his political and military movement, the largest in the 19th century in Central America, led to the emergence of a large revolutionary party throughout the region, which opposed ideas against ideas and advanced its ideas of change by the force of the federalist weapons. Then the struggle was not between Hondurans and Salvadorans nor between Guatemalans and Nicaraguans, but between liberals and reactionaries, between the armed revolutionaries of that period and obscurantist clerics and feudal landlords and a gloomy Central America of the friars of the Inquisition and the lords of the gallows and knives. And Morazán, like Washington and Bolívar, was a great exporter of revolution, of subversion, and of extremism because he wanted to change reality.

So for the Sandinistas, who are repeating the revolutionary feats of Morazán in the 20th century, it is impossible to prevent their idea of revolution from being exported. We export ideas, ideas of change and renovation, ideas that provide a foundation for a new world being born, we export the proven possibility that an armed people, when they set about to do so, can overthrow tyranny and establish a nascent and innovative world on the wastes of that tyranny; we export the news that in Nicaragua the revolution has brought with it literacy, agrarian reform, an end to poliomyelitis, the right to life and hope. How can one prevent a peasant from another Central American country from hearing, from finding out, from realizing that in Nicaragua land is given to other poor and barefoot peasants like him? How can you avoid his realizing that here children—not his children—are being vaccinated while his children still die of gastroenteritis and polio?

Now, like then, the struggle is not between Nicaraguans and Hondurans, but between peons and bosses, between the New Man and the specters of the past, between those who struggle for a better order and those who try to maintain for all eternity the worst of orders.

In that sense, we export our revolution.

"The Sandinistas Have Betrayed Their Original Revolutionary Project."

The original revolutionary project of the United States began to be betrayed very early, such that James Madison himself, father of the American Constitution, already feared by 1829 that the perpetual expansion of the new nation, controlled by manufacturers and businessmen, would end the experiment of a republican government.

Soon after, Madison's fears were changed into Manifest Destiny and the Americas in revolution, a continent lit by the bonfires of change, were soon turned into the America on top and the America on bottom, the oppressors and the oppressed, the plunderers and the plundered, the expansionists and the occupied. And the sons of Washington and Jefferson not only took the huge territories of Mexico in that first great push to dominate but also took the name of America, and since then the dream of liberty and justice has been turned into a nightmare of hegemony. The United States of 1898 were no longer the same United States of 1776; the original revolutionary project had been left behind and in its place was started the expansionist counterrevolution that swallowed up Cuba and Puerto Rico and prepared to assault the entire Caribbean, including Nicaragua and Panama. This was carried out, not in the name of that old republican ideal for which so many soldiers during the struggle for independence spilled their blood on the snow covering the battlefields, but instead in the name of that imperial ideological aberration of Manifest Destiny, an aberration which would later be veiled by Pan-Americanism—the United States allied with the rest of the continent in a crafty and opportunist way, only to destroy the possibilities for identity and identification of nations that now appear conquered or conquerable. All the scaffolding of constitutional law, division of power, and courts of justice began to succumb under the worst elements that those weak and poor countries could offer, the political dealers and dark exploiters who divided up presidential gangs, who negotiated with the grandchildren of the founders of that first liberatory republic, already hidden among the shadows of history.

We know what the original revolutionary project of the United States was. But when they talk about the Sandinistas' betrayal of our original revolutionary project, what project are they talking about?

During Reagan's 1980 Presidential campaign, the New Right's spokesmen—who had already conquered the positions of ideological leadership within the Republican Party—declared that the United States would never again commit the mistake of not fighting to the end for an ally like Somoza; they felt guilty and ashamed for having abandoned him. Later they confirmed preferring Somoza a thousand times over the Sandinistas. And even later they armed the old supporters of the Somoza regime—the Guard no less—to destroy the Sandinista revolutionary project and to retake power through the counterrevolution's arms.

The original project that the United States government refers to is not ours. Their project is the same one as always—not changed or even retouched—it is that of the National Guard created in 1927 by the United States itself to replace the Yankee occupation army in 1933, which sustained the Somoza dictatorship for almost half a century.

The United States' project intends to reinstall the National Guard as the decisive force within the country, to be faithful to North American interests in the region, like the army of General Alvarez in Honduras is faithful to those interests.

Why do they want the National Guard to occupy Nicaraguan territory again like they did for almost 50 years? To give us Jefferson's Constitution and George Washington's political model? To fulfill the American Dream of 1776 in Nicaragua? That dream doesn't exist but the National Guard does, thanks to the Reagan administration.

The Reagan administration's miracle workers cannot really think that we have betrayed our original revolutionary project because they radically and viscerally reject all revolutionary ideas. The word revolution is incompatible with their views and conception of the world. Of course, the revolution that we have been unable to make and from which we have separated ourselves they will entrust to the Somocista Guard's colonels and paid assassins, who murdered thousands of young people and peasants, who bombed neighborhoods and villages, who raped women and filled the jails.

But it's not only the Reaganite ideologues who declare that we have betrayed the original revolutionary project. The people who feel materially and ideologically affected by the revolution also say that they don't see, in its path or its actions, what they thought was the original ideological project; that is to say, their original project which would impetuously ignore the privileges that they had for so many decades, their excessive riches, their feudal plantations, their businesses, and corporations with the dictatorship. It would have been impossible to make a revolution with so much sacrifice and blood that could fit that model, a selfish, not very Christian, and not at all altruistic model. We have truly betrayed this meaningless idea of revolution.

However, one must not forget that we Sandinistas did not make fundamental promises to the United States—to whom we never made any type of promises—nor to Nicaragua's privileged groups. The basic promises were made to the country's poorest people, the promises that they have defended with weapons and their heroism. The original project is still there, growing and being multiplied for those people, in the cooperatives, schools, health centers: land, dignity, and sovereignty. There was never any other revolutionary project besides this one; this was the original project.

We believe that the United States is the one which should return to its original project of liberty and democracy, the project of Washington, Madison, and Jefferson, that beautiful revolutionary project that was betrayed by capitalist greed, by the wanton accumulation of riches and by this perverse expansionist will that has forced the United States' borders so many times to our border, as they are once again doing by pushing it to the Honduran border.

"The Sandinistas Have Copied a Model Of Revolution That Is a Totalitarian Model."

The same ideological device that justified the invasion of these lands of the Americas and the confiscation of our free destiny also created the pretext of the invader's racial superiority and that of the invaded people's inferiority: if we as marginalized people were perpetually condemned to live off the rich's crumbs, it was because of our own historical inabilities. The adventure of the Yankee conquest thus became an adventure for the white race, master of initiative and spirit of conquest, capable of dominating nature and of creating all science and technique, machinery and unceasing progress; we not only became the conquered but also the slow and lazy mestizos and were illiterate because of desire and inertia, poor due to our hopeless destiny, violent and anarchical, quarrelsome and vengeful.

God was associated with the United States and with its prophetic mission to conquer the world; the people of the Second Coming found their promised land wherever they could lay down their claim to conquer frontiers and tame the tumultuous savages, who according to William Walker's beliefs, only deserved slavery because they were racially inferior.

Since then, our country has been subject not only to divinely dictated submission, but also to a model of political conduct which meant accepting foreign domination along with all that conquering race's superiority and their advantages which were never trusted: civilization and progress were gifts offered to us, but under that ideological condemnation to which we were subjected, they were impossible to obtain.

Therefore, the dogma of a political and cultural domination could not inspire hope to aspire toward any independence or individual thought; the North American political system which our forefathers coveted and fought for turned into the permanent expansion of the armed Puritans to conquer, and this was a destiny that had to be accepted, no matter how bitter it was. The triumph of the business of domination presupposed the draining of all our national identity and ideas, of any hopes of creating a political model or developing our own creative capacity. The almighty, strong, and wise Yankees owned all initiative and the future; we, the cause and product of underdevelopment, could only own our misery, our poverty which created more poverty, condemned to live off the ideological leftovers of the perfect model of Yankee democracy that elects a President every four years among colored balloons, willing nonetheless to tighten the screws of domination in our countries in the name of the bankers and financiers whose claws neither Jefferson nor Madison envisioned.

That is why when the New Right, which now governs the United States, hears us talk about our own model in Nicaragua, they raise their eyebrows disdainfully and unhappily, and their first reaction changes from surprise to fury. "Their own model, they do not have the historical capability to generate models, they can only aspire to have an immutable role in the ideological and political division of labor!" For such a mentality, the initiatives, whatever they may be, and historical projects can only be generated in the metropolitan centers and never in the periphery, as if the United States itself had not originally been on the periphery, where the new model of bloody revolution emerged.

But as Madison bitterly lamented, political models also waste away when they begin to serve interests they were not intended for. For us, the efficacy of a political model depends on its capacity to resolve the problems of democracy and justice. Effective democracy, like we intend to practice in Nicaragua, consists of ample popular participation; a permanent dynamic of the people's participation in a variety of political and social tasks; the people who give their opinions and are listened to; the people who suggest, construct, and direct, organize themselves, who attend to community, neighborhood, and national problems; the people who are active in the sovereignty and the defense of that sovereignty and also teach and give vaccinations; a daily democracy and not one that takes place every four years, when at that, or every four, five, or six years when formal elections take place. The people don't go as a minority but in their totality, and they consciously elect the best candidate and not one chosen like a soap or deodorant, a vote freely made and not manipulated by an advertising agency, a vote for change to improve the nation and not in favor of a transnational finance company or an industrial military trust.

Maybe when Madison wrote his Constitution, he was thinking about this type of democracy, which no longer exists in the United States.

On the other hand, for us democracy is not merely a formal model, but a continual process capable of solving the basic problems of development and capable of giving the people that elect and participate in it the real possibility of transforming their living conditions, a democracy which establishes justice and ends exploitation.

Because a political model emerges from concrete reality and from the needs that that reality imposes in order to change it, the Sandinista model—our own model—emerges from the long period of U.S. domination in Nicaragua, a domination that was political, economic, and even military as well as social, ideological, and even cultural. It is in the face of this domination that our model responds and establishes a vital necessity that independence be our own model, and together with this national independence, the recovery of our natural resources and of the will to develop an economic project that while transforming the nation, will give us the possibility not only to generate riches but also to distribute them fairly.

When they speak about copying models, we must remember that during half a century Somocismo slavishly copied the model imposed by the United States. Nicaragua was branded with the most radical capitalist model, a market economy which impoverished the country and ravished the possibilities for its true development. With this destructive capitalist model came the destructive dependency on markets, raw materials, and financial resources; Nicaragua became a satellite of the United States; Nicaragua was behind a true iron curtain with a solid, triple-locked bar. Of course, the Somoza family also imported the political model of elections every four years, and elections existed here, a bi-partisan system existed here, and there was a two-chamber legislative system, a supreme court, and a constitution with laws. And it was all a bloody hoax.

And this imported, copied, and imposed model historically failed, and we are now seeking our own model. We are no longer a satellite of the United States, we are no longer behind the United States' iron curtain. We are free, sovereign, and independent, something that was always deceptively written into all the Somoza constitutions and only now is true, even though we still have not written our constitution.

To consolidate this national project, this genuine project of a sovereign revolution, we are willing to meet any challenge and make any sacrifice. To make this idea possible and to nurture it, the people of Nicaragua are ready to defend their project and their model of revolution with arms. They are ready to achieve a definitive peace so that this model may flourish, a model which we do not want to impose on anyone. Because it has real political borders, Nicaragua's borders. We are not a people chosen by God to fulfill any manifest destiny, we don't have capital to export or transnational corporations to defend beyond our borders. Our dreams are not to dominate, expand, or conquer but rather our dreams are the humble dreams of a humble people who aspire to true justice and independence.

That is why we want to live in peace and grow in peace, that is why we want to spread the news of our sovereign people's example in peace, a people who never thought to ask anybody for permission to make its revolution and will not ask anyone for permission to defend it.

Free Homeland or Death!

Intervention and Negotiation in Central America

Pablo González Casanova

Pablo González Casanova is the former rector of the Universidad Nacional Autónoma de México (UNAM), and a leading sociologist, currently at the Instituto de Investigaciones Sociales of UNAM. In recent years his writings have had particular importance in relation to the revolutionary struggles in Central America. He has contributed to two previous issues of Contemporary Marxism.

Power, Politics, and Diplomacy

In the history of ideas, there are moments of rupture when old concepts take on new meanings that are difficult to discern.

The concepts of nonintervention, self-determination, and democracy are cases in point. In Latin America, and particularly in the Caribbean and Central America, they have undergone such profound changes that not even their own proponents fully realize that these concepts now refer to radically different realities and ideas. Needless to say, semantic differences, with their practical implications for hemispheric politics, do not seem to have been identified by most North American experts, or by U.S. politicians who consider the continent to be the natural sphere of U.S. influence.

The principles of nonintervention and self-determination, as well as the ideal of democracy, have a long tradition among intellectuals, internationalists, and journalists in Latin America. Of the many significant changes in their meanings, the most original flows from the way in which the phenomena corresponding to these concepts are conceived simultaneously within a logic of power and within a logic of political negotiation and diplomacy. The change has been deepened and refined most particularly in Nicaragua and El Salvador.

Generally, it can be said that until the end of the Guatemalan Revolution* in 1954, the concepts of nonintervention and self-determination were

---

* The reference is to the democratic and anti-imperialist governments of Arévalo and Arbenz, 1944-1954, ended violently by the U.S. intervention of 1954—Eds.

thought of more in political and diplomatic terms than in terms of the logic of power. Even when the logic of power was considered, it contained no clear concept of the logic of class. Something similar occurred with the ideal of democracy. When an attempt was made to achieve democracy through political and diplomatic action generally, these actions frequently lacked any logic of power. When the logic of power was present, the logic of class—and above all the linkage among classes, with their interactions, their alliances, their coalitions—was absent.

From the Cuban Revolution to the revolution in El Salvador to the new one in Guatemala, and including that of Nicaragua, the problems of nonintervention, self-determination, and democracy have been posed not only in terms of a (necessarily revolutionary) logic of power and of class. In addition, in the struggle for power and for the consolidation of power, *a policy* and *a diplomacy* are also necessary, conceived as forms of negotiation and struggle for principles and ideals, in which confrontations are combined with alliances and coalitions. From positions of *power* and *class,* desirable or necessary compromises are considered, [that] delay the enemy's objectives and, at times, one's own. We are speaking of delays in the sense that one does not struggle to impose objectives immediately, but rather seeks to achieve them within a policy of constructing *the very mediations of power,* within a policy of approaching the structural changes and changes in social, political, and economic relations that permit a higher level of democracy and social justice.

The conceptual novelty of the principles of nonintervention and self-determination and of the ideal of democracy reflects a *general unification of theories,* in which power and negotiation, power and politics, power and diplomacy are combined with the problems of class struggle and negotiation, class struggle and politics, and class struggle and diplomacy. In these multiple combinations are found the strength and at the same time the flexibility for political and diplomatic concessions or negotiations that consolidate power or prevent its loss.

The necessity for national and international alliances or coalitions implies different forms of ideological pluralism, of conciliation, tolerance, or even of political and ideological integration, as well as the establishment of mixed economies (which approximate or are a transition to socially oriented systems of production and distribution). It implies the development of all this without losing sight of the fact that there is a class struggle, in the sense that there is a struggle for both private accumulation and for public and social accumulation. All of this determines the shifting alliances in which private or collective interests may win. Such a necessity moves revolutionary leadership to forge or encourage worker-peasant-popular coalitions formed in the common interest, and to seek international alliances with the nonaligned nations, with the democratic and social democratic governments among the highly industrialized nations, and with the socialist countries—all through a series of measures which follow the general articulation of theories. These theories, these explanations, in practice and in struggle, are applied flexibly, always within the perspectives of power and of the common interest, structured in the form of *peoples* and *fronts.*

When we have, on the one hand, the politics of power and its touchstone, the logic of class, and on the other the politics of negotiation, negotiation (considered as a form of compromise and mediation) is not left to chance. Negotiation becomes a matter of strategic and tactical considerations (revolutionary and political, using very precise terminology) *so that self-determination and democracy cannot be co-opted;* so that the coalitions, alliances, pluralism, and mixed economies do not serve as an instrument or a means of interventionist policies on the part of the hegemonic power and its allies, of monopoly capital, the oligarchies, the dependent bourgeoisies. Instead these become *instruments of the coalition* representing the working people and their national and social interests.

To the *rights of self-determination, democracy, and nonintervention,* understood within a logic of power and of class, we can add: the *right to a politics of coalition* (without the classic game of parties, which never existed as a reality and does not exist in current or future reality); the *right to a politics of international alliances* (the right to struggle for one's own existence in the international arena); the *right not to have everything reduced to a Manichaean struggle between East and West* (in which one's people, state, and nation count only as *pawns* in a supposed game between at the most two players); the right to oppose a simplistic Cold War ideology; the right to resist that colonialism in which liberation means merely a struggle between the great powers, which negates the identities of peoples and small and medium-sized countries, and denies the right to their historical, political, and legal personalities, the right to sovereignty (in these same areas).

The foregoing rights, demanded by peoples and small and medium-sized countries, arise from the system of justice and also of power, corresponding to the ideals of liberty and equality of peoples, but also to the correlation of forces in the world in relation to the liberation of peoples, to their sovereignty and democracy. To these rights is added the *right to reforms,* a right that has the same normative or power-derived meaning, capable of achieving *real* social and structural reforms. Finally, there is the *right to a new type of negotiation* that does not limit the historic process, but carries it by successive approximations and transitional steps toward a more social, public, sovereign, and democratic system.

Out of so many new and rich elements contained in the rights to self-determination and democracy, one fact should be underlined, and that is the force or power that lies behind both rights. This force is measured not only by the prestige that the ideals of self-determination and democracy have among the people and their leaders, but also by the close ties existing between the former and the latter. The strength of these ties is difficult to comprehend when one is accustomed to the frustrating experience of a pseudo-democratic or populist rhetoric; but when it becomes an operative reality, it explains the power underlying the national and democratic struggle against the powerful empire.

If it is true that in El Salvador the FMLN "is in fact the people," as its members claim, then this is not a mere phrase. It is a reality, which explains why Reagan's policy is a failure. That policy was directed against a proposition falsely interpreted by its enemies, who tried to reduce it to rhetoric and dogma, while in fact it was a reality. Upon encountering this reality, the Reagan administration, employing an excess of military force and land and naval blockades, encountered a shattering and *quite unexpected* failure. The new reality must be understood very precisely. Anyone who understands it will recognize and respect it as a political, military, and diplomatic fact.

The Power of the Nation-State

The totality of the Central American peoples' rights, with their *norms and forces,* has elicited at least three reactions: the first, one that is not new, is opposition by the U.S.; the second, somewhat more recent, is the failure to comprehend the need for a change in the politics of negotiation conducted between "a great power" and "a small nation"; the third, which is totally new, is recognition of the political-military impossibility of victory by the great power over the small nation.

What is really new here is that the U.S. cannot defeat the people of El Salvador. And this novel phenomenon is as difficult to comprehend as is the new negotiation—as difficult to comprehend as the English people's right to petition was in the 17th century, which incited such fury and incomprehension that it was necessary to cut off the head of a king in order to drive home to the others the fact that the English people had the *right to petition.* In this sense, El Salvador is experiencing in the 20th century what the English experienced in the 17th. And just as the passage from a policy of imposition to one of negotiation spelled, at that time, the end of an epoch, today the passage from a policy of negotiation that corrupts and ultimately destroys the processes of popular democracy, to one that acknowledges and consolidates those same processes, constitutes a historic breakthrough in the terms of negotiation.

The old and rigid reactionary resistance from Washington, its increasing incomprehension of the need to change its policy towards Central America, and the unfamiliar notion that the empire cannot win the war against El Salvador pose a set of problems in all areas, both in regard to negotiations and in regard to the power to impose the new and the old forms of negotiation, or to impose a sovereign and democratic revolution as opposed to corruption and interventionist/dictatorial repression.

The problem is fundamentally one of democracy. The new democracy is developing as a local process that tends to be universalized. What happens in Nicaragua is not only for the Nicaraguans; it can also be (changing what needs to be changed) for the people of the United States. With all its implications, the new democracy is a force that defends Central America and threatens the North American oligarchy.

The new democracy manifests itself not only as a multiplicity of parties, and respect for the ballot, but also as an articulation of forces in relation to the state that arose from the democratic revolution. These forces are joined within the new state and in civil society, within the nation-state besieged by the empire and its dictatorships. The institutions linked to the state apparatus arise from revolutionary coalitions and alliances. The revolutionary coalition is already an embryo of the state, integrating the nation into a front for political, ideological, and military struggle. Upon the triumph of the coalition, the right to opinion and criticism is maintained, but more importance is given to participation of the citizenry in the activity of government, in the military and civilian, economic and social executive organs of the state, and in its judicial and legislative organs. Complementing this structural and institutional achievement, with its coalition dominated by the worker-peasant alliance (which is also the center of power and of social and political activity for those sectors of the middle classes committed to the movement), the strength of the *institutionalized coalition* and its majoritarian worker-peasant base give the nation-state and state power an ideological coherence that strengthens it considerably. In so doing, it gives almost all of the dissident groups the civic option of giving *critical support,* or the sinister option of joining the interventionist and counterrevolutionary groups among that sector of *civil society* backed by the transnationals, the colonial oligarchy, and the imperialist state.

The coalition integrates the nation into a combative political, economic, ideological, and military totality. It is an embryo of the nation as a state. From a Machiavellian point of view, the state-nation predominates over the nation-state. From a political-military point of view, the nation is integrated into a state in order to struggle and to win. When triumph is achieved, a state of the civil society emerges, a state permeated by civil society — democratic, popular, and progressive. The people, inserted into the state, are the state. The task of the people, more than commenting on the state, is to act within it in a way that serves both them and their functionaries. This situation arises from the threat of intervention against the nation and of the imposition of an anti-democratic dictatorship sponsored by that part of "civil society" composed of historically decadent forces, such as the old landowners, plantation owners, colonial transnational merchants, their defeated and defeatable armies and politicians, their hired and supported mercenaries and bandits. Added to these forces are those who claim to struggle for liberty and religion, doing so from reactionary, interventionist, and ultimately sham positions in which liberty, religion, and democracy are directly linked to a policy that longs for marines, gunboats, and the magic of Vietnam-style experts — like some technological miracle, which will again win only to lose. In practice, it means massacres and innumerable crimes that only make the process of struggle for sovereignty and democracy more painful.

Faced with this kind of "civil society," mystified by the press at times with liberal terminology and at other times even with a Marxist one, a civilian society-state takes shape, a people-state in which society and people do not merely have opinions, do not merely vote and have representation;

in addition, they become integrated into, joined with, and form part of that emergency state, that state-nation or that nation-state in which, curiously, one can find the extreme discipline implied by liberation combined with the most diverse moral, religious, popular, and civilian currents of a war that involves the *entire* "civilian population."

A democracy that is integrated with its worker-peasant contingent and with its bases and cadres among the middle classes, both civilian and military; a democracy with a state of which more than 90% of the population considers itself, and indeed forms, a part; such a democracy acquires an ideological, political, and military strength that is considerably superior to any previous democratic project.

It is true that this state, like any other, has its weaknesses. From the point of view of the government and the relatively privileged groups that form it—its functionaries, professionals, and trained workers—the major weakness lies in the danger of imitating and reproducing patterns of consumerist behavior and of the oligarchical/middle class culture of the "Yankeefied" parts of Latin America, alienated from the old and the modern cultures. From a global or national point of view, the major weakness lies in the urgency of satisfying *the needs of the majority with production systems for the minority,* within an international capital goods and financial market that is generally unfavorable and that is strong enough to apply economic, political, ideological, and military pressure on popular governments that constitute a serious threat to the continuity of colonialist methods of accumulation. The awareness of this and other possibilities (such as those inherited from a reactionary interpretation of religion or from tribal cultures that have traditionally used colonialism against all processes of liberation and democratization in the Third World) permits the implementation of a policy that is the opposite of "destabilization." That policy is achieved with a popular base so solid and extensive that the nation-state is an organization capable politically and ideologically of confronting imperialist intervention.

If from an ideological and political point of view, the nation-state or state-nation has a high probability of victory against any imperialist intervention, from a military point of view the probabilities are even higher. The war for liberation in Central America is waged with 20th-century methods. It is an organized war *of the people,* a war in which the people participate in an organic and majoritarian way. They face a war waged with 19th-century methods by oligarchical and imperialist armies organized and led by North American soldiers and technicians.

The characteristic of wars in the 20th century, wars that mobilize all those capable of fighting, is found particularly in wars of liberation, in which there are few limitations on age, sex, and physical ability. The people/coalition wages a revolutionary war with political-military-economic-ideological organizations that involve mass organizations and actions. The people/state wages war with an organization that is even larger and more perfect. In both cases, it is highly unlikely to be defeated by isolated armies, recruited and trained by the local military oligarchy and by North American experts.

It is true that the invading forces try to compensate for their weaknesses in human resources with their military superiority in technical personnel, and this results in the use of tactics such as scorched earth, total warfare, and genocide. However, these tactics not only run the risk of extending the war and turning it into a worldwide conflagration, they also could repeat the sufferings of the North Americans in Vietnam. Both outcomes would provoke strong political resistance within the United States itself.

The fact is that in Central America a power structure of the people has arisen, and it cannot be disregarded. This power appears before the taking of state power and once the new state is established. "The civilian population has become guerrillas," said Comandante Pedro Guerra Alegría. He explains the fact: "These masses were obliged to create mechanisms for self-defense, because they were being massacred; armed self-defense was a response to a necessity." This armed population united with the guerrilla movement to the point that "it isn't clear where one ends and the other begins." The people from some districts incorporated with others, and with organizations similar to family clans; they then related with yet other districts, and small politico-military nuclei began to be formed, progressively extended, and generalized. The phenomenon is that of war for power, a war of the real people who are there.

"The people's own way to wage war" is through social structures. This is a change from all previous wars, and of course, this war has nothing to do with wars reducible to small groups. In effect, "the war is transformed not into a fistful of long-haired, bearded communists but rather into the action of a whole people." "Zones that are impregnable to the enemy have sprung up, with the combination and development of armed detachments of the masses and the guerrillas. . . ." The new territory of the emerging state is born. "The zone of control is converted into a small state." The clans, cantons, and towns turned embryo of the state do not pretend to be "independent republics." They organize production, justice, the war, and the union with other control zones. It is the heart of the new state. The linking together of these elements of the people explains a strength and a power that has had no precedent in other revolutions and other states. And this power is willing and ready to negotiate.

What Is Nonnegotiable

With all the necessary force to resist and with a high probability of victory, the coalitions and states that are fighting for national sovereignty and social and political democracy in Central America are willing to negotiate. In actuality, these forces have repeatedly proposed dialogue and negotiations, but they will accept only "a form of dialogue and negotiation that will not be injurious to popular interests." Dialogue or negotiations that tend "to gain political-military time," that permit "a regrouping of counterrevolutionary forces" so they can operate more effectively, that "take away the political and social base of the revolutionary forces"—these are interventionist dialogue and negotiations in the style of 1950s Pan-American politics, "whose objective is not in any way the real solution to the conflict, that is, the solution to the country's serious problems." They in fact result in a mere trap, the inevitable effect of which would be first to isolate and later to annihilate revolutionary forces. Since 1954, in Guatemala it has been known clearly that a "negotiated solution" favorable to U.S. and oligarchical interests is the basis for repression against the masses that can last several decades. To an awareness that this form of dialogue and negotiation only leads to defeat is added the determination to achieve a new type of dialogue and negotiation in accordance with historical experience and with strength, with power.

The new democracies, which have arisen out of new revolutions that take into account the experiences of previous failures, set as a priority in their strategic plan the need to preserve and not to break up the worker-peasant-popular alliance that tends to favor public and social over private accumulation. The right to this predominantly worker-peasant-popular alliance becomes *nonnegotiable,* and is the correlate of a policy of power and moral action that confronts conservative, liberal, or populist coalitions and the various forces that would break this alliance and the power of the workers and peasants, the social and public forces within it.

The confrontations take place not only between coalitions, but inside each revolutionary coalition, to prevent its deterioration, its moral, intellectual, and emotional corruption; its consumerist tendencies, its irresponsibilities, fears, and insecurities in the face of the real vivid force of the liberating revolution.

It has been discovered that the dominant class governs with a form of conservative coalition, which of necessity must be confronted by a revolutionary and democratic coalition, capable of undertaking the social and political reforms that the progressive forces have struggled for in their more diverse ideological manifestations. That discovery of the struggle of coalition against coalition, with its undercurrents of people against oligarchy and of workers-peasants-community members against the bourgeoisie, not only leads to the *revolutionary* basis of the struggle and the *revolutionary* character of democracy. It also permits one to decipher the present manifestations (the mediations) of the struggle, the revolution, and democracy, and with these the *necessity for unity* (beyond sectors and factions), even though the decentralization of control is maintained by sectors or regions, and lines and philosophies or different interpretations of the same ideology are preserved. Popular unity *is not negotiable.*

The discovery of what is necessary is the discovery of what is non-negotiable. This is a many-faceted and common-sense discovery. Unity is not negotiable, the overall popular control is not negotiable, the alliances are not negotiable.

Perhaps among the most important discoveries of what is necessary is the discovery of the necessity of alliances and of the right to internal and international alliances (a right that by common sense is not even questioned in the case of the big powers). In Central America that right appears not only as the right of countries to be recognized in their capacity as countries, but also as the right to exist. *It is not negotiable.* If the identity, the base for the struggle of power, and power itself are acquired, through internal alliances, it is through international alliances that the recognition of that identity and the fortification of that identity in the face of foreign intervention is achieved. Instead of yielding, of reducing the ties to natural allies, or of concealing them as in the democratic governments of the past, those ties are maintained and strengthened. They are not negotiable.

The organization of the people and their coalitions, and the recognition of the latter and of their belligerence, or of their governmental and state representation, are nonnegotiable requirements. The representation of the people is not negotiable. The right to a policy of internal and international alliances is not negotiable under any pressure or pretext. This stems less from principle than from previous historical experience, in which every negotiation that led to the shattering of alliances with forces smeared as "communist" or "subversives," every concession that untied those forces of internal and international alliances was used precisely by those who demanded concessions against those who granted them, in order to defeat them once they had been isolated and their alliances broken. Today the "moderates" do not sacrifice the "radicals" in order to be sacrificed afterwards. Based on the common sense of survival, the "radicals" are not negotiable.

Another nonnegotiable objective, and without doubt one of the most difficult to achieve, consists in not permitting the private sector to dominate the mixed economy. The correlation of internal and international forces, the scanty development of industrial and productive forces, the necessity of resorting at least in part to the capitalist finance market and its centers of production and consumption—all those and other factors determine the pace, often very slow, at which social and economic reforms are undertaken. When the displaced centers of power do not harass the democratic-revolutionary project to the point of rupture, but accept the new character of the state and the new character of the negotiation and of the negotiable, the nonnegotiable character of the dominance of the public and social over the private economies—paradoxically—appears to permit a slower rhythm in the deepening of the reforms that facilitate the predominance of the public and social. On the other hand, when the counterrevolutionary pressures are greater and imperialist intervention more intense, that same dialectic seems to lead to radicalization and deepening of the reforms, to measures that not only tend to socialize the means of production and the whole economy, but also strengthen the worker-peasant-popular bases and the alliances with the socialist countries.

The old form of domination and mediation of the mixed economy, which led to the forging of neocapitalism and neocolonialism through the corruption of the revolutionary processes and their popular or nationalist leaders, certainly continues to threaten the new type of revolution. But that threat encounters an entire historical experience and awareness that any concession permitting the dominance of the private over the social and public not only begins a process that distances revolutionary governments from their proposals of change in favor of the people, the peasants and workers, but also begins a process by which the leaders first distance themselves from their people. They later place themselves in contradiction to them and finally are defeated and liquidated or become the new governing overseers, supported by the oligarchies, by the new bourgeoisies, by the transnationals, and by the imperial state, which they serve consistently and abjectly, and with which they are associated in their business or in their corrupt practices, while they finish off any vestige of democracy. For that reason the dominance of the public and social sectors in the economy *is not negotiable*.

The new democratic currents in Central America, in particular those of Nicaragua, are found in the advances of a revolutionary democracy that cannot be overthrown because its leaders, cadres, and mass organizations are determined to defend the hard-won gains of a prolonged and painful popular war: all the freedoms of religion and opinion that they need, and all forms of respect for the human being, be they oppressed or oppressive minorities; a new concept of mixed economy which favors social over private interests; pluralist alliances in politics and in the military open to all friends of the new democracy, of national sovereignty, of self-determination and nonintervention. This is the real application of the modern ideals of democracy, freedom, equality, and the sovereignty of peoples.

The incomprehension of this democratic current by neoconservative thought dominant in Washington today will force the Central American people to demonstrate that they are not only right but powerful. Willing to negotiate what is negotiable, but not to negotiate democracy, a socially oriented economy, or national sovereignty, the peoples and governments that lead the struggle for democracy in Central America are also ready, if necessary, to win a painful war. This does not mean they threaten the security of the United States, as Washington pretends. However, they do threaten the oligarchy that governs the United States, and for that reason, Washington fears them. They portend a new type of democracy for the U.S.; and it is precisely democracy that Washington fears.

Unfortunately, the problem is not limited to the conservative party that governs the United States today. The Democratic Party does not seem to understand the new realities either. The majority of its members and leaders are trying to return to the *interventionist negotiation* of the past; that is, they want to impose the kind of negotiation that was the basis for the development of neocapitalism and neocolonialism in the countries of Latin America, Africa, and Asia. There the empire obtained by force the negotiation of [what should be] nonnegotiable. Today that type of negotiation is as far from being successful as the type of repression and war that the Reagan administration is organizing. But, in Washington, they do not see the new history or the new kind of negotiation. The conservative and Democratic politicians are divided. The former believe that negotiation which relies on corruption is no longer possible, and, therefore, that repression is the only solution. The latter try to return to an interventionist negotiation. As a matter of fact, both sides are incapable of meeting history as true statesmen. Both want to repeat past history, that of repressive interventions and that of interventionist negotiations. On the other hand, the peoples are forging *a new history.* They do not accept negotiations that will necessarily lead to their defeat. Today they have the power and the experience to impose the terms of a democratic and sovereign negotiation.

When the crisis of Reagan's repressive policy in Central America comes, as it inevitably will, Democrats or social democrats, if they want to succeed, instead of proposing or supporting *interventionist negotiations,* need to allow a policy of sovereign negotiation to win out. Curiously, this is the only realistic alternative today. Only a certain historical idiocy would call it romantic, idealistic, or naive.

To struggle with realism and within the logic of power for a negotiation that respects the sovereignty of the Central American peoples will be the role of the most advanced democratic forces in the United States, and of the governments of Mexico, Venezuela, and Colombia, if they want to forge the one negotiation that will open up a history of peace in Central America and the world.

Today the Democratic Party in the U.S. is so weak because it does not propose, either domestically or internationally, a democratic alternative to the policy of the conservative party. If it had a minimal creative impulse, the Democratic Party should "look for a way to end the war in Central America politically and achieve a dialogue leading to a mutually agreeable solution, [and find] the path leading to peace with social justice. . . ." It should explore the road to a new democracy in the United States itself, and new international relations of that democracy with Central America and with the world. If the Democratic Party does not do it, other truly democratic forces in the United States will. Meanwhile, Central America will impose [upon the U.S.] the minimum rights to which the peoples of contemporary history aspire.

A Call From Artists and Intellectuals of Nicaragua to Artists and Intellectuals of the World

The following statement was drafted on Friday, November 11, 1983, by a group of Nicaragua's leading artists and intellectuals at the Casa Fernando Gordillo during a meeting called by the Sandinista Association of Cultural Workers (ASTC). The meeting was presided over by Father Ernesto Cardenal, Minister of Culture, and Rosario Murillo, General Secretary of the ASTC. The statement was read in the United States at a series of teach-ins and speaking engagements in mid-November, 1983, by representatives of the ASTC, including several events sponsored by the Institute for the Study of Labor and Economic Crisis. It was translated in Nicaragua.

Since it is not yet too late, since zero hour has still not come, and in order that it never come, we ask you, artists and intellectuals of the world, to build a wall against aggression, through words and concrete actions.

At a time when the specter of another war threatens us; when the attacks fomented by U.S. imperialism continue mercilessly against this free land; when their violence reaches levels of madness so tragic and disproportionate as the invasion of Grenada; when innocent lives are criminally taken every day; when the insanity that Reagan has brought to the White House persists in invading us, even knowing that an intervention against Nicaragua would ignite Central America and then the world, to leave it destroyed by nuclear fire—this is the time when we artists and intellectuals of Nicaragua, imbued with our patriotic responsibility, appeal to the artists and intellectuals of the world, so that we may come together immediately and raise the banner of peace, which is the banner of culture and the most complete symbol of justice and liberty.

May it go down in the history of humanity that one day during this 20th century, in the face of the gigantic aggression that one of the smallest countries of the world, Nicaragua, was about to suffer, artists and intellectuals of different nationalities and generations raised along with us the banner of fraternity in order to prevent our total destruction.

Day by day, night by night, death stalks our borders. For us war is horrible and abhorrent, but our rejection of that which is abominable must never be confused with cowardice, because for us life is synonymous with self-determination and sovereignty. We can conceive of no other way of living than being free, and ultimately we prefer struggle, the greatest expression of all songs, and if necessary, death.

We are not suicidal. We struggled and triumphed in order to live in peace and constructive liberty. What person in the world with a minimum of honesty and at the risk of losing his/her own dignity, can remain indifferent in the face of the real possibility of a holocaust against a small people as a gloomy preamble to a world holocaust. . . ?

If we have already said that our true frontiers are defined by our forebears Rubén Darío and Augusto César Sandino, today we proclaim that the universal consciousness represented in the people of the world, in the intellectuals and artists of the world, will widen without limits our moral frontiers.

From the very heart of anger, and also from prudence which knows the value of peace, we repeat that we are not aggressors, but rather the victims of aggression. We are not a military threat to anyone's security, as our enemies' lies allege. Our great and only crime, in the eyes of the U.S. administration, is to have planted on firm ground an example of dignity and creativity born of the people and put at the service of that same people. It has been amply demonstrated that revolutions are not exported, they grow out of the very heart of those peoples who can no longer tolerate suffering, corruption, exploitation, and submission. The political and social problems of the Central American region will not end with our genocide—although it seems that such a "final solution" is the one chosen by the desperate Reagan government, faced with a series of defeats in all its plans to destabilize us, to crush us with all the weight of its resources, whether by the training, arming, and financing of the counterrevolutionary task forces, applying its sophisticated sabotage techniques against us, blockading us with its fleets, violating our airspace and territorial waters, provoking confrontations among the peoples of Central America, or reactivating the death apparatus known as the Central American Defense Council (CONDECA).

The truth is that not even by assassinating all the people of Nicaragua could they assassinate the Sandinista People's Revolution, which due to its undeniable contributions is already part of the patrimony of humanity, of that creative humanity to which the artists and intellectuals of the world are committed.

By defending peace in Nicaragua, we are defending life, including the lives of those North Americans who would come to invade us, dragged in by their government's grave historic error. Only in the heat of the combat that would be fought inch by inch in this land of ours, would those North Americans come to fully understand the meaning of our slogan— Free Homeland or Death!

The tone and urgency of this fraternal call to artists and intellectuals of the world is a response to the destruction and annihilation which the U.S. government wishes to impose on Nicaragua, where the right of a small people to decide their own destiny must not only persist, but must also grow and flourish.

Managua, Nicaragua, November 11, 1983

SERGIO RAMIREZ MERCADO

ERNESTO CARDENAL

CARLOS TUNNERMANN BERNHEIM

ROSARIO MURILLO

CARLOS MARTINEZ RIVAS

JOSE CORONEL URTECHO

GUILLERMO ROTHSCHUH TABLADA

MICHELE NAJLIS

BELTRAN MORALES

OCTAVIO ROBLETO

CIRO MOLINA

GLORIANTONIA HENRIQUEZ

ILEANA RODRIGUEZ

FRANCISCO DE ASIS FERNANDEZ

MILAGROS PALMA

ARMANDO MORALES

ORLANDO SOBALVARRO

ALEJANDRO AROSTEGUI

ROGER PEREZ DE LA ROCHA

PABLO BETETA

LEONEL VANEGAS

LUIS URBINA

ARNOLDO GUILLEN

CESAR IZQUIERDO

MANUEL GARCIA

GENARO LUGO

DAVID OCON

JUAN RIVAS

EFREN MEDINA

WILFREDO ALVAREZ

LEONCIO SAENZ

LUIS ENRIQUE MEJIA GODOY

FERNANDO SILVA

LIZANDRO CHAVEZ ALFARO

LUIS ROCHA

ERICK BLANDON

OMAR CABEZAS

GIOCONDA BELLI

JUAN ABURTO

CARLOS MEJIA GODOY

RAMON FLORES

PABLO BUITRAGO

MARIA MONTENEGRO

OTTO DE LA ROCHA

GRUPO "PANCASAN"

GRUPO "MANCOTAL"

GRUPO "IGNI-TAWANKA"

CORO NACIONAL

ORQUESTA DE CAMARA

ALEJANDRO CUADRA

BLANCA GUARDADO

IRENE LOPEZ

GRUPO "MACEHUATL"

GRUPO "TEPENAHUATL"

TALLER DE DANZA MODERNA

JOSE DANIEL PREGO

SALOMON ALARCON

ROLANDO STEINER

COLECTIVO DE TEATRO "NIXTAYOLERO"

COLECTIVO DE TEATRO "JUSTO RUFINO GARAY"

COLECTIVO DE TEATRO "TEYOCOYANI"

TALLER DE TITERES DEL SSTV

COLECTIVO "MIGUEL DE CERVANTES"

MOVIMIENTO "MECATE"

Index

About the Editors

Marlene Dixon has extensive experience as a leading organizer in the civil rights, anti-war, and women's movements. She has been a professor of sociology at the University of Chicago and at McGill University in Montreal, Canada. She is Director of the Institute for the Study of Labor and Economic Crisis in San Francisco and is the editor of its journal *Contemporary Marxism*. Dixon has written or edited numerous books on issues facing the socialist, women's, and workers' movements, including *Revolution and Intervention in Central America*, *The Future of Women*, *Grassroots Politics in the 1980s*, *World Capitalist Crisis and the Rise of the Right*, *Health Care in Crisis*, and *Things Which Are Done in Secret*.

Susanne Jonas is an internationally known expert on Latin America, particularly Central America. She co-edited the books *Guatemala* and *Revolution and Intervention in Central America* and has also published numerous articles. She holds degrees from Harvard University, Massachusetts Institute of Technology, and the University of California at Berkeley. A former staff member of the North American Congress on Latin America (NACLA), she is now with the Institute for the Study of Labor and Economic Crisis in San Francisco.

Other Titles from Synthesis Publications

Guatemala: Tyranny on Trial	032-1 cloth	$19.95
Susanne Jonas and Ed McCaughan (eds.)	024-0	$ 9.95
Revolution and Intervention in Central America	029-1 cloth	$19.95
Marlene Dixon and Susanne Jonas (eds.)	027-5	$10.95
The New Black Vote: A Look at Four American Cities		
Rod Bush (ed.)	038-0	$ 9.95
Black Socialist Preacher: The Teachings of Reverend George Washington Woodbey	026-7 cloth	$19.95
Philip S. Foner (ed.)	025-9	$ 8.95
The Future of Women	031-3 cloth	$14.95
Marlene Dixon	021-6	$ 7.95
Grassroots Politics in the 1980s: A Case Study *Institute for the Study of Labor and Economic Crisis*	017-8	$ 6.95
Contradictions of Socialist Construction *Marlene Dixon and Susanne Jonas (eds.)*	008-9	$ 4.95
Karl Marx Remembered: Comments at the Time of His Death *Philip S. Foner (ed.)*	020-8	$ 9.95
The New Nomads: From Immigrant Labor to Transnational Working Class *Marlene Dixon and Susanne Jonas (eds.)*	018-6	$ 8.95
Proletarianization and Class Struggle in Africa *Bernard Magubane and Nzongola-Ntalaja (eds.)*	019-4	$ 8.95
World Capitalist Crisis and the Rise of the Right *Marlene Dixon, Susanne Jonas and Tony Platt (eds.)*	016-X	$ 8.95

ISBN Prefix: 0-89935
Order from your local bookstore or directly from the publisher. Send payment plus $1.50 for the first book, 50¢ for each additional book to **Synthesis Publications**, Dept. 128, 2703 Folsom St., San Francisco, CA 94110